Haptic Modernism

For Randall Stevenson, who made a modernist of me.

Haptic Modernism

Touch and the Tactile in Modernist Writing

Abbie Garrington

EDINBURGH
University Press

© Abbie Garrington, 2013, 2015

Edinburgh University Press Ltd
The Tun – Holyrood Road
12 (2f) Jackson's Entry
Edinburgh EH8 8PJ

www.euppublishing.com

First published in hardback by Edinburgh University Press 2013

This paperback edition 2015

Typeset in 10.5/13 pt Sabon by
Servis Filmsetting Ltd, Stockport, Cheshire

A CIP record for this book is available from the British Library

ISBN 978 0 7486 4174 1 (hardback)
ISBN 978 1 4744 0142 5 (paperback)
ISBN 978 0 7486 8253 9 (webready PDF)
ISBN 978 0 7486 8254 6 (epub)

The right of Abbie Garrington
to be identified as author of this work
has been asserted in accordance with the
Copyright, Designs and Patents Act 1988,
and the Copyright and Related Rights
Regulations 2003 (SI No. 2498).

Contents

Acknowledgements

Many friends and colleagues have assisted in the completion of this project. In particular I would like to thank Randall Stevenson, Lee Spinks, Chris Baldick and Laura Marcus for comments on the earliest papers that led to this manuscript. Susan Manning and the Institute for Advanced Studies in the Humanities (IASH) at the University of Edinburgh awarded me the postdoctoral fellowship that allowed me to begin in earnest my haptic investigations. Anthea Taylor provided assistance and encouragement during my time there. David Trotter, Jeff Wallace and Scott McCracken helped with part-chapters, related articles and thorny issues. Alexandra Harris's enthusiasm for an earlier incarnation of my reading of *The Years* was much appreciated, prompting the extended version given here. At Newcastle, Andrew Shail has offered observations on early film, and Alison Light has allowed me to raid her bookshelves for Woolfian treasures. My students in the 'Modernisms' and 'Metropolis' courses let me drag our conversations towards matters haptic on a weekly basis. Danny Kielty gave me his very interesting thoughts on D. H. Lawrence. Douglas Fraser contributed an experienced psychiatrist's view of schizophrenia, and graciously allowed me to follow psychoanalytic readings instead. The British Association for Modernist Studies, the Scottish Network of Modernist Studies, the Northern Modernism Seminar, the North East Modernist Research Initiative and the Dorothy Richardson Society have provided events, encouragement and connections at various stages of writing and redrafting. Churnjeet Mahn, Sarah Gamble, Mal Bell, Ella Dzelzainis and the Ladies of Arden (Nicki Dennies and Helena Gray) have offered moral support/cheerleading services. Ash Fusiarski provided inspiration despite being consigned to Antarctica. Mrs Cuthbert was in charge of biscuits.

Permissions

Chapter 1

Haptic Modernism

Modernist manicures

In Sinclair Lewis's 1922 novel *Babbitt*, we first meet our eponymous hero at rest in his sleeping-porch, where his recumbent body may be read: 'He was not fat but he was exceedingly well fed; his cheeks were pads, and the unroughened hand which lay helpless upon the khaki blanket was slightly puffy. He seemed prosperous, extremely married and unromantic' (Lewis 1950: 2). Babbitt's choice of bed, in a space related only tangentially to the main body of the house, and removed from the conjugal chamber, leads the reader to suppose he may not be as 'extremely' married as the narrative voice would have us believe. For Rebecca West, this initial approach to a slumbering Babbitt is part of Lewis's exhaustive study of an inconsequential man, for 'we know the poor fatuous being in his standing up and his lying down' (West 1987a: 272). Lamenting the 'planless' quality of the novel, West states that 'its end arrived apparently because its author had come to the end of the writing-pad, or rather, one might suspect from its length, to the end of all writing-pads then on the market' (271). Whatever the meanderings of the story, West concedes that *Babbitt* constitutes 'a triumph of impersonation' and 'a bit of character-exhibition comparable to [Charles Dickens's] Mr. Micawber' (271). To the detriment of the world's paper stocks, then, Lewis achieves an insight into the (vertical and horizontal) life of a suburban estate agent in the year 1920. Yet it is the second protagonist of that opening sleeping-porch scene that takes centre stage in the novel – Babbitt's 'unroughened', 'helpless' and 'slightly puffy' hand. It is through his hand that we come to know the man – as a synecdoche of Babbitt's agency, his organ of intentional touch, and the point at which his skin both defines him (his continent skin contains him; his fingerprints are his alone) and most conspicuously extends to meet the world (in an array of manual practices). Dermatoglyphics, the study of the 'writing' or ridges of the fingers, was established following the discovery by Sir Francis Galton in 1872 that the finger print of the human being is unique to each (Jablonski 2006: 100–1). If Babbitt's hand reads the world, gathering impressions of shape, texture, temperature and solidity, it can also be read, and read in such a way as to establish its owner's identity. In Lewis's novel it is most often the behaviours of the hand rather than its skin inscriptions that are available to be deciphered – making *Babbitt* a kind of study in haptoglyphics (from *haptesthai*, of the grasp). If a literary sleight-of-hand has occurred here, where I seem to be treating Babbitt's puffy paw as an independent entity, then in my defence I must argue that Lewis's novel encourages me to perform this manoeuvre. In fact, the adventures of the human hand and related sensations of touch and the tactile constitute a substantial tranche of the literature of the modernist period, as this study aims to demonstrate.

Babbitt does not always take care of his dermatoglyphs. His motorcar is most often depicted by Lewis as a positive prosthesis, extending his physical capabilities, enabling his inhabitation of the commuter belt community of Floral Heights, and marking out his importance within the overtly masculine central business district of his city, Zenith. Washing his car, however, temporarily allies Babbitt with the feminine – not through an association with the domestic cleaning tasks customarily overseen by Mrs Myra Babbitt, but through the regrettable femininity of his hands. A masochistic scrub of those hands rounds off the motorcar washing procedure: 'He used up many minutes in washing his hands; scoured them with gritty kitchen soap; rejoiced in hurting his plump knuckles. "Damn soft hands – like a woman's. Aah!"' (Lewis 1950: 267). By 1932, advertisers had created the condition 'Domestic Hands' and were selling balms for its alleviation: balms which returned a woman's hands to their proper softness after the rigours of domestic care (Armstrong 1998: 100). Babbitt's traffic is in the opposite direction, in that he punishes his hands for their womanly softness, scouring the skin with grit. He does well to try and control the way his hands might be read by fellow citizens of Zenith. Lewis subtly but consistently links Babbitt's manual condition, and manual practices, to his newly arisen discomfort with his place in the Zenith hierarchy. Masculinity here is carefully circumscribed and regulated through manual decorum. One must obey the rules of the Boosters Club or Athletics Club in terms of hearty handshakes and slaps; one must fold one's hands in prayer at the Chatham Road church on Sundays; one must not let one's hands stray, either towards the wives of others, or towards undesirable (or too desirable) young girls. Babbitt's troubles begin when he cannot keep his hands to himself, both in terms of sexual straying, and in terms of failing to use those hands in ways agreed by the community. The situation gets out of hand, we might say, when Babbitt loses his sense of orientation with regard to his place in Zenith and his socio-political identity, when his plangent longing for the amorphous 'fairy girl' (Lewis 1950: 37) leads him in dangerously unbusiness-minded directions. Zenith, as its name suggests, attempts to reach the celestial heights via the thrusting, phallic, glistening towers of modernity. With another hubristic attempt to reach the heavens in mind, that of Babel, we know that collapse comes from a failure to speak a common language. Babbitt's language of the hand goes awry, and he falls out of touch, both literally and meta-phorically, with his surrounding community. Lewis's novel can there-fore be read as the story of one man's drift away from manual decorum, later corrected by a return to the fold, or to the enfolding hand, of club members, churchmen and wife.

Babbitt's relationships with women other than Myra are mediated through the touch of his hand. Playing on the intertwined understanding of the terms 'touching' and 'feeling' as both physical and psychological experiences, the trope of the touch of a loved one's hand is a familiar one. In Babbitt's trinity of extra-marital relationships, however, touch always means more than sexual and emotional connection. His party girl neighbour Louetta Swanson is the recipient of his first forays into unlicensed contact (and we should note that the 'tact' within con*tact* here refers to both the skin-to-skin connection of a tactile act, and the recognition of social niceties – niceties with which Babbitt dares to tamper). Giving Louetta the benefit of 'that sonorous Floral Heights gallantry which is not flirtation but a terrified flight from it' (124–5), Babbitt stumbles into the realisation that she is a fellow traveller, tacitly dreaming of escape:

> 'Well, when you get tired of hubby, you can run off with Uncle George.'
> [. . .]
> 'Anybody ever tell you your hands are awful pretty?'
> She looked down at them, she pulled the lace of her sleeves over them, but otherwise she did not heed him. She was lost in unexpressed imaginings. (Lewis 1950: 125)

Babbitt and Louetta touch hands on a number of occasions (125, 276, 278), touches that speak most clearly of psychological desperation:

> He had [. . .] the impression of a slaggy cliff and on it, in silhouette against menacing clouds, a lone and austere figure. [. . .] He grasped Louetta Swanson's hand, and found the comfort of human warmth. Habit came, a veteran warrior; and he shook himself. [. . .] He patted Louetta's hand,

to indicate that he hadn't meant anything improper by squeezing it. (Lewis 1950: 128)

Reaching for a point of anchorage, Babbitt grasps her; shaking himself, and resetting his somatic sensibilities, he 'comes to his senses' and reinstates gestural propriety in a pat. It is at a party attended by Louetta that one other form of getting in touch is depicted, that of 'spiritualism and table-tipping!' as Mrs Frink describes it (125). Foregrounding the touch/communication connection, this attempt at spiritual contact will be mediated by Chum Frink, whose hands are monitored carefully for misleading raps of the table (125). Mrs Orville Jones requests that they attempt to contact Dante, whom she has studied at her reading circle, and whom Babbitt memorably glosses as 'the fellow that took the Cook's Tour to Hell' (126). Even the prospect of making contact with the poet is overshadowed by the licence this event provides for married men and women to hold one another's hands in the gathering of the séance: 'They [the wives] laughed, "Now, you be good or I'll tell!" when the men took their hands in the circle. Babbitt tingled with a slight return of interest in life' (125). Spiritual contact with Dante, then, takes second place to the thrill of manual contact that teeters on the brink of impropriety – it is the 'other side' of extra-marital romancing that is the real journey beyond the bounds of Zenith in this scene.

After these initial experiments in transgressive touch, Babbitt finally succumbs to a philanderer's affair with Tanis Judique, a woman whose suitability is first registered through her own sense of manual propriety. She refers to 'these women that try to imitate men, and play golf and everything, and ruin their complexions and spoil their hands!', prompting Babbitt to state that he 'never did like these mannish females' (282). The use of the present tense by both parties suggests that there is a type of woman now abroad who offends social dignities, with the result of conspicuous manual ruin. Babbitt's own feelings on the gender-appropriateness of certain hand characteristics were made clear in his masochistic scrubbing, and they recur when he meets Tanis, whose wonderfully feminine hands lead him to believe that she must surely play the piano – an excellent feminine accomplishment – 'like a wiz' (282). Neither is Tanis ignorant of the statements being broadcast by her precious hands: 'He glanced at her smooth hands [. . .]. She caught the glance, snuggled her hands together with a kittenish curving of slim white fingers which delighted him' (282). Babbitt's own manual movements are made awkward by the sight of 'her fragile, immaculate fingers' (327) and his sexual desire is strangely diverted toward a yearning felt in his own digits: 'he was restless with desire to touch her hand', he is 'agonized with need' of the opportunity of a clasp (328). While this ballet of tactile negotiations conspicuously stands in for other, future physical manoeuvres ('"I'll have to take you in hand!" "Wish you would!"' (325)), it is curious that initial attraction and partner selection, desire, decision-making and the ultimate dissipation of resolve all seem to be displaced to the end of the arms.

Given all the 'manual labour' that Babbitt undertakes, both in the pursuit of women and in the bonhomie of the gentlemen's clubs and associations he frequents, he can perhaps be forgiven an indulgence that he has in common with many protagonists of modernist texts: a regular manicure. While Babbitt's own office is part of the Reeves Building, fully equipped with a barber shop of its own, he slopes off with not a little guilt to 'the glittering Pompeian Barber Shop in the Hotel Thornleigh' (33), conspicuous as the 'largest and most dynamically modern hotel in Zenith' (284). The curiously named Pompeian employs forty barbers and nine 'manicure girls' working at a desperate pace (285), and its steam-filled basement (buried?) position prefigures the underworld of Fritz Lang's *Metropolis* (1927).[1] The latter's combination of futuristic technology and Egyptian stylistic flourishes is pertinent here too since, for all its dynamic modernism, the Pompeian's clients sit in their pomp amongst a sumptuous array of preparations that seems to owe more to classical Arabia:

> About him was luxury, rich and delicate. One votary was having a violet-ray facial treatment, the next an oil shampoo. Boys wheeled about miraculous electrical massage-machines. The barbers snatched steaming towels from a machine like a howitzer of polished nickel and disdainfully flung them away after a second's use. On the vast marble shelf facing the chairs were hundreds of tonics, amber and ruby and emerald. It was flattering to Babbitt to have two personal slaves at once – the barber and the bootblack. (Lewis 1950: 285)

While the violet-ray treatment, massage-machines (an example of sensuous touch being mediated by a newfangled mechanism) and battle-ready howitzer of a towel machine ally the Pompeian with technological modernity, the plenty of the jewelled tonics and the personal attention of 'slaves' suggests a multisensory manipulation belonging to far older a time. Later, 'the barber obsequiously rub[s] his wet hair and b[i]nd[s] it in a towel as in a turban, so that Babbitt resemble[s] a plump pink calif [*sic*] on an ingenious adjustable throne' (286). As Laura U. Marks reminds us, Arabic philosophers' association of happiness of body with happiness of mind led to toleration of moderate indulgences in bodily pleasures, in societies otherwise carefully regulated in relation to the carnal. The aesthetics of multisensory stimulation is in particular associated with 'the luxurious courts of the Abbasid caliphate in Baghdad' (Marks 2008: 127). Babbitt is, then, a votary of trans-historical sensuous indulgence and yet at the same time thrilled to find himself amongst the markers of modernity. Both the turban and the ingeniously mechanised 'throne' establish him as a man of importance, one whose masculinity seems at first imperilled by bodily care (Tanis's tended fingers marked her femininity, after all) but is ultimately reinstated by this caliph's marshalling of slaves to his needs.

Votaries of dame fashion

Lewis's deployment of the term 'votary' links his novel to a modernist milestone also published in 1922, James Joyce's *Ulysses*. In the latter's 'Nausicaa' episode, Gerty MacDowell is described as a 'votary of Dame Fashion', language lifted from the pages of Gerty's prescriptive and exacting women's magazines (Joyce 2008: 335). Naomi Wolf's study *The Beauty Myth* observes that the use of religious rhetoric to describe and promote women's hunger for beauty products may be traced across the twentieth century (Wolf 1991: 86–130). Gerty's role as a 'votary' or specifically religious supplicant is underscored by the presence behind her on the Strand of Father Conroy's church, a church whose persuasive propositions inspire the adman Leopold Bloom. For Gerty, herself a product on the marriage market, the business of looking after one's physical assets is important enough to inspire devotion. Magazines such as the *Lady's Pictorial*, *Pearson's Weekly* and the *Princess Novelette* (Joyce 2008: 335, 338, 334) ensure that the connections between physical beauty, beauty products, the allure of romance and the prospect of marriage are tightly drawn – beauty advice and advertisements (and slippery combinations between the two) being interleaved with romance stories and society announcements concerning marriages and engagements. Gerty's reading diet is filled with injunctions to care for one's bodily resources; Joyce has carefully replicated the language of her favourite publications. For example, the *Lady's Pictorial* for 18 June 1904 (dated, that is, two days after Gerty's fictional moment) is stern with a correspondent:

> Louise – It is the cold winds, I am sure, that are making your face so uncomfortable, and evidently you have a very sensitive skin; send to the chemists [*sic*] for a bottle of Rowland's Kalydor Lotion, and bathe your face in it directly you come indoors. (Anon. 1904: 1,162)[2]

In this context it is no surprise that Gerty has hands 'of finely veined alabaster with tapering fingers and as white as lemon juice and queen of ointments could make them though it was not true that she used to wear kid gloves in bed' (Joyce 2008: 333). Gerty's use of a home-made preparation ('lemon juice') suggests that 'queen of ointments' is not always affordable, although in both cases we presume she has been advised by 'Dame Fashion', 'Madame Vera Verity' and their ilk (335, 334). Her alabaster skin is an aspect of her appearance that allies Gerty with statuary, a form of beauty contemplated using the caressing touch of the eye, as we will see. Reference to her 'Greekly perfect' mouth (333) can be read in this light. Her presentation of her beauty to Bloom is largely static or statue-like, and is broken when she begins to move and he perceives that she is lame: 'Thought something was wrong by the cut of her jib. Jilted beauty' (351). There is little Gerty can do to correct this aspect of her physical stock (the result of 'an accident coming down Dalkey Hill' (348)); nor can she do much about fingers that fail to taper, for all that their signalling of feminine power would be useful to her (as it is to Tanis). The restrictions of her hereditary lot aside, Gerty keeps herself in good order. The narrative voice, which we presume to be in free indirect discourse here, echoing Gerty's own exercises in magazine-influenced self-reflection, notes that 'there was an innate refinement, a languid queenly *hauteur* about Gerty which was unmistakably evidenced in her delicate hands' (333). Barring recourse to bed-time gloves, Gerty is keen to ensure that her exercises in manicure, meaning literally 'care for the hands', result in a correct reading of her manual assets.

Gerty's beach scene will be discussed further in Chapter 2. For now, it is pertinent to observe that, through her 'queen of ointments', Gerty returns us to Babbitt's Zenith caliphate, but also to biblical incidents of salving touch or the application of balm, often associated with Mary Magdalene. If religious rhetoric and strategies are useful in bids to convince women to spend on secular beauty products, it is equally the case that activities of care for the skin have further, spiritual resonances when read in a religious context. In an oft-quoted letter to Frank Budgen, Joyce designates the 'Nausicaa' episode one concerned with 'mariolatry' (Joyce 1966: 135), and in so doing primarily intends to emphasise the importance of the mother of Christ. However, other Marys of the New Testament, often erroneously conflated (Anzieu 1989: 144), hover around the beach, each of them in some way reiterating a link between the application of a 'salve' and the notion of 'salvation'. It is of course Mary of Magdala who first sees the risen Christ in the Garden of Gethsemane, and who, taking him initially for a gardener, reaches forth a hand and is told 'noli me tangere', or 'do not hold on to me' (John 20:17; Mark 16:9). Christ's injunction to Mary may be contrasted with his insistence that 'doubting' Thomas 'reach out [his] hand and put it in my side. Do not doubt but believe' (John 20:24–9). We return to Thomas's need for manual verification, and his unlikely compatriots amongst the modernists, in Chapter 3. Mary Magdalene arrives in the Garden on a mission of anointment, attending alongside another Mary, the mother of James, to apply unctions to the body of Christ (Mark 16:1). It is Mary of Bethany, sister of Lazarus, who anoints the feet of Christ, a gesture he reads as preparation for his coming embalmment and therefore for his resurrection (John 12:3–8). In a biblical context, then, the application of a balm may nourish the skin and invigorate the living body, it may form a carapace for the carnal remnants of life, and it may – as with Lazarus's sister – anticipate the reanimation of the carnal, a further reincarnation. We should also consider the anonymous woman, often referred to as Mary, who attends the banquet of Simon the Pharisee, and who anoints Christ's feet – an honour he receives with gratitude despite her feared status as a prostitute (Luke 7:37–47). Mixed up amongst the Marys, Gerty has her own interest in anointing – in this case in relation to hands rather than feet (although there is mention of a 'milk footbath' (Joyce 2008: 333)) – in preparation for the Christ/'dreamhusband' figure she takes the watching Bloom to be: 'there were wounds that wanted healing with heartbalm', she observes (342).[3]

Given that Joyce's most famous image is one of manicure, we should not be surprised to find him alert to the importance of care for the hands, and the application of balms to the human skin, in the early twentieth century. For Stephen Dedalus, 'the artist, like the God of the creation, remains within or behind or beyond or above his handiwork, invisible, refined out of existence, indifferent, paring his fingernails' (Joyce 2000a: 233).[4] The image most obviously conveys Stephen's belief in the artistic creation of a world entire, but it also emphasises the fact that to write is to undertake manual labour, an effort of the hand. Both of those points lead us towards Stephen's namesake, the mythical inventor and sculptor Daedalus, of whom Diodorus of Sicily writes:

> In natural ability he towered far above all other men and cultivated the building art, the making of statues and the working of stone. [. . .] In the carving of his statues he so far excelled all other men that later generations invented the story about him that the statues of his making were quite like their living models; they could see, they said, and walk and, in a word, preserved so well the characteristics of the entire body that the beholder thought that the image made by him was being endowed with life. (Diodorus 1939, vol. 4: 76, 1–3)

In confrontation with his own writing hand, Joyce recognises its power to create and animate, to endow life, in a way which calls to mind the work of the sculptor, whose manual endeavours create work in three dimensions, available to the imagined touch of the eye. Joyce's 1904 essay 'A Portrait of the Artist' in fact contains an explicit conflation of the literary artist and the sculptor. He writes, attempting to sketch his own practices: 'His judgement was exquisite, deliberate, sharp; his sentence sculptural' (Deane 2000: ix). Yet Joyce's consideration of the hand of the sculptor-author also allows his artist proxy Stephen to ruminate on the question of its careful, habitual maintenance. He was not alone. 'Molly the Manicure Girl' was a syndicated comic strip series, released in the US, by the artist Virginia Huget. One strip of 1928 sees Molly meet her friend Gertie on the beach ('those girls, those girls, those lovely seaside girls', as Blazes Boylan sings, and Bloom recalls while watching his own Gerty (Joyce 2008: 354)). Molly and Gertie are wearing bathing costumes, and would to readers of the twenties be taking their parts as familiar advertising tropes – 'shapely bathers on golden strand', as Bloom has it (Joyce 2008: 115; see also Richards 1990: 205–48). 'Exercise is making a new girl out of me, Molly,' says Gertie. When did she start exercising, Molly wonders. 'Tomorrow,' comes the reply (Huget 1928). The seaside girls playfully refer to the hard slog of personal maintenance, work that Joyce's Gerty takes to with great alacrity as a true 'votary'. Yet it is also significant that Huget's Molly, a young woman of the 1920s, is a manicure girl, attending the beach with friends rather than family, and (as far as we can tell) unchaperoned. The manicure girl may be seen to form a kind of unholy trinity alongside the department store assistant and the typist, each being a job a young woman might take to maintain her financial, and therefore social, independence in an urban environment. Questions of sexual impropriety haunt all three. Émile Zola's *The Ladies' Paradise* of 1883 is the most detailed account of the department store life and the perceived purchasability of the women who worked in such places, but 'a grubby shrieking cash-girl from Parcher and Stein's' who has allowed herself to be 'picked up' also gets a mention in Lewis's novel (1950: 342). T. S. Eliot's 'typist home at teatime' and her failure to fend off the attentions of the 'young man carbuncular' give us an evocative account of the dangerously unchaperoned working woman (Eliot 1963: 71, 72; see also Rainey 2004). The manicure girl, if she works in a hotel barber shop, shares with her department store saleswoman compatriot a liminal status in a semi-domestic space. She shares with the typist the dependency of her trade upon nimble, dextrous hands. But the potential for impropriety is intensified inevitably in the case of the manicure girl, since the recipient of the manicure treatment is, rather than an inert mechanism (as with the typewriter), a sentient, feeling hand. She therefore operates in a position of considerable social vulnerability, as *Babbitt* makes clear.

Gentleman or cigar-store sport?

Ida Putiak, 'Babbitt's' manicure girl, joins Tanis and Babbitt in their habit of connecting care for the hands to gendered social status: 'You always ought to go to a manicure. [. . .] There's nothing looks so nice as nails that are looked after good. I always think that's the best way to spot a real gent' (Lewis 1950: 287). Ida has a pecuniary interest in Babbitt's regular attendance at the Pompeian, making this putative model of gentlemanliness an oblique exercise in advertising. In fact, Ida's experiences lead her to believe the very opposite of her declared conviction – a manicure is no indicator of the gentleman at all: 'these cigar-store sports that think because a girl's working in a barbershop, they can get away with anything. The things they saaaaaay!' (288). Babbitt's sexualised enthusiasm for the manicure (procedure) and manicure (practitioner) suggests he might have much in common with such sports:

> With quaking eagerness he saw that his manicure girl was free. [. . .] When she withdrew his wet hand from the bowl, it was so sensitive from the warm soapy water that he was abnormally aware of the clasp of her firm little paw. [. . .] He had a certain ecstasy in the pain when she gnawed at the cuticle of his nails with a sharp knife. He struggled not to look at the outline of her young bosom and her shoulders, the more apparent under a film of pink chiffon. (Lewis 1950: 286–7)

With their hand-to-hand contact intensified by the film of water, Babbitt again shows masochistic tendencies, this time thrilled by the gnaw of a knife, rather than the scrape of gritty soap. His 'certain ecstasy' may be read as a simple indicator of arousal, but it also suggests that he experiences *ecstasis*, the state of being beside oneself. The reiteration of the surface of his skin through pain receptors around his cuticles leads to the transcendence of that skin as the frisson of legitimised contact with a relative stranger moves him outside the realms of his body. Thus invocation of the bodily border, the human skin, reinforces Babbitt's status as a fleshly being, even as it allows him to imagine the slipping of that skin, an escape from his incarnation.

Ostensibly Ida, for her part, has inferred that something distinguishes Babbitt from the 'cigar-store sports', hence her decision to confide in him about the impertinent behaviour of the latter. However, it is equally the case that the description of bad behaviour, of inappropriate things said, is a bid to create consensus, and protects Ida from another client's attempts to 'get fresh'. If this is her strategy, it works in the first instance, as Babbitt imagines the ways in which he might be superior to less kind-minded fellow citizens of Zenith, since 'there were some roughnecks who would think that just because a girl was a manicure girl and maybe not awful well educated, she was no good, but as for him, he was a democrat, and understood people' (287). Such self-justification continues when Babbitt makes the decision to invite Ida to dinner, since he can see no earthly reason 'why he shouldn't have a quiet dinner with a poor girl who would benefit by association with an educated and mature person like himself' (289). The dinner is no great success, Ida's chatter being confined to lively tales of her mistreatment at the Pompeian. Babbitt steals a post-prandial kiss – 'there was no sense of struggle and transition; he kissed her and simply she responded' (291) – but the clinch is broken by Ida. It becomes clear to Babbitt that while he 'h[o]ld[s] out hungry hands' (291) to her, Ida is simply hungry; this is not the first time a wealthy client has provided a meal in exchange for a kiss. Babbitt's wounded pride results in some ugly insults imagined for Ida, including 'gutter-pup' and 'darn immigrant' (she has mentioned a Polish grandfather and described her name as 'kind of kike') (292, 292, 288). It is the first of these insults that most clearly emphasises the manicure girl's precarious social position, a position of which both Babbitt and Ida herself have shown themselves to be aware in their references to the impertinent assumptions of 'cigar-store sports' and 'roughnecks'. Ida knows how her present employment is interpreted, and also that it is a kind of self-fulfilling prophecy, in that she cannot access good dinners without accepting at least some of the propositions reaching her across the manicure table. In this way Ida connects to Babbitt's political insecurities, which have seemed intertwined with his new-found interest in romancing. He fulminates about 'agitators' out on strike, and yet when he reads that 'even on their former wages the telephone girls had been hungry, he was troubled' (312). The 'telephone girls' are a neat choice for Lewis, since their strike inevitably leads to a breakdown of the communication networks operating across Zenith, and from Zenith out to the wider world, foregrounding the disorder, disarray and backwardness of strike action, in contravention of Zenith's civic mythology as a city of the world. But the telephone girls are also the sisters of the shop girls, typists and manicure girls – the 'girlish' (which is to say unmarried), the socially vulnerable (unchaperoned), the hungry, the alluring and the new.

The figure of the manicure girl crops up at one other important moment in Lewis's novel. Eunice Littlefield, daughter of Babbitt's neighbour Howard and eventual bride of Ted Babbitt, is incorrigibly interested in the movies:

[she] read the motion-picture magazines, those extraordinary symptoms of the Age of Pep [. . .] illustrated with portraits of young women who had

recently been manicure girls, not very skillful manicure girls, and who, unless their every grimace had been arranged by a director, could not have acted in the Easter cantata of the Central Methodist Church. (Lewis 1950: 225)

Here the job of manicure girl functions as a typical holding pattern for the under-talented wannabe actress, the 1920s equivalent of today's Hollywood waitress – a job for the would-be glamorous, a temporary affair, and one carrying a hint of availability for manipulation, directorial, sexual or otherwise. In 1925, the role of manicure girl dreaming of more actually found itself in the movies in Frank Tuttle's *The Manicure Girl*, starring Bebe Daniels in the title role. Daniels's appearance echoes that of Ida, her sharp-cut dark hair, slim figure and propensity to wear chiffon bespeaking her status as a woman of a new generation, a proto-bright young thing. Babbitt eventually becomes entangled in 'the Bunch', Tanis Judique's social circle, and something of a fast set. Their status as social outsiders and rebels within the restrictive expectations of Zenith behaviour is underscored by their association with 'bouncing young women whom they picked up in department stores and hotel coatrooms' (342). The manicure girl could, to her detriment, find a home in such company.

Rebecca West's hands

Elsewhere in the literature of the modernist period the reading of manicure practices follows the paths discernible in *Babbitt*. In Rebecca West's autobiographical novel *Sunflower* – which, although published posthumously in 1986, was written, and abandoned, in the mid-1920s – Liberal politician Francis Pitt's dubious associate John 'Jack' Murphy is legible through his hands. Giving an account of his rough-and-tumble upbringing in Liverpool, a somewhat drunken Murphy conveys the family's situation thus: '"Twelve of us there were," he said, beaming at her with a face suddenly grown soft in contemplation of the domestic virtues, "and all double-jointed"' (West 1986: 99). Much to his listeners' disappointment, this bizarre claim comes with a demonstration, as Murphy bends back each of his fingers until cracking point. Mercifully, he loses interest while wrangling with the eighth digit. His performance affords an opportunity for Sunflower, herself an actress and an acute observer of physicality, to read the hands before her, 'which had more character than most hands, since they were exquisitely shaped, dark brown with sunburn, grained and horny like shagreen, and adorned, even over-dressed, with gleaming rose-pink nails' (99–100). Perceptively, Sunflower finds the man in the manual, or rather in the manicure. The jarring discrepancy between Murphy's gnarled hands and the manicure to which they have been treated suggests that he is grasping at gentlemanly status, and gives a presentiment of the ultimate realisation that he is a drunk and a manipulator, a 'dirty devil with his gab about friendship', as Pitt puts it (210). Pitt's own outsider status as a not-quite-gentleman Australian whose fortune has been made in California may be seen echoed in his own unlikely manicure: '[Sunflower] saw the light shining on his funny fingernails that were so wranglingly bitten and so glassily manicured' (157). Pitt's gentleman status is an overlay, a purchased add-on, and he is referred to repeatedly as having 'paws' or 'paw-hands' beneath the sparkling show of his nails (73, 85, 111, 119, 122). Pitt does not refer to his cumbersome and leonine paws, unlike Babbitt, who makes self-deprecating mention of coming to get his 'mitts done' by Ida (Lewis 1950: 287). In West's novel, the social position of the manicure recipient is at issue, shifting from Lewis's focus upon the status of the manicure practitioner to home in on the man behind the mitts.

West can be read as something of an authority on the many potential resonances of the manicure, and elsewhere in *Sunflower* an image of the practitioner herself does in fact appear. At a tedious party at Pitt's Hampstead mansion, Sunflower is left watching the tennis:

> It made one sick to watch Lord Canterton go out on court, carrying his racket in one large oblong red hand [. . .]; wearing the pompous and meaningless impression that is affected by the statelier and less efficient sort of manicurist when she carries her dish of soap and water across the room, the eyebrows raised, the chin dropped but the mouth closed, the whole advertising a state of bored superiority over somebody who was not here in an issue which was purely imaginary. (West 1986: 174)

This is a peculiar broadside, and the reader may presume that West had the misfortune to attend a very pretentious salon. However, the scene is interesting for its 'pompous' and ritualised aspect, leading us back once more to Babbitt's Pompeian indulgences. The 'statel[y]' manicurist, carrying aloft her bowl of lather in a mock ritual of obscure imaginings, recalls that more famous 1922 novel, echoing the morning processional of Joyce's 'stately, plump Buck Mulligan' who 'came from the stairhead' of the Martello tower 'bearing a bowl of lather on which a mirror and a razor lay crossed. [. . .] He held the bowl aloft and intoned: – *Introibo ad altare Dei*' (Joyce 2008: 3). Lord Canterton's own nails are not remarked upon, implying that his status as bona fide gentleman prevents him from lowering himself to such glittering appearances, or to worship at such altars as the Pompeian provides. Elsewhere, West represents a regular recipient of care for the hands in *Harriet Hume* (1929), whose eponymous heroine, as a pianist, spends as much time in contemplation of her own digits as any writer. Given that she shares with Sunflower a stage-based vocation, her hands must please an audience too, and she is as anxious for their proper maintenance as Gerty MacDowell:

> she had come downstairs after half an hour spent in making ten moons of her nails, and discovered [her lover] sitting at his ease by her hearth, toying with the long gloves which she had left on her piano. She had chided him for coming in with neither knock nor ring, and for laying his rough paws on the fine leather. (West 1980a: 53)

While Harriet is engaged in some self-manicure here, we gather this is a rare effort of budgeting, since her lover (Arnold Condorex) later suggests that she record an occurrence between them 'in that little book you keep for things it is useful to know. You have given over far too many pages in it to the addresses of manicurists, considering you have but two hands' (210). Condorex's paws indicate that in his ruthlessness he will echo his precursor, Pitt. Harriet's touch is, by contrast, delicate, as one would expect of a concert pianist – this is, after all, a profession where quality of touch is highly prized. Harriet and Tanis Judique are considered alongside other pianists in Chapter 6, where the former's abandoned gloves will also be addressed.

It is in *The Return of the Soldier* (1918) that West makes most extensive use of her fascination with the many meanings of hands, manicured or otherwise. Hands are deployed schematically in this short novel to connote class, social standing and spiritual worth, and are also used by Chris, the soldier of the title, to initiate a tactile remembering process. The contribution of touch to memory and the moment will be explored in Chapter 3. For our present purposes, we must note one further, peculiar resurfacing of the manicure trope. Our narrator, Chris's cousin Jenny, recounts the history of his inheritance, Baldry Court:

> when Chris rebuilt Baldry Court after his marriage, he handed it over to architects who had not so much the wild eye of the artist as the knowing wink of the manicurist, and between them they massaged the dear old place into matter for innumerable photographs in the illustrated papers. (West 2010: 7)

Jenny's slippery narrative contains only glimpses of her true sentiments, and it is through the scant implications of the phrase 'knowing wink of the manicurist' that we gather, aside from an apparently customary mistrust of the latter, that she does not like the changes that have been wrought upon the 'dear old place'. Beyond the province of the manual, the term 'manicured' is perhaps most often applied to lawns, suggesting that the massaging of Baldry Court relates to neatness, improvement and order, and contrasting in the strongest terms with 'the brown rottenness of No Man's Land' where, in Jenny's fevered imagination, Chris steps on a severed hand in the mud of war (8). Jenny, alongside Chris's wife Kitty, makes further changes to the Court while Chris is in service, changes with which Jenny is better pleased: 'I reflected that by the contriving of these gardens that lay, well-kept as a woman's hand, on the south side of the hill, Kitty and I had proved ourselves worthy of the past generation' (9). Upon his return from the conflict, Chris disagrees, fleeing the manicured aspects of Baldry Court, and most often retreating to an unmaintained pool and wooded area of the estate. Given that Chris returns suffering from the short-term memory loss of shell shock, we might simply suggest that he instinctively moves towards those aspects of his home that have not been changed in his absence. However, extrapolations from West's other uses of the manicure trope lead the reader to suppose that the untended regions of Baldry Court have a sincerity that is ill-masked by the overlay of a manicure, the landscape equivalent of the unnerving glassiness of the nails of Murphy and Pitt.

Babbitt, then, keeps eclectic company when he treats himself to the indulgence of a manicure. His well-tended hands ultimately become the means of registering his reincorporation within the power structures of the Zenith community, and within the sanctity of his marriage to Myra. At the Chatham Road church, Sheldon Smeeth 'imprison[s] Babbitt's thick paw' and expresses his delight at Babbitt's return to the fold after his political and romantic philanderings (Lewis 1950: 379). The 'affectionate clasp' (379) of Sheldy's handshake is a reinstatement of brotherhood – as Jennifer M. Barker reminds us, 'the handshake at its most basic is a gesture of reciprocity' (Barker 2009: 93). Another clasp ensures the reciprocal nature of affection in the Babbitt marriage since, when Myra is suddenly taken ill with appendicitis, her husband sits 'on the edge of her bed, holding her hand, and for the first time in many weeks her hand abode trustfully in his' (Lewis 1950: 383). In circling back to beds and hands at the close of his story, Lewis has *Babbitt*'s manual protagonist in its rightful place at last – in the environment of the bedroom, not the sleeping-porch, and enfolding the hand of his wife, not grasping at dreams of the 'fairy girl'. Babbitt's hand eclipses its owner even in the novel's closing moments. As Myra is driven to hospital for the operation that will save her life, her husband's 'damn soft hand' is flung against the over-heated radiator in the ambulance's rear: 'So, as they drove up to St. Mary's Hospital [. . .] it was she who consoled him and kissed the place to make it well' (387). Babbitt's carefully manicured 'mitts' strike again. For Lewis's novel, the human hand is an agent and recipient of care (most obviously through the manicure encounter), a facilitator of spiritual mediumship, partially literalising the notion of 'getting in touch' (here, with Dante) since hand contact between members of the séance circle is the earthly portal for messages from the 'other world', a symbol of prayer or communion, a shaker of other hands in a gesture of reciprocity crucial to carefully monitored social relationships, a facilitator of the act of anointment, in turn making it a node of contact with other geographical and historical realms (through its involvement in multisensory indulgences in the Pompeian caliphate), a point of contact with the complex prostheses of the piano (Tanis) and the motorcar (Babbitt), a sexual connector, an indicator of class and social status as well as of a point upon the newly recalibrated masculine/ feminine continuum, a means of knowledge-gathering or affirmation (here most obviously in relation to desire and love), an imaginatively conceived lone adventurer, and, crucially, a synecdochic stand-in for the tactile experiences of the whole body, the most widely culturally recognised symbol of skin-to-skin contact. As such, and by considering *Babbitt* amongst other modernist manicures, the human hand can be read as the 'poster boy' for a set of somatic experiences which we can call the haptic – a set undergoing a crucial phase of adaptation and theorisation in the modernist period.

Histories of the haptic

The word 'haptic' should be understood as an umbrella term denoting one or more of the following experiences: touch (the active or passive experience of the human skin, subcutaneous flesh, viscera and related nerve-endings); kinaesthesis (the body's sense of its own movement); proprioception (the body's sense of its orientation in space); and the vestibular sense (that of balance, reliant upon the inner ear). Every aspect of that quartet of somatic experiences is troublesome to define, isolate and understand. Also problematic is the notion that 'the body' is the experiencing entity here, opening up questions of what constitutes a self – the possession of the body, the ability to perceive oneself as something in excess of that body (a thing which may 'possess' a carnal envelope, in terms of both ownership and inhabitation), a sense of the 'lived' body rather than 'my' body, or an objective carnal reality beyond the subjective set of somatic experiences. Vivian Sobchack outlines this important notion of the 'lived body', describing it as 'a phenomenological term that insists on "the" objective body as always also lived subjectively as "my" body, diacritically invested and active in making sense and meaning in and of the world' (Sobchack 2004: 60). Sobchack's definition is helpful in its insistence on the mutually constitutive relationship between the self (here tied to the carnal) and the world beyond that self. The haptic is intimately connected to the constitution of the self, and it is so by virtue of its very intimacy, its operation on the carnal border between self and world. Our attempts to define the haptic as a broad sense modality incorporating the foregoing somatic quartet are also hampered by an inevitable slippage towards the metaphorical register since, as was evident in Babbitt's adventures, the physical and psychical aspects of touching/feeling are often attendant upon one another in a complex intertwining. In the literary realm, the flicker between physical reality and psychical reflection has an artistic value, and this study will largely follow its texts in allowing references to haptic experiences to operate in both literal and metaphorical senses, while wherever possible making clear the direction of intellectual traffic. My concern here is to identify an orientation toward the haptic in the literature of the modernist period, and to explore the reasons why an unprecedented level of interest in what we can more colloquially call simply 'touch and the tactile' is discernible at this time. I trace the history of physiological and philosophical exploration of this sense modality, and find modernist thinkers peculiarly alert to its ramifications, in relation to concepts of selfhood and aesthetics in particular. I also consider the technological and social changes of the modernist period and seek to establish their contribution to a renewed interest in matters haptic. As we will see, modernist literature both responds and contributes to a kind of 'hinge point' in the multi-stranded history of the haptic, drawing on theorisations from the eighteenth and nineteenth centuries to consolidate a notion of the role of touch for the perceiving subject, and therefore providing the groundwork for the many purposes to which the notion of the haptic is put in the later twentieth- and twenty-first-century world.

J. Lionel Taylor, writing in 1921, claims that 'the greatest sense in our body is our touch sense. It is probably the chief sense in the processes of sleeping and waking; [. . .] we feel, we love and hate, are touchy and are touched, through the touch corpuscles of our skin' (Montagu 1978: 1). There is an echo of Babbitt's 'standing up and lying down' (as West had it) here, that flicker between feeling (corpuscular registrations) and feeling (love and hate; touchiness), and finally the important suggestion that touch is the 'greatest sense' within the human sensorium. The phrase 'are touchy and are touched' refers not only to psycho-physiological conflations, however, but also to the reciprocal nature of touch experiences. 'Touchy' commonly connotes being irrationally available to emotional hurt, but here it also carries the sense of being *abroad with an interest in tactile contact*, a Babbittian appetite. One is an agent with the capacity to touch, and one is also the passive recipient of the touch of others. Giuliana Bruno reminds us to look to the Greek etymology of the term haptic, which 'means "able to come into contact with." As a function of the skin [. . .] the haptic – the sense of touch – constitutes the reciprocal con*tact* between us and the environment, both housing and extending communicative interface' (Bruno 2007: 6). The notion of 'housing' here tells us that the skin is a thing which we inhabit, and as such constitutes a border vital to the notion of an individuated self, even as it forms the possibility of an 'interface' with an 'environment' into which its sense experiences extend. The title of Claudia Benthien's *Skin: On the Cultural Border between Self and the World* (2002) reiterates the status of the skin as a culturally contested, and culturally reimagined, mediator between the bodily and the body's environment. The etymological origin to which Bruno refers, in *haptesthai* or the gesture of grasping (Paterson 2007: 4), suggests that the human hand plays a central role in touch experiences. Looking at Taylor's quotation, then, it is apparent that the attempt to assign touch to a physiological element is problematic – is it an experience of the body, the skin or the hand? Might its psychological registration be of paramount importance? Yet such questions must be answered for, by 1921, it is possible for Taylor to raise touch to the status of 'greatest' bodily sense.

In his study *De Anima* (c. 350 bc), Aristotle creates a hierarchy of the senses, assigning touch to the lowest position, a base sense (Aristotle 1907: Book II). While at first glance this claim seems to stand at odds with Taylor's 'greatest' label, the latter in fact chimes with Aristotle's account, if 'greatest' is taken to mean 'fundamental' or 'involving the largest expanse of physical receptors'. For touch is, in the Aristotelian schema, 'base' in its connection to erotics and the obscene, but also in that it is a kind of grounding, a scaffold on which the other senses are built. Given that Aristotle proposes all senses be attributable to a sense organ, a medium of sense and an object, touch presents a problem, as it seems to be the province of no single organ (Paterson 2007: 1). As the philosopher expresses it, 'tangible objects we perceive not by any action upon us of the medium, but concurrently with it' without recourse to an organ (Aristotle 1907: 101). Frans Floris's allegorical painting *Touch* of 1561 includes the caption 'tactus sensorium per totum corpus expansum est, ac proinde etiam organum', which may be translated as 'the sense of touch is spread out over the entire body, and therefore it is also its organ' (Benthien 2002: 188). Edith Wyschogrod concurs with Floris's claim, stating that 'the whole body is the tactile field. The body

[. . .] is the primordial ground of existence as incarnate' (Wyschogrod 1981: 26). To study touch, then, is to study the whole body in its carnal, fleshly reality; yet that body is represented most conspicuously by the human skin, the 'cultural border' of 'reciprocal con*tact*'. The skin, site of sensations of pressure, temperature and texture, presents its own problems of description. Steven Connor notes that the dermis can be conceived of as a kind of protection or dermatological shield, a concept present in the skin-shield or aegis of Zeus (Connor 2004: 32; see also Anzieu 1989: 44). However, the term 'aegis' is used in contemporary parlance to mean not only 'under the protection of' but also 'under the control of', confused in its deployment with the term 'auspices'. In this way we can read the skin as a means of control, indicating that a continent epidermis is essential to the imaginative projection of a coherent selfhood. We are back to the mutual constitution or contingency of the skin here since, as Michel Serres reiterates, 'through the skin, the world and the body touch, defining their common border. Contingency means mutual touching: world and body meet and caress in the skin' (Serres 1998: 97). Despite the psychological need for a skin that is continent in its contingency (from *contigere*, 'to have contact with' (Marks 2000: xii)), Connor observes that the skin is often a 'base' sense in one further extrapolation from Aristotle's claims, in that its 'fundamental condition is to be that on top of which things occur, develop or are disclosed. The skin is the ground for every figure. [. . .] a setting, a frame, an horizon, a stage' (Connor 2004: 38). The skin, then, is *hypothetical*, a ground on which stories unfold. The hypothesis of this study is that the haptic, of which the experiences of the (in this strict sense) hypothetical skin form such a substantial part, does not just matter to modernism, but is a peculiarly modernist matter. Further, the centrality of the haptic in modernist literature can be illuminated, or rather excavated, by drawing attention to the skin beneath the stories.

Benjamin, Riegl and the Kunstwollen

Writing in 1950, Geza Révész, then professor of psychology and laboratory director at the University of Amsterdam, notes that 'our knowledge of the haptic world is very bare [. . .] in respect [. . .] of leading principles. Haptics [. . .] has always been a stepchild of Psychology' (Révèsz 1950: 5). The professor's observation suggests that, for all the complexities of attempting to isolate touch, or the wider set of somatic experiences we can designate 'haptic', to an aspect of human physiology, the self/world questions set in train by any enquiry into sense perceptions make the haptic a psychological as much as a biological concern. For Walter

Benjamin, perhaps modernism's best-known interrogator of the haptic, any understanding of human sense perception will have existential implications. In a passage from his widely analysed essay 'The Work of Art in the Age of Mechanical Reproduction' (1936), Benjamin states that:

> During long periods of history, the mode of human sense perception changes with humanity's entire mode of existence. The manner in which human sense perception is organized, the medium in which it is accomplished, is determined not only by nature but by historical circumstances as well. The fifth century, with its great shifts of population, saw the birth of the late Roman art industry [. . .] and there developed not only an art different from that of antiquity but also a new kind of perception. The scholars of the Viennese school, Riegl and Wickhoff, who resisted the weight of classical tradition under which these later art forms had been buried, were the first to draw conclusions from them concerning the organization of perception at the time. [. . .] They did not attempt – and, perhaps, saw no way – to show the *social transformations expressed by these changes of perception.* The conditions for an analogous insight are more favourable in the present. (Benjamin 1999b: 216, my emphasis)

It is the thinking of Viennese art historian Aloïs Riegl with which Benjamin is conjuring here, and Riegl is vital in the establishment of a history of the haptic. Crucial for Benjamin, whose failed doctoral thesis on tragedy in German drama attempted to incorporate the thinking of Riegl (Lant 1995: 48; Iversen 1993: 15), is the latter's concept of the *Kunstwollen*. Comparable to the notion of a cultural zeitgeist, the *Kunstwollen* explains shifts in the artistic styles of historical civilisations as they relate to shifts in the spatial perceptions of those civilisations, perceptions mediated through the senses. The art historian's claim is, essentially, 'by their sensory experiences shall ye know them'.

Riegl's area of special study was Egyptian art, which he read as stimulating the tactile rather than the optical sense in hieroglyphic conflations of figure and ground (Riegl 1988: 183). 'Only by means of shadow', Riegl claims, 'does the presence of depth become recognizable; however, shadow is an optical element, which as such stimulates the visual faculty and thereby detracts from the utilization of the tactile sense' (Riegl 1988: 181). This unshadowed *Nahsicht* or 'nearsightedness' of Egyptian art (Lant 1995: 63) invited the imagined touch of the eye; a relationship ruined by the appearance of shadow, perspective and foreshortening. For Gilles Deleuze, Riegl's understanding of the 'Egyptian assemblage' can be understood as follows:

> Bas-relief brings about the most rigid link between the eye and the hand because its element is *the flat surface*, which allows the eye to function like

the sense of touch; [. . .] it confers [. . .] upon the eye a tactile, or rather *haptic*, function. (Deleuze 2002: 99)

Riegl's *Kunstwollen* teleology therefore posits a shift from the tactile to the optical in the move towards modernity. Antonia Lant suggests that this interest in Egyptiana at the turn of the twentieth century expresses a 'dual desire to locate ancient Egypt both as the powerful but limited source from which modern culture has traveled an enormous and valuable distance, and as a[n] [. . .] eternal beacon from the past, reassuring in the grip of modernity's fluctuations' (Lant 1995: 51). Riegl's *Problems of Style* (1893) and *Late Roman Art Industry* (1901) are important texts within the history of the haptic as a result of this influential positing of the *Kunstwollen*, and its attendant establishment of Egyptian hapticity as an 'eternal beacon'. His interest in questions of touch and tactility were perhaps inevitable given that he spent much of his professional life, prior to his death in 1905, as a curator of textiles at the Museum of Art and Industry in Vienna (Bruno 2007: 247), a job which required him to spend hours 'inches away from the weave of a carpet' (Marks 2000: 168); 'nearsight' indeed. In addition to inspiring Benjamin with his suggestion of historical revolutions in sense perception, Riegl gives us an early reference point for the term 'haptic' itself, remarking in a footnote to the 1902 essay 'Late Roman or Oriental?' that:

it has been objected that this designation [tactile, from *tangere*, 'to touch'] could lead to misunderstandings [. . .] and my attention has been drawn to the fact that physiology has long since introduced the more fitting designation 'haptic' (from *haptein-fasten*). [. . .] I intend henceforth to use this proposed term. (Riegl 1988: 190)

Yet, however important Riegl's contribution to theorisations of the haptic sense, he does of course argue against the notion that it is haptic perception that is the essence of modernity. It is in his inheritor Benjamin's work that we see Riegl's *Kunstwollen* teleology dismantled, such that touch is fundamental not only to Egyptian but also to modernist existence, persisting within the optical onslaught of the cinema.

Benjamin's central claims in 'The Work of Art' are two-fold. First, sense perceptions clustered under the banner (or aegis) of the haptic are an observable aspect of life in modernity. Second, the haptic may be seen as *symptomatic* of modernity, implied in his suggestion (given above) that the social transformations of an age may be read in the sense perceptions to which – via the model of the *Kunstwollen* – they are seen to give rise. At Benjamin's suggestion, then, this study will consider the social transformations of modernity that might contribute to haptic experiences, seeking to trace both those transformations and those experiences in literary texts of the time. Benjamin quotes the film theorist Abel Gance, whose *L'Art cinématographique* of 1927 states that 'by a remarkable regression, we have come back to the level of expression of the Egyptians' (Benjamin 1999b: 220–1), suggesting that Riegl's teleological model has in fact become cyclical. It is through the cinema that Benjamin comes to his conclusions regarding the fundamentally haptic nature of modernity, stating that the art of the Dadaists, which 'hit[s] the spectator like a bullet' (231), creates an appetite for film which 'is also primarily tactile, being based on changes of place and focus which periodically assail the spectator' (231). The sensory bombardment of cinema, its 'Egyptian' tendency to call upon what Virginia Woolf conceptualised as a licking eye (Woolf 1950: 166), will be tackled in Chapter 4. For now we should note that Benjamin incorporates the haptic into his argument in one further, curious manner. For him, the film cameraman may be compared to the surgeon rather than the magician, for while 'the magician heals a sick person by the laying on of hands; the surgeon cuts into the patient's body' (Benjamin 1999b: 226–7). The image, seeking to convey the bodily response of the film spectator, reminds us that surgery or *chirurgie* comes, as Jacques Derrida notes, 'from the Greek *kheir* (hand) and literally means the "work of the hands"' (Derrida 1993: 5). Derrida returns to this notion in *On Touching – Jean-Luc Nancy*, in his description of surgery as a 'handmade [. . .] operation' (Derrida 2000: 124). The touch of the surgeon, the touch that (with the aid of the scalpel) cuts, is discussed in Chapter 6.

In their haptic speculations, Benjamin and his fellow modernist thinkers can be seen to be influenced by two periods of philosophical history, both of them concerned with the connection between human sense perception and aesthetics, the latter derived from *aesthesis*, referring to active sensing and feeling (Paterson 2007: 10; see also Gaiger 2002: 7), and therefore to the affective aspect of the contemplation of art, as well as to that psycho-physiological flicker noted above. The most conspicuous or overt of these two contributory periods is late nineteenth and early twentieth-century art history under the influence of Riegl, including Adolf Hildebrand's *The Problem of Form in Painting and Sculpture* (1893) and Wilhelm Worringer's *Egyptian Art* (1928). This is an era in which the discipline of art history is itself being consolidated, perhaps explaining Riegl's footnote hinterland of physiological exploration (and we should note here that John Shaw Billings's *The National Medical Dictionary* lists the term haptic, 'pertaining to touch, tactile', as early as 1890, and declares it to be 'in current use'). Yet the modernist period is also in the philosophical lee of a still earlier time, in its engagement with debates initiated by eighteenth-century proto-art historical studies written in response to the Molyneux question. The latter contributory strand will be explored in relation to the myth of Pygmalion in my Excursus, and to the question of blindness in Chapters 2 and 5. For Benjamin, these two phases of thought are consonant with his own, since they seek to ally human sensory capacities with aesthetics and, in particular, to determine the varying calls upon the senses made by different art forms. In fact, with Benjamin in mind, we can suggest that it is the appearance of the cinema, an additional art form or, as Laura Marcus puts it, a 'tenth muse' (Marcus 2007), which prompts a reinvestment in questions regarding the senses and aesthetics that had gripped the thinkers of the previous two centuries. If cinema undergoes its 'second birth', as a medium rather than simply a mechanism, around 1910 (see Gaudreault and Marion 2002), it can be read as the catalyst for Benjamin's attempts to analyse the 'human apparatus of perception' at the 'turning point' of the modernist period (Benjamin 1999b: 233). Benjamin is picking up a thread first traced across sculptural form in the eighteenth century, woven through the textiles of curator/theorist Riegl and his acolytes, and thence found tracking across (or exploding ballistically out of) the modernist screen.

Benjamin, invoking Riegl, suggests that 'the conditions for an [. . .] insight' into the 'social transformations' sitting behind the shift toward the tactile are 'more favourable' in his 'present' moment (Benjamin 1999b: 216). While his essay spins off to consider, as its title suggests, the fate of artistic expression in a time of mechanical reproduction, we would do well to attempt to identify some of the 'transformations' foregrounding haptic experience in the modernist period. The new artistic form of the cinema functions, as noted above, as a catalyst for aesthetic debate, but it does so because of the peculiar invocations of the haptic brought about by a screen which at first seems to have nothing to offer to any somatic sense but vision. Chapter 4, tackling Dorothy Richardson alongside Woolf, returns to this matter. Other aspects of scientific and technological modernity will be considered in future pages, including atomic structure, the motorcar, the X-ray apparatus and the typewriter. For now, we focus on the notion of selfhood, most obviously reimagined in the modernist period by the establishment of psychoanalytic practice under Sigmund Freud. The notion of a 'skin ego', formed, troubled and traduced in the modernist period, can be read as one of these 'social transformations' encouraging a shift toward consideration of the haptic – a reading made possible by the problematic relationship between selfhood and the human skin.

Skin, self, schizophrenia

In Paul Valéry's 'L'Idée fixe: ou, Deux hommes à la mer' of 1933, he famously claims that

> that which is most profound in the human being is the skin. [. . .] The marrow, the brain, all these things we require in order to feel, suffer, think [. . .] to be profound [. . .] are inventions of the skin! [. . .] We burrow down in vain, doctor, we are [. . .] ectoderm. (Valéry 1957: 214–16)

This statement, echoing Aristotle's notion of the skin as the medium of the fundamental (here, profound) sense of touch, has been widely quoted (see Anzieu 1989: 60; Benthien 2002: 6–7; Connor 2004: 28; Ellmann 2010: 154). Feeling, suffering (in terms of *paschein* or the active undergoing of pain (Paterson 2007: 19)) and thinking, which we take to be psycho-physiological experiences belonging to other body parts, are 'inventions of the skin', such that the human being is reduced to its rind. This, it turns out, is no reduction at all, since the essence of the human exists in the ectoderm. Valéry's declaration of ectodermic essentialism has its basis in physiological reality, since 'the skin provides the medium in which the other sense organs are located, and the element of which we feel they are largely made', and thus 'the other sense organs exist as particular kinds of convolutions or complications in the skin, the labyrinthine turning inward to produce certain kinds of sensitivity' (Connor 2004: 34). Modifications of the skin are therefore responsible for the formation of the mouth, eyeball and sphincter, for example. The claim that 'we burrow down in vain' implies the injunction, again directed at the rhetorical doctor figure, to look to the skin. As Connor remarks, 'it is a striking coincidence that so much of the pioneering work in dermatology should have taken place in Vienna during the years in which Freud began to develop the theory of psychoanalysis', leading to a concern with 'the mind's complexion' (Connor 2004: 49). Freud's most famous patient, Serge Pankejeff, known as the Wolf Man, lived up to his name in suffering not only from the delusion of a scarred face, but also from *lupus* (Latin, 'wolf') *seborrheus*, a form of acne said to bite into the skin (Ellmann 2010: 70), suggesting that Freud at least would have to resist the urge to 'burrow' and instead confront the ectoderm. Further dermatological considerations might have crept into the consulting room, given that both the Wolf Man and Freud himself were born with a natal caul, an additional skin covering at birth (Ellmann 2010: 71), and that Freud's Vienna consulting couch was covered in richly tactile textiles (see Gay 2006: 176) in an unintentional nod to his compatriot Riegl. That ectoderm orientation is present in the twenty-first-century field of psychodermatology, which concerns itself with interactions between mind and skin, and seeks to analyse and treat 'psychophysiologic disorders' (skin problems reacting to emotional states), 'primary psychiatric disorders involv[ing] [. . .] cutaneous manifestations' and 'secondary psychiatric disorders' associated with the psychological problems attendant upon 'disfiguring skin disorders' (Koo and Lebwohl 2001: 1,873). Psychodermatologists often find themselves confronting a figure familiar to psychoanalysts and psychiatrists of the modernist period: the schizophrenic. The latter's struggle with the skin/self relationship makes him or her an important figure for any exploration of the haptic aspects of modernist life.

Connor tells us that the Greek *enchroi* 'means right up close to the skin' (2004: 10). Echoing around that word is the notion of encroachment, in this context the contravention of the skin boundary and the impingement upon a continent, stable sense of individual identity. We can usefully return to the term *contigere* here since, in addition to its primary meaning of 'to have contact with', it is also at the root of the term 'contagion', denoting as it does 'to pollute' or 'befall' (Marks 2000: xii). The schizophrenic is apt to prise open the skin/self relationship, in that his or her etiolated identity repeatedly manifests as an absence of 'ipseity' or the basic sense of experience as one's own (Sass and Parnas 2003; Ferri et al. 2012), an abnormal response to tactile experience, and a confusion as to whether skin experiences themselves belong to one's self or another (Ebisch et al. 2012). Anzieu has suggested that an appetite for masochistic flagellation might be the result of insufficient tactile engagement with the parent in childhood, or 'an episode of actual physical injury to their skin [in youth]' (Anzieu 1989: 41). These mooted causal explanations offer further evidence that the reiteration of the skin in acts of touch, and the sense of skin-inhabitation, are inherent to the development of a notion of selfhood, and further that a frayed sense of self may result in a problematic relationship with one's own skin. One of the possible manifestations of schizophrenic disorders (and the reason why schizophrenics might find themselves and their epidermis at the psychodermatologist's) is cutaneous hallucinations such as formication or crawling skin, also known as 'delusions of parasitosis' (Koo and Lebwohl 2001: 1,874), where the cutaneous sensation experienced is one of infestation (by lice) or of skin surface besiegement (by, for example, the crawl of ants, giving the symptom its name, via *formic*, 'of the ant'). Freud was wise to this fundamental connection between the psychological experience of a continent self, free from encroachment or pollution, and the physiological experience of a continent dermis. In 'The Ego and the Id' (1923), he states that the formation of the ego seems to be related to the fact that:

a person's own body, and above all its surface, is a place from which both external and internal perceptions may spring. It is *seen* like any other object, but to the *touch* it yields two kinds of sensations, one of which may be equivalent to an internal perception. [. . .] The ego is first and foremost a bodily ego; it is not merely a surface entity, but is itself the projection of a surface. (Freud 1995: 637)

First appearing in a footnote of the English translation of 1927 comes the clarification that 'the ego is ultimately derived from bodily sensations, chiefly from those springing from the surface of the body' (Freud 1995: 637). This is Freud's formulation of what later thinkers have called the 'skin ego', establishing the reliance of the individual human consciousness on the subcutaneous or internal experience of a dermic shell, and on the sensory experiences of the epidermis through touch, pain and so on. It is Didier Anzieu who has done most to enlarge upon this theory, writing in *The Skin Ego* that 'the development of a Skin Ego is a response to the need for a narcissistic envelope and guarantees the psychical apparatus a sure and continuous sense of basic well-being' (Anzieu 1989: 39–40), and going on to emphasise the fact that 'the Skin Ego finds its support in the various functions of the skin' (40). As Benthien has noted, Robert Musil's use of the term *Hautich* ('skin ego' or 'skin self') in *The Man Without Qualities* as early as 1930–32 anticipates Anzieu's observations by many years (Benthien 2002: 208). Musil's efforts in fact make the 'skin ego', in terminology as well as concept, a modernist coinage. The schizophrenic's failure to form a single, unified concept of selfhood may be read, then, as a failure to form this 'skin ego', a reading reinforced by the symptomatic presentation of sensations of formication, an ostensible loss of dermic control. Colloquially, the declaration that one's skin has been made to crawl implies a feeling of dread or disgust, with the hint that one's sense of self has been made to quake by confrontation with a disturbing 'other'. Further, a crawling skin contains the implication of the *ecorché*, the flayed skin that forms a second self, and moves independently. Fantasies of second selves created through ghostly skin apparitions are, suggests Connor, at the very root of horror, since 'horripilation' or the flaying/ lifting of the skin may well share an etymological origin with the term 'horror' itself (Connor 2004: 12). While schizophrenia is categorised as a psychiatric condition, the schizophrenic's problematic relationship with his or her own skin suggests that, rather than burrowing down to the mind in vain, we read the ectoderm to find the hypothesis, or skin grounding, of this illness. In fact, the skin/psychology connection is of the most fundamental type since, as Anzieu tells us: 'In the embryo [. . .] the sense of touch appears first [. . .], and this is doubtless a consequence of the development of the ectoderm, the common neurological source of both skin and brain' (Anzieu 1989: 61).

An unnamed schizophrenic patient, cited in Paul Schilder's *The Image and Appearance of the Human Body*, reiterates the problematic relationship between skin and self in the recollection of a schizophrenic episode:

> When I am melting [having an episode] I have no hands. I go into a doorway in order not to be trampled on. [. . .] In the doorway I can gather together the pieces of my body. It is as if something is thrown in me, bursts me asunder. Why do I divide myself in different pieces? I feel [. . .] that my personality is melting and that my ego disappears [. . .]. Everything pulls me apart. [. . .] The skin is the only possible means of keeping the different pieces together. There is no connection between the different parts of my body. (Schilder 1935: 15)

The patient's painful description draws a connection between a dissipated sense of selfhood, an atomised body (or anatomised, in its reduction to constituent parts), a failure of ego, and the limited continence, the fragile protection, of the aegis of the human skin. That the 'melting' self has no hands indicates that not only does the skin's border seem a tenuous means of keeping oneself together, but the manual gestures which most obviously manifest intentional touch are impossible under schizophrenic conditions. The diagnostic concept of schizophrenia was first outlined by Emil Kraepelin, under the term 'dementia praecox', in 1896, although Kraepelin's thorough exploration of the condition, *Dementia Praecox and Paraphrenia*, achieved its first English edition as late as 1919 (Sass 1998: 13). It is Eugen Bleuler who coins the term 'schizophrenia' in 1908, taking it to refer to a 'specific type of alteration of thinking, feeling, and relation to the external world' (quoted in Sass 1998: 14). The language of this definition echoes Valéry's ectodermic injunction, recalls the operation of the skin as a 'cultural border between self and the world' (in Benthien's terms) and brings us back to the thinking and feeling of *aesthesis*. Skin in the modernist period is, then, a ground for philosophical discussion of selfhood, for psychiatry and psychoanalysis, and for aesthetics, a triangulated relationship which is fascinating to track on its own terms, but even more illuminating when drawn across (or traced beneath, hypothetically) the literary texts of the period. Indeed Louis A. Sass has suggested that we consider the cultural output of the modernist period, very broadly conceived, as consonant with the experience of schizophrenia. Sass's study states that 'modern art has been said to manifest certain off-putting characteristics that are reminiscent of schizophrenia', including 'a quality of being hard to understand' and 'acute self-consciousness' to the point of 'hyperreflexivity' (Sass 1998: 8). While these comparisons are suggestive, Sass does not address the question of touch and the skin; burrowing, he ignores the ectoderm. It is the contention of this study that skin experiences connected with schizophrenia are the most useful features of that condition in any attempt to understand the self/world border of the touching skin in the literary texts of the modernist period.

A gesture of prayer

Beyond the bounds of schizophrenia, there is one human gesture that most encourages the contemplation of that self/world border: the act of self-touching. The sexual implications of the act are considered in Chapter 2, where I tackle the business of masturbatory modernism with the help of Leopold Bloom. For now, we make a more chaste turn toward phenomenological theory, and to the work of Maurice Merleau-Ponty. In the latter's *Phenomenology of Perception* (1945) comes a description of the human gesture of touching one's hands together, a gesture which in fact prevents *both* hands from simultaneously achieving the status of active toucher:

> When I press my two hands together, it is not a matter of two sensations felt together as one perceives two objects placed side by side, but an ambiguous set-up in which both hands can alternate the rôles of 'touching' and being 'touched'. [. . .] in passing from one rôle to the other, I can identify the hand touched as the same one which will in a moment be touching. In other words, in this bundle of bones and muscles which my right hand presents to my left, I can anticipate the integument or incarnation of that other right hand, alive and mobile, which I thrust towards things in order to explore them. (Merleau-Ponty 2004: 106–7)

The activity of self-touching, approximating to the gesture of prayer, results in two important observations: first, that the skin may actively touch or be passively touched, both experiences resulting in skin sensations; and second, perhaps appropriately given the prayerful gesture here implied, that the body's fleshiness or meat (recalled in the French *carné*) may be subject to *reincarnation*, that is, the spirit or will may be reinserted into its 'bundle of bones and muscles' in order for it to become the animate, active toucher. To mutually touch or enfold one's hands is, then, to recognise the power to caress, and to experience caress, but also – in the manner of a *memento mori* – to be reminded of the fleshly bundle that constitutes the human sensorium. Merleau-Ponty returns to this matter in 'The Intertwining – The Chiasm', in which he remarks that 'our body is a being of two leaves, from one side a thing among things and otherwise what sees them and touches them' and as such attains a 'double belongingness to the order of the "object" and to the order of the "subject"' (Merleau-Ponty 1968: 137). The *chiasmatic*, or crossed, sensation referred to here identifies the peculiar status of the self-touching human body as the – to borrow a Derridean phrase – 'touching-touched' (Derrida 2000: 159). Elsewhere, the *chiasma* turns up in the history of optics, being the 'point behind the eyes where the nerve fibers leading from the retina to the brain cross each other', explored by physiologists of the late 1820s (Crary 1992: 119). This notion is adapted by Derrida to form that of the *chiasmus* or 'crossed look' of two eyes with the power of sight, an idea that brings us back to Merleau-Ponty, since Derrida contends that an eye with the capacity for looking can never truly be seen; only in blindness is the human eye exposed to the eye of others (Derrida 1993: 57) – this is the 'looking-looked at' relationship.

These investigations in the *chiasmatic* operation of the senses are useful because they encourage us to think about the role of the human skin as a kind of *chiasm* writ large – a medium of sense experience that at once separates the self from the surrounding world and facilitates the perception of that world, both as existent, and as distinct from the self, further reiterating the skin boundary at the very moment of realising its limits. Maud Ellmann, considering the complexities of the human navel, has proposed the use of Derrida's term 'brisure', which she understands as 'a term from carpentry denoting both a break and a junction', and which might find a bedfellow in the less precise 'cleavage' (Ellmann 2010: 5). The skin and its touch sensations make appropriate such terms, and also call for concepts such as butterfly (recalling Merleau-Ponty's 'two leaves') or hinge. With the hypothetical skin – that running beneath the story – in mind, we could also consider skin sensations as the spine of a book, from which two leaves/pages unfold, a borderline between interoceptive and exteroceptive sensations. The fact that a folio would originally, as its name implies, have been bound in skin forms a neat ending to these self/world speculations, encouraging us to search for their traces in literary texts themselves.

Poster boy of the haptic

Babbitt proposes, through its central protagonist's manual escapades, that it is the human hand that provides the most effective means of considering the haptic experiences of the somatic system. Derrida concurs, suggesting that the hand 'could well be [. . .] the *best* rhetorical figure, or a trope among others to expose what an "organ of touch" or tactility is in general' (Derrida 2000: 154). Such a figure is necessitated, as Aristotle makes clear, by the dissipation of touch across the skin and through the flesh and viscera, making the bodily surface (and attendant subcutaneous sensations) a medium rather than an organ of touch. The hand, then, *stands in for* the diffuse and mysterious set of somatic responses we can attempt to gather beneath the aegis of the haptic. Derrida suggests that the hand may be seen as 'the *best* example of what characterizes the *human being*, at the top of an ontological hierarchy – for attaining, taking [*prendre*], comprehending, analysing, knowing [. . .] and so forth' (Derrida 2000: 159). The comprehending (*prehendere*) or grasping hand, the hand that *knows*, is hymned by D. H. Lawrence when he asks:

> Why should I look at my hand, as it so cleverly writes these words, and decide that it is a mere nothing compared to the mind that directs it? [. . .] My hand is alive, it flickers with a life of its own. It meets all the strange universe in touch, and learns a vast number of things, and knows a vast number of things. (Lawrence 1985b: 193)

We return to Lawrence in Chapter 5, and to the unnerving sense that the hand might have its own mind in Chapter 6. Lawrence's claim here, that the hand is a learner and knower, supports Derrida's contention that it can usefully stand in, metonymically, for a broader set of somatic experiences, those which I refer to as a haptic sense modality (Derrida 2000: 159). I propose an understanding of the human hand as a synecdoche, a kind of 'poster boy' for the haptic, since it not only participates in active and passive touch sensations of temperature, texture, solidity and shape – that is, as a functioning element of the human body – but also operates as a symbol of other, more obscure and difficult to decipher haptic experiences. The fact that 'all hands on deck' is typically given as an example of synecdoche is useful to us here – it is the hands (sailors) that will labour on the deck, knowing, learning and doing; the hands of the 'hands' have elided the fact of the participation of the rest of the sailors' bodies; and the hands therefore come to symbolise both a set of somatic practices involved in deck work, and the personhoods of the summoned sailors. The more colloquial notion of 'poster boy' for the haptic is supported by the enthusiastic exploration of the human hand and its capacities by modernists themselves – modernists seeking to understand the haptic quartet, but coming back, time and again, to the manual functionaries making their writing possible.

Writing in 1925, Fernand Léger states that 'the hand is an object with multiple, changeable meanings. Before I saw it in the cinema, I did not know what a hand was! The object by itself is capable of becoming something absolute, moving, and dramatic' (Léger 1973: 65). The artist does not reveal which films have brought about this revelation of the status of the hand although, were he feeling romantic, Léger could have attended *The Manicure Girl* in this same year. It is curious that, having been in possession of two since birth, he becomes aware of the power of the hand only when it is projected on a cinema screen, a technological intervention that ostensibly prevents the involvement of his tactile faculties. The previous year, fellow artist F. T. Marinetti had been at work on just this irony, as shall be seen in a moment. For Révèsz, it is the hand that 'enables us to master nature and to establish the material foundation for culture and civilization', the very essence of man, with a literal grasp that permits the deployment of tools, and a metaphorical grasp or reasoning process which is the foundation of intellectual life (Révèsz 1950: v). Henri Focillon, writing unequivocally 'In Praise of Hands' (1948), is fulsome in that praise. Echoing Lawrence in his engagement with immediate perceptions in the writing room, he claims that:

> even as I begin to write, I see my own hands calling out to my mind and inciting it. [. . .] Through his hands man establishes contact with the austerity of thought. They quarry its rough mass. Upon it they impose form, outline and, in the very act of writing, style. (Focillon 1948: 65)

We are back to the Daedalus/Dedalus connection here, where the forbidding marble block of thought is given form by the chisel/pen of the sculptor/author. The hands, then, sculpt thoughts, an act of crafting which contains the suggestion (as in Lawrence) that thinking is occurring in the manual as well as, or instead of, the mental arena. Focillon's use of the term 'quarry' refers to the carving process, as well as to the initial extraction of his metaphorical thought-marble. Yet 'quarry' also implies 'that which is hunted', suggesting that the hands are engaged in a chase for the thoughts of the writer, a tracing which results in the legible tracery of the written word. As we will see, the contemplation of the hands is common amongst writers of the modernist period. It is perhaps inevitable that a writer, in daily confrontation with his or her own digits, and most often working in isolation, might attempt to people that solitude with sentient hands; Focillon refers to 'these tireless companions' (65). A second 'peopling' is also occurring in the case of the author, however, in that figures are being 'quarried' which must seem, in their imagined three-dimensionality, plausible things, apt to run away, as Daedalus's excessively lifelike statues were said to do. Focillon certainly suggests, like Lewis, that those characters might be best read, apprehended or grasped through their hands:

> The aptitudes of hands are written in their curves and structure. There are tapered slender hands expert in analysis, with the long and mobile fingers of the logician; prophetic fluid hands; spiritual hands whose very activity has grace and character; and tender hands. (Focillon 1948: 65)

This is a peculiar form of palmistry, with the aim not of divination of the future (although 'prophetic hands' hints in that direction), but of character analysis. Focillon's list also gives us a literalisation of the 'grasp' of mental analysis in his long-fingered logician; he reminds us of the symbolic meaning of 'spiritual' hands, presumably self-touching in prayer; and he gives a mention to the tender hands ('soft [. . .] like a woman's. Aah!') which may caress.

Focillon also anticipates Révèsz in his claims that hands have been crucial to the development of civilisation. We can find in our palms, he suggests, 'handwriting' (bringing us back to Galton's dermatoglyphics), a 'strange landscape' that seems to contain the world, and – in another nod toward palmistry – 'the pattern and as it were the memories of our lives otherwise lost to us, and perhaps as well some even more distant inheritance' (66). Memory of our own lives becomes embodied, then, in the tributary creases of the human palm, but that 'distant inheritance' reminds us that our hands are the product of evolutionary processes. Focillon returns to this point in stating that 'man has created his own hands – by which I mean he has gradually freed them from the animal world, released them from an ancient and innate servitude' (67). Meanwhile, 'hands have also created man', in that their role in knowledge-gathering has made possible the scientific acumen of the contemporary world, Focillon's example here being fluid dynamics (67). The hands have long had a role in scientific measurement, given that 'surface, volume, density and weight are not optical phenomena. Man first learned about them between his fingers and in the hollow of his palm. [. . .] Without hands there is no geometry' (68). Mark Paterson has considered at length the role of the manual in the origins of metrical and geometrical measure (Paterson 2007: 59–77), and we return to this issue in Chapter 3. Focillon's understanding of, and praise for, the human hand involves this potent mixture of evolutionary theory and palmistry, alongside Anaxagoras's suggestion that not only is man the most reasonable of animals because he possesses hands, but he also possesses hands because he is the most reasonable of animals (Aristotle 2001: 686). If the hand is taken to be indicative of our mammalian status and yet our distinction from the apes, we might expect these speculations to occur in a post-Darwin world. Yet here is another way in which the modernist period can be considered a hinge point, brisure or cleavage in relation to questions of the haptic. Modernist writers perceive the civilisation that has been wrought by the dexterity and motility of the human hand, using it as an indicator of the end-point of a teleological trajectory. However, this is also the period in which the 'rule of thumb', the attempt to know – mathematically, geometrically, scientifically – using the touch or shape of the hand, is being most conspicuously outmoded. Scientific exploration, mediated by, for example, the X-ray and the calculations of atomic analysis, is moving far beyond the powers of the hand. Further, technologies synonymous with the modernist period, including the typewriter and the telephone exchange (when not hit by strike action), use the hands as ancillary devices, a quite different relationship to the pen/chisel/hammer tool set, which may be read as at once symbiotically connected to the hand and echoing its operations in their form. The modernist period is therefore one which posits the hand as the ultimate indicator of contemporary civilisation, and which sees its power wane, set aside by scientific and technological discovery. In both cases, or at the hinge, a resurgence of interest in the haptic is discernible, joining Focillon in his fulsome praise, lamenting the supersession of the hand, exploring the alterations to the body's haptic capabilities when confronted by new media and technologies, and panicking about split skins, incapable grasps and hands inexplicably run amok.

Going to the feelies

Think of modernist literature and the question of touch and the tactile, and Aldous Huxley's 'feelies' will perhaps come most readily to mind. In *Brave New World* (1932) Huxley presents a form of cinematic entertainment that seeks not only to thrill the eye, but also to stimulate the haptic responses of the human body, mediated through the grasp of the viewer's/feeler's hand. While the multisensory stimulation of the feelies presents the reader with an insight into bodily pleasure in the year A. F. (After Ford) 632, Huxley has a precursor in the year 1921, in the form of F. T. Marinetti's 'Tactilism: A Futurist Manifesto', originally delivered at the Théâtre de l'Oeuvre. In his later refinement of that piece, 'Tactilism: Toward the Discovery of New Senses' of 1924, Marinetti outlines the present contribution of tactile values to modernist art and life, and speculates about their further exploitation. He states that the roots of his interest in matters manual may be traced to experiments made in 1911, and later recalled when he found himself crawling through 'the subterranean darkness of the trench where my battalion was billeted' in 1917 (Marinetti 2006b: 377). Santanu Das has traced the impact of trench warfare on the tactile responses of participants, pressed against the limits of the human body by virtue of their proximity to flesh, mud and vermin (Das 2005); this is 'life feeling its way' (Marinetti 2006b: 378). Marinetti, while declaring that 'a sense of the tactile has been in existence for a very long time' in 'both literature and plastic art' (Marinetti 2006b: 377), corrals his experiences and experiments into an impassioned claim for the recognition of this sensibility, a recalibration of the human sensorium which will afford 'the perfect spiritual communication between human beings through the epidermis' (Marinetti 2006a: 376). He is in full manifesto mode here, with that form of writing being manual (as the product of the hand)/a manual (in its listing of observations, rules and injunctions), but also engaged in a kind of conjuring (a term also hand-associated) in that it seeks to *make manifest*. Tracing that which already exists as a trend within aesthetic production, it also issues a call-to-arms (or -hands) in its request that we now live, or make art, differently.[5]

Marinetti recalls a summer's day spent at Antignano, where a swim in the sea inspired the theorisation, and later physical manifestation, of the 'first tactile panels' (Marinetti 2006a: 370). 'I was naked in the silken waters lacerated by foaming rocks, sharp-edged like scissors knives razors, swimming among beds of seaweed saturated with iodine,' claims the author; 'I was naked in a sea of flexible steel, rippling against my body in an animated, manly, fertile fashion. [. . .] The sun [. . .] vulcanized my body and bolted the keel of my brow, in full sail' (Marinetti 2006a: 370). The images deployed here recall those of Marinetti's more famous Futurist manifesto, with its suggestive associations between the mechanism of the motorcar and the animal life its capacity for movement implies (Marinetti 2006c: 13). Here, the steel sea has a muscular ripple comparable to the snorting motorcar, but more important is that the steel sea-skin is torn by four kinds of tool created from its own waves, that it in turn caresses the bather's skin ('silk[ily]'), and that the sun 'vulcanize[s]' and 'bolt[s]' the human body until it too takes on the quality of a mechanical apparatus. While the skin of the sea is that which is flagellated (by the wind), or which self-flagellates (using its waves), Marinetti's repetition of the word 'naked' suggests that he too is vulnerable to the cutting tools described, at least before his own transformation into steel. This combination of sea-bathing and masochism suggests that Marinetti may, in writing on tactile issues, have had in mind the work of Algernon Charles Swinburne, whose unfinished work *Lesbia Brandon* (1859–68) contains recollections of sea-swimming. In the latter, the sea is transformed by the wind into a tool of potential punishment (Swinburne 1952: 6), while also forming a body with 'fingers of foam and tired eager lips' (9); meanwhile, the vulnerable skin of the swimmer struggles to remain continent: 'the soul of the sea entered him and filled him with fleshly pleasure [. . .]; he felt the fierce gladness and pleasure and glory of living stroke and sting him all over as with soft hands and sharp lips' (9). Swinburne's fame as a masochist and author of such works as *The Whippingham Papers* (1888) has dominated his literary reputation.[6] Yet for Joyce's Buck Mulligan, it is his sea writing that is crucial: 'Isn't the sea what Algy calls it [in 'The Triumph of Time' (1866)]: a great sweet mother?' (Joyce 2008: 5). It is in the realm of the masochist that both Swinburne and Marinetti are operating in penning sea-bathing scenes, in that both authors play upon the dangerous caress of the sea – a caress that threatens the body with its wind-whipped potential for scarification, and in doing so reiterates, paradoxically, the boundary of that skin. Yet the 'great sweet mother' is present in Marinetti's 1924 piece, since here he speculates on the healing potential of touch between mother and child, and the *'maternal bodily sense'* (Marinetti 2006b: 380) – a potential rejected in the most fierce terms by Brave New London, as we will see.

Thigmophilia

Marinetti recommends sea-bathing as a means of training one's tactile sense, suggesting that the reader 'try [. . .] to distinguish by touch the mingling currents and different temperatures' (Marinetti 2006a: 375). He also prescribes 'wear[ing] gloves for many days, and in that time the brain will focus one's desires on different tactile sensations in the hands' (375), a fascinating suggestion implying that manual thigmophilia, or hunger for touch, is an appetite that can be increased through periods of deprivation or abstinence.[7] Of course, the wearing of gloves does not prevent tactile sensations, since the sheathed hand can continue to determine temperature, shape, solidity and (to a degree) texture, not to mention perceive the sensations of the glove itself. Marinetti's implication is that a covering and unsheathing, as with a giant nerve, increases sensitivity – a practice allied to Babbitt's stringent scrubbing, although the latter's aims were otherwise. Marinetti's trinity of sense-educative undertakings is completed by the recommendation that the reader 'every night, in total darkness, count and be aware of all the objects in [his or her] bedroom' (375). This more familiar trope suggests that the tactile faculties will be sharpened by the absence of the visual sense, a claim common to theories of blindness in this period, as we note in Chapters 2 and 5. Following this training phase, a reader will be ready for engagement with Marinetti's 'scale[s] of tactile values' which further educate the touch, and also form a set of 'values', implying an equivalence with colour values, for 'the Art of Touch' (372). The two scales contain six categories in total, each of which seeks to engage a type of touch, described in terms associated with psychological attitudes or approaches. The first, aiming to stimulate 'very sure, abstract, cold' touch, contains sandpaper and silver (emery) paper (372). The fifth, associated with 'soft, warm, human' sensations, contains 'suede. Horse or dog hair. Human hair and body hair. Maribou [*sic*]' (373). Humanity and warmth, then, involve a relationship with the skin and hair of humans and their companion animals, as skin-to-skin contact is seen, once again, to be vital to human identity. Marinetti further seeks to categorise tactile values, and to calibrate human touch capacities, when he spatialises his tables according to geography, via associations with landscape and region. His first 'abstract or evocative tactile panel' is named '*Sudan-Paris*' and, with its mix of sandpaper, wool and wire brushes, seeks to evoke African visions in the mind of the toucher (373). Paris's silk and velvet is 'very delicate' (373). Value seems to have moved a long way from its colour-value meaning here, as Marinetti suggests that, via tactility, a 'vision' (mental projection or recollection) may be conjured up in the feeler, and that culturally determined connections between silk and the civilised will be played upon.

While Marinetti includes a reference to Boccioni (375), he later states that sculptors are 'unlikely to have [a] gift' for creating tactile panels due to their habit, alongside painters, of 'subordinat[ing] tactile values to visual ones' (375), a claim with which Joyce's Bloom will be seen to disagree. Far better, states the Futurist, to leave the construction of such tables to poets, pianists and typists (375), three figures we have already associated with hand-confrontation above. Marinetti catches the zeitgeist, amongst wild claims and startling images, in his suggestion that the distinction between the five senses is arbitrary, that it is tactilism or, in our terms, a focus upon the haptic that enables this discovery, and that the 'confusion of interlacing senses' of the human sensorium 'can be better observed at the epidermic frontiers of our bodies' (Marinetti 2006b: 379). This interest in human skin and its breach, in emotional and intellectual responses to tactile sensations, and in touch as the grounding sense modality for all forms of somatic perception, ties Marinetti into the lineage of skin thinkers already outlined in this book, as well as establishing him as an important contributor to Huxley's thinking regarding the feelies. However, the feelies find their closest corresponding description in Marinetti's 1921 manifesto, where he proposes the creation of 'tactile theaters' in which seated spectators will 'place their hands on long, tactile conveyor belts which will produce tactile sensations that have different rhythms. One will also be able to mount these panels on turntables and operate them to the accompaniment of music and lights' (Marinetti 2006a: 374). These 'tactile conveyor belts' flowing beneath the sensing hand suggest an apparatus poised between the braille-reading hand of the blind or partially sighted reader, the flow of film through a projector, and the rotating pins of a music-box mechanism, in addition to their more conspicuous allegiance with the A(fter) F(ord) factory. Huxley's feelies – appropriately enough, since they occur approximately 574 years after Marinetti's proto-feelies (that is, 632 years after the birth of Henry Ford in 1863) – utilise a more mysterious means of operation. However, Huxley's investment in the somatic experiences of those living in Brave New London reverberates with echoes of the two tactilism manifestoes as it makes manifest the peculiar role of touch in a society hedged about with alarming prohibitions and permissions of the flesh.

Bear skin

The Assistant Predestinator asks Henry Foster if he will be going to the feelies tonight: 'I hear the new one at the Alhambra is first-rate. There's a love scene on a bearskin rug; they say it's marvellous. Every hair of the bear reproduced. The most amazing tactual effects' (Huxley 1994: 30). While Henry replies that he 'shall make a point of going', Bernard Marx, struggling with life under the World State, presents a 'contemptuous' face (31). Henry's intention to indulge his senses at the feelies associates him with carnal appetites and with the pleasures of contemporary mass entertainment, while the reader gains an early taste of Bernard's discomfort with the World State's prescriptive attitude toward individual identity. The feelies are produced at the largest scale, in terms of both their sensory onslaught and the enormous reach of their distribution. The Hounslow Feely Studio covers 'seven and a half acres' (55); the Bureaux of Propaganda by Television, by Feeling Picture, and by Synthetic Voice and Music range across 'twenty-two floors' (59). The College of Emotional Engineering boasts a Professor of Feelies (141). The scope of this operation – to make, distribute, promote and analyse/legitimate feelies – makes that 'mass entertainment' tag an appropriate one. Meanwhile Dr Gaffney, Provost of Eton, explains that the school library 'contains only books of reference' (147), with distraction to be provided not by books but at the feelies, further boosting attendance at the latter. The library's limited holdings are a result of the fact that 'we don't encourage them [the pupils] to indulge in any solitary amusements' (147). As indicated by the media employed by the multiple bureaux of propaganda, it is communal entertainment that is encouraged – 'mass' entertainment, that is, at the moment of consumption, as well as by dint of the scope of its distribution. The categorisation of reading as a 'solitary amusement' carries an implication of the 'solitary pleasure' of masturbation (see Laqueur 2003), and a prohibition against the latter at first seems to stand at odds with the startling sexual openness of London in 632, in which children as young as seven are encouraged to perform al fresco sexual congresses (Huxley 1994: 27), and in which promiscuity has become the norm from which one dare not deviate (38). Yet it is the solitary nature of the masturbatory act, and its engagement with an individuated selfhood (through the *chiasmatic*, touching-touched gesture of self-touching), that must be avoided, rather than the sexual engagement of the act itself. The masturbator, particularly if undertaking skin-to-skin contact (that is, without the aid of a supplementary prosthesis), is involved, as the cliché has it, in an act of self-love – an act predicated on the notion of an individuated identity, despite its frequent dependence on fantasies of the touch of another. Eton's limited library suggests that reading, that other solitary pleasure, also reiterates the self/world border, both putting forth and appealing to individuated identities, and must be restricted accordingly. It is the voracious reader of *Brave New World*, the Shakespeare-quoting 'savage' John, who forms Huxley's reader's best guide to the prohibitions upon enfleshed selfhood operating in pan-sexual London in the post-Fordian world.

With Lenina, carefully emotionally calibrated member of the World State, and John, former resident of the New Mexico Savage Reservation, we make our first trip to the feelies, and watch that feely of the 'amazing tactual effects' that had so impressed the Assistant Predestinator. While they are waiting for the film to begin, 'the scent organ [. . .] play[s] a delightfully refreshing Herbal Capriccio – rippling arpeggios of thyme and lavender, of rosemary, basil, myrtle, tarragon; a series of daring modulations through the spice keys into ambergris' (150). This synaesthetic conflation between sound and scent mixes the distance sense of hearing with the proximal sense of smell, in anticipation of the sight (distance) and touch (proximal) combinations that are to come in the central filmic performance. The passage also incorporates the slightest nod toward the figure of *Hamlet*'s Ophelia, whose emotional expression becomes displaced into the symbolism of herbs and flowers ('there's fennel for you, and columbines' (IV, v, 177)), and whose presence in this scene anticipates the tragic conclusion to John's love for Lenina. The despairing request of Ophelia's brother Laertes that his tears 'burn out the sense and virtue of mine eye!' (IV, v, 155) echoes Huxley's interest in relationships between sense (intellect or sanity), sense (the body's capacities for perception), and virtue or morality, evinced also in the labelling of John as 'savage'. Huxley concludes the performance of the scent organ by observing that 'the final blast of thyme died away', a phrase carrying a hint of the apocalyptic within its homophonic joke, again striking a note (or scent) of unease beneath the glitter of entertainment. The scent organ as a contraption may have its origins in the experiments of Louis-Bertrand Castel (1688–1757), whose 'ocular harpsichord' was to play 'music' consisting of displays of colour and light, building on contemporary interest in the Aristotelian suggestion that colour, too, might have its own harmonies (see Gage 1993: 233–4). Huxley is, then, engaged in aesthetics, in the affective, sense-provoking aspects of his brave, new (although post-Castelian) art forms.

The lights eventually go down on Lenina and 'the Savage', and 'fiery letters' whose three-dimensionality makes them seem 'self-supported' proclaim: 'THREE WEEKS IN A HELICOPTER. AN ALL-SUPER-SINGING, SYNTHETIC-TALKING, COLOURED, STEREOSCOPIC FEELY. WITH SYNCHRONIZED SCENT-ORGAN ACCOMPANIMENT' (Huxley 1994: 151). Lenina instructs John to 'take hold of those metal knobs on the arms of your chair [. . .] otherwise you won't get any of the feely effects' (151) – as in Marinetti's theatre, it is the touch of the hand that will form the gateway, the point of contact, enabling a range of somatic experiences to flow from the (undisclosed) mechanism attached to the knobs. On the screen appear, 'dazzling and incomparably more solid-looking than they would have seemed in actual flesh and blood, far more real than reality [. . .] a gigantic Negro and a golden-haired young brachycephalic Beta-Plus female' (151). Huxley's 'far more real than reality' here recalls Woolf's description of the cinema, in an essay of 1926, as 'more real, or real with a different reality' (Woolf 1950: 167). Huxley's date night for Lenina and John can in fact be seen as an imaginative extrapolation of Woolf's opening claim that, in order to truly understand the operation of the cinema in her moment, we must consider 'the savages [. . .] watching the pictures' (Woolf 1950: 166). For Woolf, the state of savagery is one of intellectual disengagement when confronted with the movies' dazzle; Huxley's alleged savage, by contrast, is the only audience member who forcibly maintains his intellectual interrogation of the situation in which he finds himself. John struggles to understand how the sensations within his body are being generated through his limited manual connection to an apparatus in the dark: 'He lifted a hand to his mouth; the titillation ceased; let his hand fall back on the metal knob; it began again' (Huxley 1994: 151). The 'titillation' is tactile and erotic, and yet his six thousand fellow spectators (152) seem happy to have their senses, and their sexuality, manipulated in public.

With sound-track and scent organ at full throttle, and vibrations providing 'almost intolerable galvanic pleasure' (152), the scene reaches a multisensory climax; the sexual nature of that climax is clearest in the 'dying moth' quiver of the remnants of galvanic titillation (153). A duet has occurred in the meantime, a 'little [bare skin?] love' is made on the bearskin rug, and Lenina and John find themselves able to confirm that 'every hair' of the latter can be 'separately and distinctly felt' (152). Huxley's decision to depict a 'bearskin rug' scene does not simply foreground the sensory pleasure available to a viewer (toucher) at the feelies. As Anzieu tells us, in addition to fur's obvious status as the flayed skin of a beast, it represents, in masochistic fantasy, 'the return to contact of skin with skin – velvety, voluptuous and odorous (nothing smells as strongly as a new fur) – and to that physical embrace which is one of the attendant pleasures of physical *jouissance*' (Anzieu 1989: 42). Further, the bearskin rug echoes that which we presume is occurring on top of it, since 'fur plays a role as a fetish [. . .] on account of its resemblance to the body hair which masks the genital organs' (Anzieu 1989: 45). Via Anzieu, we can begin to unpick the ways in which the feelies, while appearing to afford physical engagement, in fact prohibit and fetishise intimate fleshly experiences, at the same time as orchestrating an elaborate distraction from desire. While these manipulations and distractions are presented as overwhelming and disorientating for John, for Woolf's savages, the picture-goers of 1926, the stimulation of their whole bodies was to be expected. Associated primarily with the visual, cinema – with only a flat screen, and without the benefit of galvanic knobs – is able to stimulate the whole human sensorium. As Siegfried Kracauer established, the film treats the viewer as a 'human being with skin and hair', presenting 'material elements' that 'directly stimulate the *material layers* of the human being: his nerves, his senses, his entire *physiological substance*' (quoted in Sobchack 2004: 55). The bearskin rug therefore forms a neat junction between romantic cliché, masochistic fetish and cinematic symbol. We return to the tactility of movies, rather than feelies, in Chapter 4.

Huxley's, and the Hounslow Feely Studio's, use of the term 'stereoscopic' to describe the presentation of *Three Weeks in a Helicopter* guides us, once more, toward the haptic. As David Trotter has declared, 'the stereoscope is the historically specific visual technology which haptic theory requires to make its case in relation to that phase of the education of the eye which includes early cinema' (Trotter 2004: 41) in that it offers the 'illusion of tangibility. The illusion is a product of the assertiveness with which objects in the foreground occupy space: the feeling that one could reach out and touch them, or be touched by them' (Trotter 2004: 41). As a proto-cinematic device, the stereoscope's presentation of scenes apparently available to the grasp reiterates the persistence of the Egyptian invitation to touch, even as it moves towards the cinema in its invocation of a space in three dimensions. It is the stereoscopic manipulation of the eye that offers the illusion that the very letters 'STEREOSCOPIC' are standing out 'solid and as though self-supported' in the darkness (Huxley 1994: 151). What is it, then, that makes this miraculous appearance of the possibility of touch, combined with the galvanic manipulation of the sensorium through the connecting hand, such a troubling experience for John? The latter's spasmodic relationship to sexual desire is the result of sense-and-virtue training (to borrow Laertes's term) which took place in the geographically proximate but historically distant Savage Reservation. The incommensurability of this upbringing and the tactile values (in terms of both Marinettian touch and related moral prescriptions) that John encounters in London comes across most clearly during his post-feelies journey home:

> In the taxicopter he hardly even looked at her. Bound by strong vows that had never been pronounced, obedient to laws which had long since ceased to run, he sat averted and in silence. Sometimes, as though a finger had plucked at some taut, almost breaking string, his whole body would shake with a sudden nervous start. (Huxley 1994: 153)

Pulled like a string between the realm of the Reservation and the World State-controlled metropolis, John is an arrow ready to fly and puncture the regulations of the flesh currently in place; this metaphor is literalised in his creation of a bow and arrow in the book's closing scene, as we will see.

Shakespearean savagery

Thrumming with tension, John realises that the mediated experiences of the feelies have been a preview/pre-feel for a proffered sexual encounter with Lenina:

> And suddenly her arms were round his neck; he felt her lips soft against his own. So deliciously soft, so warm and electric that inevitably he found himself thinking of the embraces in *Three Weeks in a Helicopter*. Ooh! Ooh! The stereoscopic blonde and aah! the more than real blackamoor. Horror, horror, horror . . . he tried to disengage himself; but Lenina tightened her embrace. (Huxley 1994: 174)

John's love for Lenina is by this time long-established, leading the reader to presume that sexual contact would be welcomed. However, in his set of 'savage' values, it is the deferral of contact, and of tactile sensations, that allows desire to be generated. Lenina's world is one in which the immediate fulfilment of desire is seen to be a social good – love, partnership and shame have all been sloughed from the sexual relationship, and one is the release of a zip away from fleshly touch, or one trip to the feelies away from sensory indulgence. Lenina's 'electric' kiss prevents John's desire through its immediate availability and its reminder of the synthetic feelings of the feelies. The 'horror' he experiences comes as the skin of her outfit is removed, or horripilated, and her own flesh becomes available to him: 'She put her hand to her neck and gave a long vertical pull; her white sailor's blouse was ripped to the hem; suspicion condensed into a too, too solid certainty' (175). The rip or slice of her white skin/blouse reveals her flesh – flesh which is too solid, too available and too certain. *Hamlet* is here again, we note, with an echo of the Prince's desire that his 'too too solid flesh would melt, / Thaw and resolve itself into a dew' (I, ii, 129–30). That the word 'solid' carries the burden of the near-homophone 'sullied' (a rendering present in the First and Second Quarto in the form 'sallied' and retained as 'sullied' in editions of the play by J. Dover Wilson (see Bowers 2002: 44)) is pertinent here, since Lenina's exposed, solid, available flesh is now tainted, and rejected by John in a fit of rage. The intertext of *Hamlet* can be read as a skin play, in fact, perhaps most clearly when Gertrude is importuned:

> Mother, for love of grace,
> Lay not that flattering unction to your soul,
> That not your trespass but my madness speaks;
> It will but skin and film the ulcerous place,
> Whiles rank corruption, mining all within,
> Infects unseen.
>
> (III, iv, 145–50)

In behaving in accordance with the norms of London in 632, Lenina provokes the 'savage' behaviour of John, and yet the latter's apparent violent madness is a response to the trespass of his beloved on his treasured experience of unquenched desire. Lenina's solid/sullied flesh is, like the feelies, or the drug-induced 'soma' holidays of Huxley's novel, a contravention of the vital human, individuating privilege to desire independently, and without immediate satiation.

It is in an earlier scene, prior to date night at the feelies, in which John approaches Lenina and does not touch her, that the connection between his desire, his restraint from touch and his individuated identity is most clearly drawn. When Lenina is staying in the Savage Reservation, John invades her temporary home:

> Opening a box, he spilt a cloud of scented powder. His hands were floury with the stuff. He wiped them on his chest, on his shoulders, on his bare arms. Delicious perfume! He shut his eyes; he rubbed his cheek against his own powdered arm. Touch of smooth skin against his face, scent in his nostrils of musky dust – her real presence. 'Lenina,' he whispered. 'Lenina!' (Huxley 1994: 129–30)

John here creates a kind of prescient enactment of the multisensory stimulation later to be provided by the mechanism of the feelies, in that he entertains his eyes, his tactile sensibilities and his capacity to smell. Anointing himself with the scent he associates with his beloved, he both reiterates his own dermic border and allows his proximal senses to fantasise about her proximity. That this involves gestures of self-touching does lead us to consider the masturbatory, although the practice of anointing gives his gestures a more spiritual, quasi-religious aspect. The fact that Lenina's scent is 'her real presence', whereas her later disrobing only reveals her 'too solid'/sullied flesh, suggests that it is in the imaginative evocation of tactile contact, and the physical deferral of the possibility of *jouissance*, that both masochistic desire and noble feeling reside. John proceeds to Lenina's bedroom, where he finds that her soma holiday, despite its bodily name, has provided her with respite from her actual somatic experiences; she is present but insensible. Kneeling beside her bed in a way that echoes Hamlet's posture at the bed of the sleeping Gertrude, John gazes, clasps hands, and quotes Shakespeare. Returning to the solitary pleasures of his childhood reading experiences, he finds a historical vocabulary for desire, and for withheld sensual experience, unavailable to 632 London. John's first recourse is to *Troilus and Cressida*, which provides a hymn to Lenina's hand, 'in whose comparison all whites are ink' and 'to whose soft seizure / The cygnet's down is harsh' (131). This choice of text leads us to Troilus's declaration to Pandarus that he is 'mad / In Cressid's love' and that any reference to the latter's beauty 'Pour'st [pain] in the open ulcer of my heart', and 'instead of oil and balm, / Thou lay'st in every gash that love has given me / The knife that made it' (I, i, 49–64). In a modification of Hamlet's statement that mendacious unctions would ill cover the ulcerous place of Gertrude's betrayal, here the potential oil and balm of an evocation to beauty knifes its way into ulcers and gashes of desire.

John next seeks to express his passion (*paschein*, active undergoing of pain) for the soma-sedated Lenina with reference to *Romeo and Juliet*. When a fly lands on Lenina's body, John recalls phrases that lead us to

Romeo's statement that 'more validity, / More honourable state, more courtship lives / In carrion flies than Romeo' since they can approach the 'white wonder of Juliet's hand' and steal kisses denied her lover (III, iii, 33–40). The fly is an interesting figure here, in that it writes a black script upon a white hand in a way that returns us to Troilus, as well as forming a further intertextual connection with John Donne's 'The Flea', in which the poet's artful persuasions famously suggest that physical union will be of no further consequence than the intermingling of bloods within the titular flea (Donne 1950: 48). The fly also facilitates the reading that Lenina is at this moment a statue, insensible of its passage, or that she is suffering a kind of imagined formication or crawl of the skin – appropriate given that, via its association with schizophrenia, formication links to the split self of the soma experience. Most strongly, the carrion fly suggests that Lenina is pure *carné*, as good as dead, since her selfhood has departed on a drug-facilitated holiday, leaving only her carcass being. The love-against-the-odds of Romeo and Juliet begins, of course, with questions of origin or family allegiance, and ends with death as the (ultimately breached) barrier between lovers. Here, John's outsider status as the savage son of a hatchery worker seems incommensurable with Lenina's alpha grading, and her 'little death' of the sexual escape to soma-land prevents her from sensing John's presence. This lengthy, complicated scene of powdering, prayerfulness and praise is crucial to a haptically attuned reading of Huxley's novel in that it establishes John as both tormented by and wedded to sexual and emotional desire, a desire which depends upon the deferral of physical gratification. John, then, swears an anachronistic allegiance to an outmoded historical tradition of direct, unmediated sensory experience, and of deferred sexual gratification, in a time of sensual over-stimulation through non-human mechanisms, and of sexual plenty. He is the last gasp, or grasp, of human-to-human contact, in a way which resonates with Huxley's 1930s reader, while baffling his fellow denizens of 632 London.

Signifying nothing

In conversation with the Controller, John is able to express some of his repulsion in the face of World State practices of touch, in doing so giving vent to some of the reader's own potential frustrations. Arguing that the feelies 'don't mean anything' and are 'told by an idiot', John is assured that they 'mean a lot of agreeable sensations to the audience', with fellow sceptic Helmholtz suggesting that feelies are 'works of art [made] out of practically nothing but pure sensation' (Huxley 1994: 201). John's 'told by an idiot' claim echoes *Macbeth* – 'It is a tale / Told by an idiot, full of sound and fury, / Signifying nothing' (V, v, 26–8) – and neatly evokes the sensory onslaught of the feelies. It also, of course, allies *Brave New World* with William Faulkner's preceding *The Sound and the Fury* (1929), to whose use of an *idiot savant* narrator Huxley's use of John, *idiot sauvage*, may be compared. The synaesthesia of the contemporary pictures – full of sound and feelies, we might say – moves from the aesthetic (sensing/feeling) manipulation of intellectual sensibilities through access to sensory capacities, to the *anaesthetic*, cutting off the sensation/intellect connection. John's revelation, as a savage watching the pictures, is that feeling (sensory stimulation) has been severed from feeling (emotional response), with the former standing in for and displacing the latter. Reduced to pure tactile sensation with his hand on the galvanic knobs, confronted with the solid flesh of a sexually available woman, John is full of fury at London's inability to permit him his own, self-defining desires. On the Reservation, he had made coil pots with Mitsima, a craft activity which nourished body and mind: 'to fashion, to give form, to feel his fingers gaining in skill and power – this gave him an extraordinary pleasure' (Huxley 1994: 122). John returns to the creative crafts of a Daedalusian inventor in his final retreat from London life, where he shapes a bow and arrow at his hermitage – a fashioning that recalls his earlier, over-stimulated resonances as a taut string ready to snap. This activity is a 'pure delight', due to its demand not only for skill but also for 'patience', that deferred gratification for which John yearns (225).[8]

The delight is not to last. Tracked down by the 'big-game photographer' (230) of the Feely Corporation, the floridly named Darwin Bonaparte, the weapon-toting John becomes the hunted. The photographer in his turn attracts a crowd, breaking the hermeticism of the hermitage: 'in the posture of an animal at bay, [John] stood with his back to the wall of the lighthouse, staring from face to face in speechless horror, like a man out of his senses' (233). Upon Lenina's appearance, John whips her, shouting 'Oh, the flesh!' (235) as he strikes her sadistically, later turning the whip on himself in acts of Swinburnean masochism that seek to enforce a return of those senses which have been mediated through the contraption of the feelies. Desperate to mark out his own right to self-determined fleshly experience through the pain of flagellation, John is horrified to find that the crowd sexualise his practices: 'they began to mime the frenzy of his gestures, striking at one another as the Savage struck at his own rebellious flesh, or at that plump incarnation of turpitude writhing in the heather at his feet' (236). In the false sound and fury of the crowd, John's attempt to claim the right of pain, and to reiterate the boundary of his own body, as well as that of Lenina's, to mortify the flesh in a direct connection to its non-sexual, carnal nature, becomes only a mime when taken up by the others. This is another show, their recreation of the scene they witness upon their own skin reducing this episode to a kind of feely *en plein air*. It is the Savage's attempt at fleshly rebellion that is in its death throes here, while Lenina's 'too, too solid flesh' refuses to resolve itself into a dew. Instead, groaning in the gloaming, she is stubbornly *incarnated*, enfleshed and available.

Intimacy and disgust

John's rebellion, then, is his insistence on the self-defining right to the experience of desire, only to be experienced if the indulgences of the flesh can be postponed, which is to say experienced imaginatively in the first instance. He also insists on the right to masochistically imposed physical pain, the true experience of the somatic system that the 'soma holiday' and the feelies seek, despite their names, to evade. Through recourse to his memories of the 'solitary pleasure' not of masturbation but of reading, John finds a means of expressing this anachronistic set of tactile expectations through Shakespeare's skin plays, folios read as having a hypothetical (sub-story) skin. Lenina's too solid flesh – flesh, that is, which is too available to immediate contact – makes her the most conspicuous example of 632 London's insistence on immediate, shared and commitment-free sexual and sensory pleasure. However, Lenina is far from alone in her lack of a selfhood dependent on a proprietorial relationship to one's own fleshly envelope. The self/skin connection has been severed intentionally through the child-rearing, or child-propagating, practices of the World State. With birth now confined to hatcheries, and the family dismantled, disgust has been attached to maternal caresses known to be essential to the formation of a sense of self. Mustapha Mond, Resident Controller for Western Europe, both expresses and inculcates this disgust when he describes to a group of students the past approach to a family life:

> And home was as squalid psychically as physically. Physically, it was a rabbit hole, a midden, hot with the *frictions* of tightly packed life, reeking with emotion. What suffocating *intimacies* [. . .]. Maniacally, the mother brooded over her children [. . .]. 'My baby, and oh, oh, *at my breast, the little hands*, the hunger, and that unspeakable agonizing pleasure!' (Huxley 1994: 33, my emphases)

It is just such disgusting intimacies, which is to say reiterations of the dermic border of the child, that facilitate the formation of a definitive sense of self – the notion of an individuated and yet coherent self that is lacking in the schizophrenic, as noted above. And it is the moment of birth itself which, via the birth canal of the mother, gives the child its first experience of skin-to-skin contact (Anzieu 1989: 61). With birth now confined to the scientific procedures or 'Bokanovsky's Process' (Huxley 1994: 3) of the hatchery, and mother-child tactility prevented by the systematic dismantling of the family unit, the touch of precocious sexual play takes its place. In this way, immediate sexual gratification is learned, even as the individual identity enabled by the inhabitation of continent skin is prevented. Such a loss of dermic identity is vital to the smooth running of the World State, carefully policing the solitary pleasures of selfhood in order to ensure that all are happy with their place in the predestined (scientifically selected) hierarchy. The notion of self-possession is vital here. We associate the attribute with decorum which, in relation to rhetorical performance, denotes language and gestural behaviour modified to suit location and audience. It also relates to 'civic mutuality' (Barnard 2001: 65). To be self-possessed is, then, to know how to control one's body, and thence how to operate that body in the realm of civil society. Yet it is also the possession of the self, where that term 'possessed' refers to the intellectual ownership of a consciousness experienced as a unity, and also retains a hint of the notion of spiritual possession, to pour spirit into a bodily housing, that is, to incarnate. To be self-possessed is, in 632 London, a great sin, for you can neither own a body (given that it must be available for work and for the sexual pleasure of others) nor conceptualise a self that might take up carnal residence, given the resistance to one's place in the social order that could follow. Considering the notion not only of feelies but of feeling – sensory, emotional and aesthetic – within *Brave New World*, it is possible to see that the transgressions of John the Savage are those made under the auspices or aegis of the haptic.

Sensuous scholarship

Recent scholarship on the sensuous has paved the way for what will no doubt be a series of studies treating the operation of the haptic sense modality within the literary realm. Discernible within this scholarly field is a shift from the distance to the proximal senses, that is, from sight and hearing to taste, touch and smell. Attempts to address the senses have typically come from the fields of sociology, anthropology, cultural studies and art history, while sensory experience has proved a meaningful way to explore the borderlines between those disciplines. Constance Classen's *Worlds of Sense* (1993) and *The Book of Touch* (2005) have been influential, alongside Paul Stoller's *Sensuous Scholarship* (1997).

Classen's monograph *The Deepest Sense: A Cultural History of Touch* (2012) considers an impressively broad historical sweep. David Howes's wide-ranging collection *Empire of the Senses* appeared in 2005, with Jim Drobnick's *The Smell Culture Reader* (2006) affording attention to an oft-neglected sense. Benthien, Connor and Gabriel Josipovici have offered fascinating studies of the skin as a sensory medium that is consistently culturally reimagined, the last in *Touch: An Essay* (1996). Within film theory, the work of Laura U. Marks has been widely taken up, with her 2000 monograph *The Skin of the Film* doing much to rehabilitate the term 'haptic', and to identify its use by Riegl and thence by Deleuze and Guattari. Other writers on film, including Giuliana Bruno, Vivian Sobchack and Jennifer M. Barker, have forged their own paths, although their work is best understood as conjuring with Marks's central tenets. As we will see in tackling film in Chapter 4, Marks's deployment of the term 'haptic' seems at first resistant to the idea of a haptic *narrative*, and David Trotter has been instrumental in opening up the possibility of haptic engagement in narrative film – an important step (see Trotter 2008). More recently, Milena Marinkova has offered a Marksian reading of the films and texts of Michael Ondaatje. Meanwhile Juhani Pallasmaa has attended to Benjamin's discussion of the haptic and the habitual in processes of inhabitation, and has explored the notion of haptic architecture. While this chapter has made use of Aristotle, Diodorus and Merleau-Ponty, a more contemporary tradition of tactile investigation exists in the field of philosophy, through the work of Jacques Derrida, Gilles Deleuze, Félix Guattari, Paul de Man and Jean-Luc Nancy. Mark Paterson, nominally within the field of human geography but ranging far beyond his discipline, has done much to track the increasing interest in touch in today's academy, while also subjecting performance art and computer technologies to haptic analysis (see Paterson 2005; 2007; 2009). Fascinating though all of this recent sensuous scholarship is, it is for the most part made up of cultural histories of aspects of embodiment, works of film theory, and philosophical meditations upon the phenomenological tradition. The *literary* representation of questions of touch, the tactile or that broader quartet of somatic experience I use to further parse the term 'haptic' is a new area of study building upon this wider engagement in the business of the bodily. Tim Armstrong (on the body) and Santanu Das (on intimate touch) are the near neighbours of this area. I cannot give a full account here of what the haptic might bring to literary studies, nor can I formulate a set of haptically attuned critical practices that will operate across all literary historical periods. I aim instead to use the haptic as a new way of grasping modernist literature, and seek to show why this book might sensibly be only the beginning of such explorations.

In what remains of this study, I make use of the histories of the haptic traced provisionally here, first to form the basis of an excursus tackling the figure of Pygmalion, and thence to shed light on four prominent members of the modernist canon: James Joyce, Virginia Woolf, Dorothy Richardson and D. H. Lawrence. In each case, these authors are of particular interest to me because they in some way prove themselves recalcitrant when chivvied into a line-up of haptic modernist authors. Joyce is perhaps my most biddable subject in this respect, since *Ulysses* in particular foregrounds its interest in bodily exploration. Trouble comes from the capaciousness of the project – as a book about everything, can we be sure that we are tackling a book about touch? Woolf is more problematic, since she is read by many critics as a writer of psychological exploration, with an interest in the body only in metaphorical terms. But I take seriously here the author's suggestion that 'the imagination is largely the child of the flesh' (Woolf 1977: xiii) and consider the moments in her writing when the body recurs, and recurs haptically, in particular looking at her treatment of the expressive potential of the human hand in a world which seems to have moved beyond its ken. Also crucial is that notion of the moment, since I argue that the hand is most often used within Woolf's *oeuvre* as an outmoded temporal marker. Richardson's *Pilgrimage* (1915–35) is doubly invested in the haptic experience, most obviously as something to be depicted at the level of content. She talks of the haptic or embodied responses of her reading protagonists, as well as exploring connections between the writing room and the human skin. Yet she also conceives of the act of pilgrimage, which structures her novel sequence in its entirety, as a haptic matter. Meanwhile Richardson's beloved cinema operates, in her own phenomenology of spectatorship, via an appeal to the epidermic eye. Lawrence stands apart from these other authors in one important way – he is sceptical about the (photographic and cinematic) camera that the others hold dear, and make use of in theoretical terms. But he *is* convinced, as we saw above, by the capacities of the human hand as a mode of sexual and spiritual contact and, crucially, as that which knows. We end with 'Horrible Haptics', a chapter that could reasonably be sub-headed 'When Hands Go Wrong'. Here I identify a set of texts that respond to their contemporary world by conjuring nightmares regarding the hand's capacities for independent thought and action. Extending Lawrence's marvelling statement that the hand *knows*, we can access texts that panic about hands run amok. Such panic can be seen to stem in a direct and legible way from the alterations to concepts of the haptic registered in the work of my four main authors. In each case, I am attempting to investigate what a haptically attuned critical practice might bring to the texts of a much-studied writer. I am also taking the opportunity to spin away from the orbit of that writer and consider a tangentially related matter of haptic experience in the modernist period. The latter strategy allows me to create further nuances in my understanding of the haptic histories that bear upon literary practice, and also to widen my canon of haptic modernists, spotting a sensuous sensibility beyond the confines of the modernist avant-garde, just as I have aimed to do in this opening chapter.

Since, as the foregoing exploration of haptic histories has established, skin is a kind of 'base' sense, a grounding, this study has the potential to become a Casaubonian key to all mythologies. To evade such a fate, I return repeatedly to the operation of that 'poster boy' of touch, the human hand, to explicitly described skin sensations and, secondarily, to renderings of kinaesthesis, proprioception and the vestibular sense. While I will consider spiritual and healing touch, mediumship, anointing, scarification, sexual touch, the 'keeping in touch' of epistolary practice, labouring hands, craft and the hand, the hands of the blind, braille, the experience of mechanised transport, the touching or licking eye of the sculpture viewer or cinema spectator, rogue hand fantasies, touch in a non-Western context and many more, I cannot possibly do full justice to each of these practices, concepts or issues. My aim is to maintain a place centre-stage for those moments when a close reading, with matters haptic in mind, can illuminate a notable preoccupation with haptic experiences in the work of my authors. I try as far as possible to filter out quotidian references to hands and acts of touch which are nothing over and above the daily use of a vital human organ/resource – often this means identifying a critical mass of haptic experiences within a text or scene. Most importantly, I want to try to answer the question of *why* it is that modernist texts – literary, scientific, philosophical and journalistic – return with unprecedented alacrity to the haptic experiences of the human body. Or, on the other hand, to identify clusters of haptic happenings within modernist texts as a means of understanding the touch-transforming social and historical contexts out of which those writings emerge.

Notes

1. Lang's film posits a triangulated relationship between head, heart and hands that will recur throughout this study in the course of exploring the psychological and emotional aspects of the physical experience of touch. Lang's

'head' is, figuratively speaking, the Club of Sons, whose privileged position in the skies of the metropolis connotes their control. The 'hands' are the workers confined to the underground city, and we return to that synecdochic use of the hand in a moment.

2. The *Lady's Pictorial* was at this time published on the Thursday prior to its cover date, meaning that the edition I cite here would in fact have appeared on the very day that Joyce depicts, and which is now drawing to a close (Gerty's scene occurring, of course, at 8pm).

3. Gerty's Homeric parallel Nausicaa, daughter of King Alcinous, offers the naked Odysseus (who has swum to shore after leaving Calypso's island) not only clothing and sustenance, but also 'olive-oil' to apply to his skin after he has bathed (Homer 1946: 108).

4. Leopold Bloom 'review[s] the nails of his left hand, then those of his right hand. The nails, yes. [. . .] My nails. I am just looking at them: well pared' (Joyce 2008: 89). In *Portrait* pared nails are a sign of femininity and/or homosexuality – Tusker Boyle is called 'Lady Boyle' for his self-manicure habit (Joyce 2000a: 43), while the disconcertingly groomed Mr Gleeson is also suspected of paring (44).

5. Marinetti's claims to the status of pioneer were challenged by Francis Picabia, who argued that tactilism was the invention of the sculptor Edith Clifford Williams, and as early as 1916. Further, Guillaume Apollinaire had given a 1918 lecture on questions of tactility, later published in the *Mercure de France*. Marinetti is explicit in his statement that his own experiments build on an interest established by other artists and thinkers; Picabia suggested he was not the first to spot and exploit the trend. (See note, Günter Berghaus in Marinetti, *Critical Writings*, 496–7.)

6. I am grateful to Heather Tilley for drawing my attention to Swinburnean sea-bathing.

7. The mortification of the senses is, additionally, allied with practices of religious devotion and penance – such mortification may involve abstinence or the withdrawal of stimulus, or the insulting of a particular sense with that which is abhorrent to it. In *Portrait* Stephen, having repented of his sexual exploits, uses sensory mortification to atone for past ills, and brings to touch 'the most assiduous ingenuity of inventiveness' (Joyce 2000a: 163).

8. Huxley finds common ground with other works of speculative fiction in his inclusion of craft practices, each considering craft in order to reassert the role of the hand in societies where many processes are now customarily given over to the mechanical. *Brave New World*'s nearest neighbours in this endeavour are most obviously William Morris's *News from Nowhere* (1890) and H. G. Wells's *When the Sleeper Wakes* (1899; revised 1910).

Excursus: Pygmalion

As recounted in Ovid's *Metamorphoses*, 'Pygmalion' is the story of a now celibate sculptor who, revolted by womankind, falls in love with his own creation – a statue of the goddess Galatea – and, begging Venus's kindness on her feast day, secures the animation of his statue/ love. The story introduces questions of the sculptor's art, the notion that art may exceed life in its beauty ('Such art his art concealed' (Ovid 2008: 234, l.252)), the peculiarities of celibate bachelorhood, the status of persons, and the moment of animation or level of sensual capacity necessary within proto-human sculpture, in order for impropriety to be perceived. It is the latter which truly animates this story of animation, since the sculpture is, we gather, naked. To caress and kiss it is, in the case of its inanimate status, a fetishistic oddity. To take such advantage of a sentient yet statue-still being is a contravention of decency in sexual and moral terms. Further, as Galatea is a product of the sculptor's own hand, the story carries the frisson of incestuous love, along with the libidinal freedoms stemming from the fact that as an artistic creation she is free from the social context of family (barring father/creator) or chaperones. 'Pygmalion' is, then, a haptic tale – one concerned with aesthetics (beauty, and also feeling, in terms of both sense and sentiment), with the contemplation of modes of art (an effort that often, as we saw via Benjamin in Chapter 1, brings the haptic into play), with the sensuous and sensual aspects of touch, and with the role of flesh and of tactile capacities in the determination of the self.

The moment of Galatea's metamorphosis or, more properly, transubstantiation into a living woman is a Venus-wrought miracle that confirms the mimetic power of Pygmalion as a sculptor. Galatea is not, in fact, a shapeshifter, as that 'metamorphosis' term leads us to suppose, since her maker's craft has shaped her to perfection. Instead, her shift is one of medium or substance, from marble into flesh and, crucially, from an inanimate artwork into a *being that can perceive shape*, which is to say one which has the capacity to move and to touch, and to distinguish in doing so both a self, and a world beyond that self. These two discoveries are, as we noted in Chapter 1, mutually constitutive. Yet Ovid most conspicuously frames the story as one of love, infatuation and desire. Pygmalion's return, to a lover not of marble but of yielding flesh, is rapturously written:

> And he went home, home to his heart's delight,
> And kissed her as she lay, and she seemed warm;
> Again he kissed her and with marvelling touch
> Caressed her breast; beneath his touch the flesh
> Grew soft, its ivory hardness vanishing,
> And yielded to his hands
>
> (Ovid 2008: 233–4, l.279–84)

While the sculptor has caressed his creation before, this is the first time that 'yield[ing]' has certainly occurred, where that term indicates both a reduction in firmness as the marble transforms into flesh, and submission beneath the imposed desires of another. Pygmalion, thanking Venus, achieves a kiss: 'at last / His lips pressed real lips, and she, his girl, / Felt every kiss, and blushed, and shyly raised / Her eyes to his and saw the world in him' (234, l.307–10). This kiss is crucial in its dramatisation of the moment of tactile reciprocity, neatly rendered in the human lips that, as one set, are already the touching-touched, and in combination with the set of a lover form the most obvious representation of romantic and libidinal contact. Galatea blushes in response to a post-lapsarian realisation that she is naked – acceptable in her former domain of art; acceptable, that is, when she is *static*, but unacceptable in contact with a new lover, and when she is *animated*, thus having the capacity to move and experience touch. In a further iteration of the reciprocal nature of the kiss, we also have Derrida's ocular *chiasmus*, in that Galatea and Pygmalion cross looks for the first time, with the latter representing 'the world', that which, through these early touching and looking experiments, Galatea has determined as the 'not me'. The moment of Galatea's looking is particularly significant since, as Derrida has noted, all statues are born blind: 'the eyes of sculpture are always closed, "walled up" in any case [. . .] or turned inward, more dead than alive' (Derrida 1993: 44). Galatea is, in her transformation, granted eyes. One final *chiasm* is relevant here, since that word's meaning of 'cross(ed)' brings us to the cross of Christ's Passion, and thence to *paschein*, the active undergoing of bodily suffering (as we saw in Chapter 1). Galatea's fall into the status of a feeling body is, inevitably, a fall into the capacity for bodily pain. In Ted Hughes's translation of Ovid's tale, the sexual implications of Galatea's awakening (the latter a term which itself carries a sexual burden) are clear: 'On his knees / He sobbed his thanks to Venus. And there / Pressed his lips / On lips that were alive' (Hughes 1997: 150). Given his kneeling position, we presume that Pygmalion is applying his oral lips to the vaginal lips of Galatea, those other organs of self-touching (see Irigaray 1986: 24), and that her blush is one of sexual arousal as well as naked shame. The move here is from Galatea's status as an aesthetic object, craft product and sex toy (in her inert provision of arousal and stimulation), to her status as a touching, feeling, enfleshed person with capacities for desire. The moment of greatest import in the story, the hinge point at which her statue history ceases, and from which her haptic life unfolds, is the one in which Galatea herself, always available as an *object* of touch, becomes a tactile subject.

Herder in the sculpture gallery

In its combination of the crucial concerns of aesthetics – form, beauty, perception, feeling – the Pygmalion story has been of great use to those considering the history of art, and those attempting to explore the nature of the human sensory apparatus. That these two endeavours are interwoven is clear within the tale itself. Perhaps the most famous utilisation of the Pygmalion myth in these theoretical terms comes in Étienne Bonnot de Condillac's *Traité des Sensations* of 1754, which achieved a renowned translation into English in 1930. The date of that republication is testament to the renewed interest in the human sensory faculties, and their role in the perception of art, within the modernist period. Condillac makes use of the Pygmalion myth as an overarching structure, imagining the statue of Galatea as she accrues her sensory faculties, sense by sense, and crucially attributing to touch the ability of the statue to recognise her status as a living being (Condillac 1930: 88). However, it is with the subsequent publication of Johann Gottfried Herder's *Sculpture: Some Observations on Shape and Form from Pygmalion's Creative Dream* – first published in Riga in 1778 – that the connections between touch and the perception of sculpture are most thoroughly explored. Herder's efforts to establish a viewer's practice, that is to convey in full the experience of perceiving sculptural work, makes a contribution to the consolidation of art historical practices written under the influence of Alexander Gottlieb Baumgarten. It is Baumgarten who is responsible for the first use of the term 'aesthetics' as it is now understood, deploying it in his *Meditationes Philosophicae* of 1735 to describe the 'science of perception' *and* 'philosophical poetics', or the study of works of art (Baumgarten, quoted in Gaiger 2002: 7). Herder's 1778 contribution was built upon his experiences of Louis XIV's sculpture collection at Versailles, and, crucially, the extensive collection of Johann Wilhelm, ultimately housed in the Mannheim Drawing Academy. In fact, Herder was not to visit Rome, where he could view many of the originals of which copies were held in Versailles and Mannheim, until 1788 – a decade, that is, after the publication of his *Sculpture*, which sang the praises of these classical works (Breul 1904: 3). Herder's bid to understand the effects of sculptural viewing upon the human sensorium have philosophical ramifications beyond this field of proto-art historical analysis, a fact perhaps best emphasised in his redrafting of the famous Cartesian statement 'cogito ergo sum' as 'Ich fühle mich! Ich bin!' ('I feel! I am!') (Herder, quoted in Gaiger 2002: 9).

Herder's speculations within the field of sensory experience owe much to the Molyneux question, also referred to as the Molyneux problem, a philosophical debate that had a considerable impact on the work of John Locke, George Berkeley, Voltaire, Condillac and Denis Diderot, amongst others. William Molyneux posed his provocative question in a letter to Locke:

> Suppose a Man born blind, and now adult, and taught by his touch to distinguish between a Cube and a Sphere of the same metal, and nighly of the same bigness, so as to tell, when he felt one and t'other, which is the Cube, which is the Sphere. Suppose then the Cube and Sphere placed on a table, and the Blind Man made to see. *Quaere*, Whether by his sight, before he touch'd them, he could now distinguish, and tell, which is the Globe, which the Cube. (Locke 1976–89, vol. 3: 482–3)

To answer yes is to suggest 'that our perceptions are amodal in their spatial systems' (Eilan, quoted in Paterson 2007: 39), whereas to answer no – in the company, that is, of Locke, Berkeley and Molyneux himself – is to argue for the independent, specific and incommensurable operation of the sensory systems of the human body. Locke incorporates consideration of the problem in the second edition of his *Essay Concerning Human Understanding* (1694) (Tunstall 2011: 4). The debate introduces the broader question of the possibility of human ideas existing prior to sensory experience. We will return to Molyneux's question within its primary field of enquiry (optics) when considering blindness in Chapters 2 and 5. For Herder, the continuing pertinence of this historical debate within eighteenth-century philosophy provides the groundwork for his attempts to establish the way in which works of art in three dimensions, which is to say the plastic art of sculpture, are apprehended by the perceiving body. These considerations lead to questions regarding the distinction between forms of artistic expression – that between painting and sculpture (*paragone*), and that between poetry and painting (*ut picture poesis*). Crucially, Herder was able to discuss with Diderot these matters regarding human confrontation with the artwork, during a visit to Paris in July 1769 (Gaiger 2002: 2). Eye problems experienced by the former may also have played their part in his fascination with the distinctions and contingencies of the senses of sight and touch. Herder was operated upon by Johann Lobstein in Strasbourg in September 1770, but struggled with failing sight throughout his life (Breul 1904: 2). Despite the parlous state of his vision, the philosopher would never-theless have been sure of his ongoing capacity to perceive beauty, since he claims (with a hint of Anaxagoras's thoughts on prehensile reason, noted above) that:

> the light that strikes my eye can no[t] [. . .] give me access to concepts such as solidity, hardness, softness, smoothness, form, shape, or volume [. . .]. Only human beings have them, because alongside reason we possess a hand that can feel and grasp. (Herder 2002: 36)

It is in this grasp that beauty can be apprehended, since true beauty relates to three-dimensionality: 'What then is beauty for the sense of touch? It is not colours! [. . .] [It is] bodies!' (Herder, quoted in Gaiger 2002: 14). Drawing tightly the connection between the beautiful and the three-dimensional – between *formosa* and form, we might say – Herder's contention is that the sculpture's beauty, truthfulness and appeal come through its invocation of the haptic capacities of the human sensorium. It is, however, important to note that Herder is not advocating actual tactile engagement with sculptural works. Rather, he suggests that our imaginative faculties, faculties educated by our prior touch experiences, generate a psychological form of touch:

> Consider the lover of art [. . .]. With his soul he seeks to *grasp* the image that arose from the arm and the soul of the artist. Now he has it! The illusion has worked; the sculpture lives and the soul *feels* that it lives. His soul speaks to it, not as if the soul sees, but as if it touches, as if it feels. (Herder 2002: 41)

There is, then, a grasp – a feeling/understanding grasp – contained within vision when it is applied to images of the human body rendered through the sculptor's art. Actual manual contact with the material reality of a statue would, however, shatter its claims to bodily status, preventing its vital illusion. In fact, a kind of reverse Pygmalionism would occur, where the apparently fleshly would be revealed as simply marble, at the expense of beauty, and of truth.

'Curves the world admires'

Chapter 1 explored the manifestations of these histories of the haptic in the modernist period, and found that matters of touch and the tactile resurface whenever aesthetics is understood in its fullest, most Baumgartenian sense, connecting sensory *and* emotional perception to the contemplation of art. One text in particular can be read as an extended conversation between a modernist author and her Pygmalion-contemplating forebears, affording an insight into the way in which haptic histories can be traced in literary work at this time. Rebecca West's novel *Sunflower*, abandoned uncompleted in 1927, was suppressed by the author in her lifetime, and published only posthumously in 1986. A conspicuously autobiographical work, it has largely been treated to critical analyses that aim in the first instance to unpick the correspondences between the novel and West's life as lived (see Glendinning 1987; Schweizer 2002), and attention to its other preoccupations has been limited. It is possible to comply with these readings, and to treat the novel as a thinly veiled attempt on West's part to work through her own experiences, in the person of our heroine Sunflower, as the mistress of H. G. Wells (whose novel proxy is the feline Lord Essington), and the infatuated lover of William Maxwell Aitken, better known as Lord Beaverbrook (*Sunflower*'s Francis Pitt). The phrase 'work through' is used advisedly here, in preference to 'depict' or 'explore', since West wrote *Sunflower* whilst undergoing psychoanalysis, in large part to understand the failure of her relationship with Beaverbrook. Victoria Glendinning has observed that the end pages of the incomplete manuscript for the novel contain notes recording West's dreams and experiences as an analysand (Glendinning 1986: 273). *Sunflower* therefore contains a knotty tangle of the autobiographical and the mythic, with psychoanalytic practices forming the means of connecting the two. However, it is by considering the novel in relation to one particular myth – that of Pygmalion – that it is best understood. This effort to trace the statue myth at the heart of the novel also serves to rehabilitate the latter from the status of the self-involved, unsuccessful or incomplete. In Ovidian terms, *Sunflower* is a thorough and fascinating exploration of beauty, touch, transformation and desire.

Sunflower is a stage actress, and an extraordinarily beautiful one, yet her beauty finds her only dwindling favour with her aging lover Essington, and rather too much favour with members of the public, for whom the combination of good looks and a long-term affair with an established figure is a compelling one – she is 'News' (West 1986: 14). While 'Essington care[s] only for thick books, for interminable talks about ideas that would go on being true if the human body had no flesh on its bones' (6), Sunflower's identity stubbornly adheres to her flesh.[1] We first meet her at a garage, where car trouble has brought her into confrontation with a small gathering of strangers: 'the look of them made her apprehensive, for though they were all smiling [. . .] there was a kind of grease on the surface of their gaze, a kind of scum of squalid feeling' (10). As an actress, a known face in the newspapers and via publicity shots, Sunflower has a body which is both her own, and available to the greasy gaze of others – a gaze which contains a 'scum' of speculations as to her domestic arrangements, as well as straightforward marvelling at the dazzle of her looks. Upon realisation that the gaze of the four people now confronting her contains the unseemly, Sunflower blushes in a way that recalls Galatea's sudden awareness of her own nakedness: 'A blush began to sweep over her face, her neck, her breasts, which had begun to smart since she realised that they were thinking of her as a sexual being' (11). Yet her appearance – with 'perfect shape, more beautiful / Than ever woman born' (Ovid 2008: 232, l.247–8) – is in a second sense not entirely under her ownership, since it is the habit of her female fans to take photographs of themselves, believing there to be a likeness, and to send these to her for verification (West 1986: 12). Sunflower's understanding of her beauty as a burden – 'she knew that her immense physical conspicuousness made her situation far worse' (13) – combined with the knowledge that she is for others an object of aesthetic contemplation, and an image to be replicated, generates a feeling of entrapment that expresses itself through recourse to images of statuary. Sunflower has, as Leopold Bloom says of the statues of Venus and Juno, 'curves the world admires' (Joyce 2008: 168). Her feelings under the gaze of the public might best be summed up by Ovid's lines: 'It seemed to be alive, / Its face to be a real girl's, a girl / who wished to move – but modesty forbade' (Ovid 2008: 232–3, l.249–51). When the actress ceases to be simply a face in the newspaper, when she dares to move, she is hedged about with self-proscriptions of behaviour, under the scummy, judging gaze of those around her. Her very name indicates not only beauty, but an orientation toward the glare of public scrutiny, and it also forms a reference to sight itself since 'the sun resembles the eye, the most "helioform" of all sense organs' (Derrida 1993: 15). The actress lives her life in the sunshine of longing, and lascivious, looks.

Sunflower's engagement with statuary begins early in the novel, and in direct response to the awkwardness arising from the garage incident:

She could not quite see how; but there gleamed deep in her mind a picture of herself as a vast naked torso, but not of stone, of living, flushing flesh, fallen helpless on its side in some public place of ruins like the Forum in Rome, with ant-droves of tourists passing incessantly round her quickly, inquisitively, too close. Sometimes it was hot, and dry winds swung against her weakly like a tired man, flung dust on her, and dropped again; and tourists crowding along in the shadow of her limbs put up their sweaty hands to experience her texture and stroked the grit into her flesh. Sometimes it was wet, and her groins were runnelled with thick shining ropes of water; and the tourists, going quicker than ever, rushed along her flanks and pricked them with the spokes of their umbrellas. [. . .] The queer things one thinks of! (West 1986: 13)

Here, Sunflower has become the toppled torso of classical sculpture, but, following a Galatean metamorphosis, she is 'flushing flesh'. The helplessness of her public position in the Forum relates in obvious ways to her sense that her living beauty is a matter for public contemplation, but the 'ant-droves' of tourists are too close: they are 'right up close to the skin', as Connor's understanding of *enchroi* had it; they are also encroaching, in that they scuttle around and over living flesh, and in doing so impose on her individuated identity. What Sunflower is experiencing is formication, here in the classic manifestation (the ant crawl) that gives the condition its name. With formication understood (as in Chapter 1) as one possible symptom of schizophrenia, we can read this bizarre imagined scene as a battle for the right to a stable, single selfhood or identity, as well as, or alongside, the battle for the right of access to flesh. Sunflower's body is also undergoing a process of tactile education of which Marinetti would be proud, since she is subject not only to sensations of the formic crawl of the tourists, but also to the touch of wind, dust, sweaty hands, grit, water and umbrella spokes. While this is certainly a 'queer thing' to think of, and while it does most straightforwardly relate to matters of conspicuousness (elsewhere, Jack Murphy's attentions are 'like having your face licked' (100)), the history of the haptic makes further sense of this scene, linking Sunflower to Galatea, and thence to questions of form, *formosa* or beauty, formication and the right to an unpolluted, unencroached upon sense of skin and self. As the novel progresses, Sunflower's imagination, haunted by statue forms, can be seen to track from the beautiful to the deathly, from pulchritude to the sepulchral, from the freeing of shape from the marble block to the entrapment of a figure in the stone of the sepulchre. The movement of the novel, read sculpturally, is from the liberation of form, to its entombment.

It is probable that, in interrogating aspects of the Pygmalion myth, West is influenced by George Bernard Shaw, whose *Pygmalion* (1912; first performed 1913) was famously adapted as the musical *My Fair Lady* (1956). The latter rendering in particular makes much of its central protagonist Eliza Doolittle's cockney vowels and colloquial phrases, problems also besetting Sunflower, much to Essington's chagrin (West 1986: 78). Shaw wrote the part of Eliza for Mrs Patrick Campbell, an actress whose social climbing was mangling both her vowels and, as a result, her career. The depiction was too close (or encroaching) for comfort – 'for I am a good ladies' tailor', wrote Shaw (Shaw 1985a: 110) – and Mrs Pat was not amused: 'She saw through it like a shot – "You beast, you wrote this for me, every line of it: I can hear you mimicking my voice in it &c &c &c"' (Shaw 1985a: 111). Eliza's residence at 'Angel Court' (Shaw 1972: 682) links her to the celestial Mrs Pat (own first name Stella), and thence to Sunflower – the beauty of all three leaves their heavenly associations in place, whatever the state of their pronunciation. Writing to Mrs Pat, Shaw is effulgent in his praise: 'you cannot really be what you are to me: you are a figure from the dreams of my boyhood' (Shaw 1985b: 185). Sunflower most importantly provides an opportunity for self-contemplation on the part of West; she too had been an actress, and in 1924 told her sister Winnie, 'I wish to heaven I had succeeded in getting on the stage. I believe it would have suited me far better [than writing]' (Glendinning 1987: 107). Actress figures from West's theatre-going youth also contribute to this portrait of a life in the public eye, since she had seen Mrs Pat on the stage when a teenager (Glendinning 1987: 32); likewise Ellen Terry, of whom *Sunflower*'s Mr Justice Sandbury is an avowed fan (West 1986: 31). Shaw's *Pygmalion*, and the real-life Eliza in the form of Mrs Pat, might lead us to suppose that West is most significantly engaged, in addition to the portrayal of aspects of her own life, in writing a novel treating matters of class and social performance. While these remain in play throughout the text, it is through the older, Ovidian iteration of the Pygmalion myth, that which leads us to contemplate the sculptural, that we can form the clearest insight into Sunflower's predicament. Shaw wrote that West could 'handle a pen as brilliantly as I ever could, and much more savagely' (Glendinning 1987: 6–7), and it is the savagery of Sunflower's shaping at the hands of her two sculptor/lovers that is the engine behind this puzzling novel.

In a return to her habit of self-conceptualisation in statue form, Sunflower considers herself as a sphinx, imagery which once again emphasises her conspicuousness (via size) and beauty, and connotes her attitude of care toward the small, mal-shaped but inescapably alluring politician Francis Pitt: 'she enjoyed among many other forms the likeness of a sphinx, crouching in a vast desert [. . .] her hands were now huge claws between which he lay in the likeness of a swaddled child' (West 1986: 204). The language here is mythic, attributing to Sunflower the power of metamorphosis, or of metempsychosis (Joyce's 'met him pikehoses' (Joyce 2008: 147)), a trans-historical ability to return and reanimate; her powers of transformation as an actress are dwarfed by this strange imagined capacity. Here the sphinx's protective function is toward the man-child, whose swaddling may recall that of the newborn Christ. But the sphinx is also famous, of course, as a figure of specifically feminine inscrutability. The associations of beauty, femininity and mystery accruing to the sphinx led to one particularly odd instantiation of the Egyptomania of the modernist period (a trend noted in Chapter 1), when publicity shots for Greta Garbo were released in the 1930s, showing the actress's face superimposed on a contemporary photograph of the sphinx at Giza (Lant 1995: 60). The image works by foregrounding the famously indecipherable expression of Garbo, but also builds on a history of images using Egyptian sites to play with matters of size without recourse to technical trickery, since 'the placement of human figures alongside the monuments enhanced their immensity and hence the images' fascination of staggering discontinuities of scale' (Lant 1995: 59). Sunflower herself has had to become comfortable with the release of publicity shots (West 1986: 68–9), a scattering of her likeness which contributes to her sense of statuary exposure in public places. A treacherous summary of her press shots and postcards is given by Essington, who recounts her efforts to match the inventive photographic scenarios dreamt up by her fellow actress Maxine Tempest. Competing in poses, settings and accessories for some time, Sunflower is ultimately trumped by Maxine's motherhood: 'A preposterous child with a photographic face, the sort of *ad hoc* baby an actress would have. And that, you see, Sunflower can't match' (69). The performance under scrutiny here is Essington's own, in a dinner party setting, but the cruelty of his reference to the 'accessory' of a child which Sunflower is now too old to mother is palpable. That Sunflower's second incarnation as a statue is as a baby-guarding sphinx should be read in this context of mystery, public exposure and the squandered chance of a child.[2]

Both Essington and Pitt are described, in their efforts to manipulate Sunflower, as undertaking the manual work of sculptors. In free indirect discourse which takes the taint of Sunflower's thoughts, the narrative instructs that we 'look at the querulous beauty of his [Essington's] long fingers, for ever restless, now kneading the stem of his wineglass, as if he hoped to change its shape, which could not be done!' (50). The imposition of Essington's egotism is later compared to the activities of a maddened masseur who has 'bec[o]me so infatuated with the mere idea of kneading flesh that he pound[s] and pound[s] the body of his patient into lifeless pulp' (154). Elsewhere the comparison is to a surgeon (*chirurgie*, 'hand-made work') whose speech is 'silver-bright and unsigned, like a scalpel [. . .] kept in the locked cabinet of silence when it was not required for real work, never treated as a toy' (53). Kneading sculptor, pounding masseur and slicing surgeon all do their work on the flesh/marble of Sunflower's identity. It is no surprise that the actress eventually reaches a 'point at which she fe[els] horror for him' (154), since Essington's exercises have been in horripilation, the lifting and shaping of the skin. Pitt's 'pressing glance' (112) can also be read in this manner, putting the two men alongside the mythic figure of Procrustes, blacksmith and bodystretcher, and also, of course, alongside Pygmalion: 'He speaks to it, caresses it, believes / The firm new flesh beneath his fingers yields, / And fears the limbs may darken with a bruise' (Ovid 2008: 233, l.257–9). Sunflower's 'horror for' Essington results in a glance at her bracelet (West 1986: 154), a band of Cartier diamonds and emeralds that is jealously admired by Pitt, since he reads it as a symbol of the ongoing attachment between Sunflower and her other lover. Ovid's description of Pygmalion's gifts to Galatea are recalled here: 'gifts / That girls delight in [. . .] Lilies and coloured balls and beads of amber, / The tear-drops of the daughters of the Sun. / He decks her limbs with robes and on her fingers / Sets splendid rings, a necklace round her neck' (Ovid 2008: 233, l.260–6). Pitt follows these Ovidian prescriptions with some care, substituting a white carnation for a lily (West 1986: 120), robing Sunflower as we will see, and clasping her hands by way of a bracelet of his own (256). These processes result in the teardrops of a flower – rather than daughter – of the sun, and they do so because of a terrifying process of reverse Pygmalionism, a move from flesh to marble in the novel's closing scenes, further explored below.

Gesture and empathy

Sunflower is self-sculpting in one crucial way – through the taking up of the lives and gestures of others in the course of her acting engagements. Essington is unconvinced of her talent, and reads even in Sunflower's own manual habits a trace of bad performance: 'She bit her knuckles. [. . .] "That thing you're doing to your hands. A silly false movement. No effect. That's how you let down the big scene in 'Leonora.' No, Sunflower, you shouldn't have been an actress"' (West 1986: 79). Sunflower's Essington-inflamed nervousness regarding her acting capabilities results in stage fright – that which German theatrical slang refers to as a '*trema*'. It is a term transposed to the psychiatric realm by Klaus Conrad, who coined its use to describe the aura experienced before a schizophrenic episode (Sass 1998: 43–4). This curiosity of psychiatric terminology links Sunflower's acting anxieties to her formicatory fantasies in the Forum – on stage, and on view as a sculpture, her sense of a continent selfhood is under threat. At first she turns to written instruction to improve her practice, accessing A. B. Walkley's book 'about acting' at the London Library after a review by the author criticises one of her performances (West 1986: 86). In this book she learns that Tolstoy, on a visit to see *Siegfried*, noted that an actor was 'betrayed' by his 'weak, white, genteel hands' (87). While Sunflower herself is often betrayed by Essington and his genteel hands, the lesson of Walkley's book, and of her reviews, is that something in her gestures is a false, presentational echo of genuine human emotion. This falseness is removed, and her acting reputation comes to be supported by her talent as well as her beauty, when her overwhelming desire for Pitt creates malleability in her flesh. She begins 'speaking and moving with a special intensity because of her need to work off that restlessness that nowadays was always tormenting her like prickly heat felt inside or outside the skin' (166). Again formication heralds the etiolation of identity, here in a positive sense since she becomes available for metamorphosis in a way that makes possible the convincing practice of her art. Sunflower's reviews improve, with one critic stating that 'in her difficult moments [. . .] she has but to sweep loveliness from the ambient air with common motions of her fingertips' (167). It is by these means that the actress achieves the emotional ramifications of gestural practice: 'If one made a gesture expressive of an emotion one felt that emotion; she knew that from her acting' (247). She has begun these speculations, which run concurrently with the impositions and manipulations of her sculptor/lovers, in the unlikely surroundings of the assizes at Packbury.

Drifting into the assizes at the invitation of Mr Justice Sandbury, Sunflower witnesses the trial of a bigamist named Alice Hester. Perceiving the goodness of the woman in her pose and gestures, she imagines that she too might attain goodness by copying them: 'she looked over at the old woman and noted how she was seated in her chair, and tried to reproduce her pose' (30). Reading the 'scuffling movements' of Alice's hands, Sunflower decides that 'this one was knitting, the other sewing', a kind of manual remembrance of domestic duties which stands in for the alternative comfort of the sign of the cross, and which indicates that 'this [is] a marvellously good woman' (30). In her conclusion that to echo the pose of a person is to take on their moral qualities, Sunflower refers not to gestural evocation, the adequate performance, but to invocation, the calling up of a different spirit, a bodily conjuring. Shaw would seem to be suspicious of the efficacy of such endeavours, given that his 'Preface' to *Pygmalion* includes the warning that 'ambitious flower-girls who read this play must not imagine that they can pass themselves off as fine ladies by untutored imitation. [. . .] Imitation will only make them ridiculous' (Shaw 1972: 664). Sunflower's faith in the invocation of the haptic echo finds a nearer neighbour in Virginia Woolf, who considers just this matter in her 'Introductory letter' to *Life As We Have Known It, By Co-operative Working Women*, written in May 1930 and first published alongside those testimonies in 1931. On 'a hot June morning in Newcastle in the year 1913' (Woolf 1977: xviii), Woolf is witness to a meeting of working women discussing matters of labour conditions, education and suffrage, amongst other topics. Her witnessing remains a visual matter since she is left unaffected by the women's plight on a haptic level:

> this demand [. . .] for eight hours instead of nine behind a counter or in a mill, leave me, in my own blood and bones, untouched. [. . .] Hence my interest is merely altruistic. [. . .] There is no life blood or urgency about it. However hard I clap my hands or stamp my feet there is a hollowness in the sound which betrays me. (Woolf 1977: xx–xxi)

The only way around this impasse, in which Woolf's privileges of wealth, class and status prevent her visceral experience of the lives testified, is 'some happy conjuring trick, some change of attitude by which the mist and blankness of the speeches could be turned to blood and bone' (xxii). Attitude is a crucial word here, for while Woolf's intellectual engagement can lead to an exercise of sympathy, it is bodily experience or physical attitude that truly connects these women to their cause:

> after all the imagination is largely the child of the flesh. One could not be Mrs. Giles of Durham because one's body had never stood at the wash-tub; one's hands had never wrung and scrubbed and chopped up whatever the meat may be that makes a miner's supper. [. . .] Something was always creeping in from a world that was not their world. (Woolf 1977: xxiii)

Woolf is, for the most part, on business other than Sunflower's here, engaged in what Alison Light has described as 'probing her sore spots' (Light 2008: xviii) in relation to questions of class; there are lives too distant from the writer's own to be adequately imagined, to be felt in the flesh. Yet Woolf does refer to the working women she observes as 'actors' (Woolf 1977: xxi), both agents and players, and to the business of attempting to share in their experiences as 'too much of a game to be worth playing' (xxiii). The language of the theatre is here and, in confronting Alice Hester, Sunflower undertakes exercises comparable to Woolf's failed attempts to feel in her body the misery and the urgent need for social change of Mrs Giles and her colleagues. Crucially, it is through physically echoing the pose of the defendant that Sunflower seeks both to understand her life, and to imbibe, and embody, some of her moral goodness.[3]

Sunflower's engagement with the figure of Alice may be read as an effort of impersonation rather than the dissembling of an actress, where impersonation is understood – via the *persona* or speaking reed of the mask of a Greek actor – as a process of sounding through (Dean 2004: 43–65). Her aim is to allow the moral rectitude of Alice to live once again in her own body. This is also, we should note, an effort of empathy, a bid to bridge the gap that Woolf reads as an impasse and make the leap into other lives. In *Between Man and Man* (1955) Martin Buber suggests that:

> empathy means to glide with one's own feeling into the dynamic structure of an object, a pillar [. . .] or the branch of a tree or even of an animal or a man and as it were to trace from within, understanding the formation and motoriality of the object with the perception of one's own muscles. (Buber 1955: 97)

The hint of the Daphne myth in this transformation into a (branch of a) tree leads us to the 'queer' playwright Miss Georgy Allardyce, who 'seem[s] to have been turned into wood' in a second coming of the battle between Daphne and Apollo (West 1986: 159). The myth recurs in *Harriet Hume*, published two years after the *Sunflower* project was abandoned, since Harriet's back garden contains three Reynolds-painted ladies transformed into trees (West 1980a: 47). The story of Daphne is also, we should remember, one of the first of Ovid's *Metamorphoses*. The question of gestural or postural reiteration-as-metamorphosis between Sunflower and the accused Alice Hester in the court room emphasises the absence of empathy in the story of another Hester accused of sexual impropriety – Hester Prynne of Nathaniel Hawthorne's *The Scarlet Letter* (1850). The wearing of the titular letter calls the eyes of Salem towards Hester in a manner with which the dock-bound Alice and the ever-conspicuous Sunflower might identify. Hawthorne's novel is also one interested in flesh, in terms of both its appetites and its punishments. One unnamed Salem gossip states that 'at the very least, they should have put the brand of hot iron on Hester Prynne's forehead' (Hawthorne 1986: 79) in retribution for her extra-marital sexual relationship. Later, spectators at the Reverend Dimmesdale's hanging believe that they see Hester's scarlet letter 'imprinted in the flesh of his breast' on the scaffold, as the 'ever active tooth of remorse' gnaws its way out of his body in a legible exscription (Hawthorne 1986: 270). While Sunflower's status as an actress most obviously leads to readings of the assizes scene which foreground theories of stage performance, retaining the Pygmalion myth at the heart of our interpretation allows us to read Sunflower's interest in Alice as one attempt to self-sculpt, that is to take up shapes of her own choosing – in acts of fleshly imagination, impersonation and empathy – in spite of the pummelling efforts of Essington and Pitt.

The right to self-sculpt

It is, however, in *Sunflower*'s closing scenes that the influence of Ovid's Pygmalion myth can be traced most easily, as the mutual declaration of love between Pitt and the actress brings into play multi-layered references to sculpting and to statue forms. The book becomes a battle for the right to be a sculptor, in terms of generative or creative practice, and in terms of self-definition; to lose the battle is to be sculpt*ed*, cast in stone. The morning following the expression of her feelings, and the revelation that Pitt loves her in return, Sunflower awakes in her own bed 'feeling as if she was already beginning to exist less definitely', fearing that she might 'fall through the bed because she was not solid enough' and anticipating a stage where she will 'seep through it like mist' (West 1986: 239). This ebbing of physical presence is not perceived negatively, however, since it is a result of the achievement of dependence on Pitt, a position of passivity with which she has become fascinated. *Hamlet*'s move from 'solid flesh' to 'dew' was a desire for atomised existence, and Sunflower is aware that her own orisons have been answered. At this moment of 'mistification', the actress engages in acts of self-touching with what at first appears to be the travelling touch of a sculptor:

> She passed her hands over her face and under the bedclothes down her body, over her round breasts, down the strong hoops of her ribs, down her flanks, admiring their beauty as honestly as if they were marble and no concern of hers. (West 1986: 240)

Her haptic engagement is a Herderian gesture of the tactile appreciation of the beauty of bodies – through touch (here real, rather than imagined, in contravention of Herder's recommended viewing mode) she perceives the marble pulchritude of her three-dimensionality. While acts of self-touching, as discussed in Chapter 1, are gestures customarily leading to sureness of self in the reiteration of the bodily border, here Sunflower's appreciation is aesthetic, her feeling belonging to the contemplation of herself as a work of art – her own body is, in its beauty, 'no concern of hers'. Touching with the touch of Pitt's look, then, her tactile experiences are remediated; in the terms of Merleau-Ponty's *chiasm*, it is the inert fleshly bundle that she registers. This morning in bed also involves a kind of haptic remembering process, where past sensations of the flesh recall the night before or, as Sunflower herself expresses it: 'remembering with all one's mind and one's flesh what had happened' (255). Her body 'ha[s] already felt his great mouth at several places, on her throat, on her shoulders' (245). It is in feeling the 'crook of her left elbow' (245) that Pitt might have been expected to witness the living woman beneath the beautiful Sunflower statue, if we have in mind Ovid's line of feast day revelation: 'she was alive! The pulse beat in her veins!' (Ovid 2008: 234, l.291). Instead, Pitt 'halt[s] at the little tangle of blue veins' and claims the apparently legible writing beneath the skin to be 'his monogram' (West 1986: 245). Therefore the pulse which indicates that Sunflower/Galatea is more than an inanimate aesthetic object is read by Pitt as marking only possession (of a beautiful thing) or, if perceived as an artist's signature, as marking creation. In either reading, the vein monogram is a kind of subcutaneous branding, with that word carrying the meaning of both punishment (as with Hester Prynne's scarlet 'A') and ownership. In Condillac's rendering of the transformation of Galatea, it is the moment of self-touching with a travelling grasp that allows her to establish her status as an 'I': 'the same sentient being will reply from one [tactile experience] to the other: this is myself, this is still myself' (Condillac 1930: 88). Touching herself, Sunflower finds only marble, making her morning realisation one of her status as a reverse Galatea, crafted by the sculptor/lover Pitt.

Love has been declared in Pitt's alley of chestnut trees, the only grace of his ugly contemporary estate, and one leading towards a statue representing love that we take to be a depiction of Cupid, a 'boy with wings' (West 1986: 256). This figure was, we might note, one among those contemplated by Herder, since a 'Psyche and Cupid' pairing was held in the Mannheim collection (Gaiger 2002: 3–4). Upon her own contemplation of Cupid, Sunflower 'stretched up her arms and moulded in the air the childish roundness of his limbs, whispering "I would like to be a sculptor . . . I would like to make figures out of wet clay . . ."' (West 1986: 257). Pitt strikes down her hands, 'not cruelly, not kindly', since he needs them 'to put to his great mouth' (257). The path of this short scene is from creation to consumption, with Sunflower's urge to sculpt representing not only creativity, but self-fashioning, and also a generative ability associated with the Creation, and with motherhood. She would like to shape/make a boy. Earth and birth have been linked in Sunflower's earlier recollection of her mother's funeral, 'when the four dark figures stood beside the hole in the ground where there lay a black box holding the body which had caused them all' (143), an interment that makes that body party to a regenerative process. The memory follows hard upon the realisation of her love for Pitt, which leads to the thought: 'The ground, the ground, she had at last become part of the process that gets life out of the ground' (143). Sunflower's yearning to be a sculptor is, then, a yearning to give birth, to give form using the resources of her own bodily clay. Meanwhile Pitt is determined that she remain an inert thing of beauty, a reverse Galatea: 'There was nothing he was not doing for her, he was putting her on a ledge in the universe where she would never be fatigued or bored, he was making her, he was saving her' (258). While 'ledge' here might simply function in the way that 'pedestal' is often used, connoting worship and devotion, both 'ledge' and 'pedestal' lead us back to statuary, an interest West demonstrates at crucial moments in her fictional depiction of relationships. In *The Judge* (1922), as Bonnie Kime Scott has observed, Ellen asks Richard to lift her into an empty niche of the temple near Roothing Castle, a manoeuvre he declines to undertake, suspecting it may also have been enacted by his own mother and father (Scott 1991: 178). *Harriet Hume*'s Arnold Condorex remarks to Harriet:

> you are different in my eyes tonight. How sculptural you appear in this metamorphosis, with your marble pallor, and the close flutings of your gown disposed about your classically perfect form! You remind me of a painted lunette in one of my own upper rooms [. . .] a young woman that stands in the recesses of a cave, all black and white, and bloodless and perfect, like yourself. (West 1980a: 208)

Pitt is allied with Condorex, then, not only through his possession of paw-hands (as noted in Chapter 1) but in his determination to cast his lover as an object of aesthetic contemplation – a marble, bloodless statue – rather than as a tactile, fleshly subject, a Galatea with a pulse.

Sunflower on the ledge

Sunflower makes one final attempt to self-define or self-sculpt when she imagines herself as a roadside saint, an effort that combines the holiness of gesture and pose that she perceived in Alice Hester with the fantasy of creative motherhood that she previously linked to the shaping of Cupid:

> It would not be so bad to be an image of a saint that stood for ever out of doors, in a shrine at the turn of the road above a valley [. . .]. She became quite still, enacting to herself how it would be to stand in rain and shine with full wooden skirts about one, while in a hollow of one's body dark buzzing principles of life built up cell upon cell of golden, feeding sweetness; and on her face she felt the sweet smile all images of holy women wear. (West 1986: 261)

Recalling the story of a wayside Madonna in which bees have made a home, the processes of those bees stand in for the cellular multiplications of human life, with the 'sweetness' of honeycomb becoming allied with the moral goodness of the saint/Madonna, visible in her smile of beatification. This is a story of fruition, and it recalls the ending of Ovid's tale, since the poet concludes with a pregnancy and the birth of a child: 'The goddess [Venus] graced the union she had made, / And when nine times the crescent moon had filled / Her silver orb, an infant girl was born, / Paphos, from whom the island takes its name' (Ovid 2008: 234, l.297–300). Yet Sunflower's fantasies of statuary – linked to moral perfection and the bringing forth of life from the 'clay' of human flesh – are ultimately to take second place to Pitt's crafting of a marble-white sepulchre, a deathly form of sculpture. As the better craftsman ('il miglior fabbro', as Eliot's borrowing from Dante has it (Eliot 1963: 61)), Pitt forces Sunflower through a reversed Galatean transformation. In fact, Ovid has Galatea's enfleshment preceded by a tale of petrification, in which the Propoetides, as punishment for denying the divinity of Venus, are 'turned with little change to stones of flint' (Ovid 2008: 232, l.239). In Hughes's rendering, Pygmalion is repulsed by women precisely because of a confrontation with the flinty Propoetides, whose acts of prostitution combine the bait of good looks with the trap of pregnancy. He sees their wickedness 'transform, as by some occult connection, / Every woman's uterus to a spider. / Her face, voice, gestures, hair became its web' (Hughes 1997: 145). Pygmalion's fear of fatherhood sits alongside his pride in his own capabilities in the sculptor's craft, the necessary skill to give birth/form to the beautiful Galatea. Further, the latter is, as we noted above, 'more beautiful / Than ever woman born' (Ovid 2008: 232, l.247–8). While this line is customarily read as a statement of mimetic mastery, in which Pygmalion claims Galatea as the most beautiful in history, it does also contain the implication of *more beautiful than ever born of woman*, a reading which places Pygmalion in the God/ Creator role, and also bypasses processes of natural, biological birth. West is a sensitive reader of the Pygmalion myth in her use of the story to explore Sunflower's longing for a child and Pitt's Pygmalionesque resistance to that longing. It is therefore possible to read Sunflower as both a reverse Galatea and a petrified Propoetide.

It is in white satin that we see Sunflower in the novel's closing scenes, a material that might most obviously be read to indicate the glamorousness of her life on the stage. Yet the narrative notes that 'white satin is a human idea, a human triumph. There is nothing like it in nature' (West 1986: 266), a fact that links the fabric to the Ovidian notion of art's *triumph over nature* ('Such art his art concealed' (Ovid 2008: 234, l.252)). Sunflower's entrapment in white satin, then, recalls marble in its colour and temperature, as well as connecting to the perfections of the sculptor's art. In its tight enclosure of the human body, recalling the 'close flutings' of Harriet Hume's gown, the satin moves us from the revelation of form in the quarrying of the sculptural act, toward the beautiful shape of the body-enclosing sepulchre:

> It held her body closely, brightly [. . .] it snarled in the hollow between her breasts, streaked the long tapering of her waist beneath them. Her body was nice enough, that was all right, but her face looked so queer. She had gone white, with the dead whiteness of a white flower in shadow, and her lips, which until now she had hardly ever needed to rouge off the stage, were very pale pink, like pink roses ruined by the rain. And there was something new about her expression. (West 1986: 267)

Ovid's 'snow-white' (2008: 232, l.245) of the pre-metamorphosis Galatea is here, a whiteness which is dead, and which recalls the 'white flower' given to Sunflower by Pitt at their first dinner together ('I've given her the flower I think she ought to have' (West 1986: 120)). Her face, in looking 'queer', recalls the queerness of Miss Georgy Allardyce, herself a Daphnean shapeshifter, partially transformed into a tree. Sunflower's lips, here apparently ruined by rain (as they would be, were she to take up the position of an outdoor statue), were already identified as feeling 'like satin' when she was self-touching with the remediated hand of her sculptor/lover in bed (248). And we presume satin to be present, too, when Pitt saw the actress on the stage prior to their intimate acquaintance:

> 'What was that play you acted in where you went to a man's rooms at night, wrapped in a great silver cloak?' He spoke gloatingly; his little hands greedily described the way the silver folds had fallen. 'You made a most beautiful picture. I have never forgotten it.' (West 1986: 138)

With a sculptor's gesture Pitt had shaped, in memory, the folds of Sunflower's drapery, a gesture prefiguring the ultimate entrapment of her body in the marble-cold satin of his artistry/love. Consideration of drapery returns us to Herder, for whom 'in sculpture a garment made of stone [. . .] is to an extreme degree *oppressive*' (Herder 2002: 47). The solution to this problem is the use of wet drapery in the studio, to allow a type of covering for the model that yet facilitates the sculptor's (and, ultimately, the viewer's) appreciation of form. In his description of the advantages of wet drapery, Herder might as well be describing the clinging white satin of Sunflower's deathly dress. In fact, satin might be said to be the wet drapery of human ingenuity, such is its ability to 'snarl' and 'streak':

In those cases in which the Greek artist [. . .] was obliged to clothe the beautiful body, which sculpture alone *can* and *should* form [. . .] could he *clothe* in such a way that nothing is *hidden*? Could he drape a body and yet allow it to retain its stature and its beautiful rounded fullness? What if the body were to *show through*? [. . .] The discriminating Greeks found an answer precisely *for the hand*. (Herder 2002: 50)

Sunflower's white satin ending indicates that she has lost the battle for the right to self-definition in sculptural terms. She cannot sculpt/create/ give birth from clay, nor can she self-fashion or self-touch with anything other than a remediated tactility borrowed from her sculptor/lover. The latter, Pitt, has 'saved' Sunflower from the pounding practices of Essington's horripilation, only to 'mak[e]' her, to trap her in the synthetic equivalent of the wet drapery of the sculpture studio. This drapery reveals her body, maintaining the painful conspicuousness she has imagined in some of her own sculptural flights of fancy, and yet it is also a shroud. Sunflower, as a white andromorphic sculpture, is a sepulchre, her beauty or pulchritude crafted into death.

Glendinning has suggested that West abandons the *Sunflower* project in part because she is chary of tackling the scene of sexual congress between Pitt and Sunflower to which the story seems inexorably to lead (1986: 275). If West's own experiences with Beaverbrook are to be drawn upon, such a scene would involve the impotence of Pitt. However, a haptically attuned reading of this incomplete novel, one that draws out the Pygmalion myth that lies, hypothetically, like a skin beneath the story, places West's work in the vital context of eighteenth-century aesthetic philosophy and its uses of that very myth. The Daphne connection, here and in the concurrently written *Harriet Hume*, puts us on the trail of Ovid, while other appearances of statue forms in West's work point us toward classical sculpture. In *Sunflower*, we begin with a nightmarish vision of public exposure and formication, with the actress as a post-metamorphosis Galatea, tumbled in the Forum to which Herder would eventually travel. Moving via attempts at sculptural self-fashioning and fantasies of birth, we finish with Sunflower as reverse Galatea, or flinty Propoetide, condemned to a sepulchral end. Placed on the ledge or pedestal proper to the public appetite for her beauty, she is entombed in satin/wet drapery/frigid marble. She will not have her Paphos. *Sunflower*'s intricate interconnections with the histories of the haptic in play in the modernist period make it a far more interesting book than a simple autobiographical reading will allow. While West's relationship with Wells does in fact connect to such histories (I discuss Wells's own 'The Country of the Blind' in just such contexts in Chapter 2), it is the story of the Pygmalion myth that really explains this novel, and which gives it a coherence, and level of completion, hitherto unacknowledged by critics. Recourse to matters haptic allows us to get to grips with a character who, despite her heliophilic moniker, meets an icy, ivory fate. Meanwhile, her sculptor/lover is a little man (West 1986: 42, 48), with 'lion's paws' (73); a little lion; a pygmy lion; a Pygmalion.

Notes

1. I adapt a phrase of Santanu Das's here: 'Vision, sound and smell all carry the body beyond its margins: tactile experience, by contrast, stubbornly adheres to the flesh' (Das 2005: 6).
2. Jane Marcus, in a literary critical obituary of West, refers to the author as 'a sphinx that spoke' (Marcus 1983: 154), a reference to her 'earthy and powerful' body and 'craggy noble face' (153). In the same piece, Marcus observes that West's writing 'reveals the well-stocked mind of an eighteenth-century philosopher' (151), an allegiance that might explain her fascination with Pygmalion. Neither the latter myth, nor *Sunflower*, is discussed.
3. The figure of Ellen Terry recurs here as a possible inspiration for Sunflower. In Virginia Woolf's essay 'Ellen Terry', the actress is described as a 'mutable woman, all instinct, sympathy, and sensation' (Woolf 1967a: 71), as being unsure of her own cleverness (68) just as Sunflower is, and as 'fill[ing] the stage' so that 'all the other actors were put out, as electric lights are put out in the sun' (67). Sunflower shares Terry's radiance and anxieties, and aspires to her talents.

Chapter 2

James Joyce's Epidermic Adventures

Masturbatory modernism

'I do not particularly like *Ulysses* or James Joyce' (West 1987b: 52). In her book-length, experimental essay 'The Strange Necessity' (1928), first published a year after *Sunflower* was abandoned and the year prior to the publication of *Harriet Hume*, West overcomes this lack of enthusiasm to offer an extended response to *Ulysses*, alongside a traveller's notes on Paris, and broad speculations on the nature of aesthetic experience. Amongst these topics, she addresses several of the haptic concerns also discernible in her fictional works of the period.[1] She refers to kinaesthesis in her observation that 'we all have a certain body-consciousness that packs away a great deal of latent information about how we feel when we move'; one which also provides 'a working knowledge of what we can do with our muscles and our nerves and all [our] other physical possessions' (99–100). She echoes Focillon's praise of the hand and attribution of human superiority to the quality of tool-related dextrousness in her claim that 'man's supremacy is due chiefly to his habit of keeping as much of himself as possible in an outhouse at the bottom of the garden', an argument against any cyborgian physical incorporation of the machinic (128). Her aesthetics, peculiarly constructed with reference to Ivan Petrovich Pavlov's psycho-neurological experiments with dogs, suggests that the human response to art is an 'organ' which is 'collective and partially external', a donation of the cortex of the artist to the waiting cortices of his audience, each contributing to a kind of suprasensual ur-brain (175–6). It is the latter interest that is of most use to us here since, while this account of aesthetics remains schematic, it does allow West the claim that '*Ulysses* is the product of the excitatory complexes of [Joyce's] time, whether derived from art and science or from straight unanalysed and unsynthesized experience, *pressing on the individuality* that is James Joyce' (179, my emphasis), a conceptualisation of the process of literary inspiration that begs the question of just what those 'excitatory complexes' might be.

This chapter initially extrapolates from West's tactile metaphor of 'pressing', in an address to the question of how one might literally or in imagined terms press, caress, grasp and trace the surface of the human skin, in order to reiterate a bodily border (one's own; another's), to test the continence of that border, but most importantly to stimulate one's own sexually or aesthetically excited response. There are two main areas of concern, both hinted at within West's sustained review: sculpture and the caress of the eye it provokes ('I had walked on the Left Bank [. . .] where one feels as if one were a stone woman, a caryatid' (184)), and masturbation. That the latter might be precipitated by the former provides a link between these two stories, and both the Ovidian figure of Galatea (see Excursus) and Merleau-Ponty's *chiasm* of self-touching (see Chapter 1) remain in play. Speculation about the sculpture/masturbation connection leads towards consideration not of the look that touches, but of the touch that looks – the touch of the unsighted, where Joyce's blind stripling proves a presiding spirit. Ultimately, Joyce's multi-faceted engagement with issues of touch and the tactile poses questions regarding the importance of the skin as a metaphor for the *Ulysses* project as a whole, as well as going some way toward explaining just what was 'pressing on [his] individuality' at this time.

West joins many of her critical contemporaries in castigating Joyce for his (to a modern eye, rather limited) use of evocative Anglo-Saxon: 'that his use of obscene words is altogether outside the aesthetic process is proved by that spurt of satisfaction, more actual but also more feeble than authentic aesthetic emotion which marks the pages whenever he uses them' (21). We are dealing with ejaculations here, linguistic and seminal, both of which escape from the body of Joyce. Sexual words result in a 'spurt of satisfaction' or *jouissance* which marks the page. While this masturbatory endeavour offers only a 'feeble' release, a deeply orgasmic response comes from the viewer confronted by a great work of art: 'Is this exaltation the orgasm, as it were, of the artistic instinct, stimulated to its height?' (196). The viewer is 'stimulated' by the reach of the artwork toward the intimate artistic instinct, a frictional excitation – we have shifted from the ur-brain to the genitals, and to their manual manipulation. For West, both the production and consumption of objects of aesthetic contemplation are therefore a masturbatory business – while the 'strange necessity' of her essay's title most conspicuously refers to the aesthetic impulse, it might just as well refer to that necessity which plagues Leopold Bloom throughout his Dublin day: sexual self-touching. Joyce's own compulsion toward what Jean-Jacques Rousseau refers to as 'the dangerous supplement' (Laqueur 2003: 42–3) is implied in his response to a fan's request to 'let me kiss the hand that wrote *Ulysses*': 'No, it did lots of other things too' (Ellmann 2010: 136). The presence in *Ulysses* of an extended scene of masturbation – when Bloom watches Gerty MacDowell on the beach in the 'Nausicaa' episode – is a primary contribution, alongside what H. G. Wells famously refers to as Joyce's 'cloacal obsession' (Deming 1970: 86), to the reputation of the novel as a 'filthy' text.[2] West's pages spattered with Joycean jism may be read in this context. Virginia Woolf's private reading notes, recorded in her diary, refer to *Ulysses* as an 'illiterate, underbred book [. . .] of a self-taught working man' (Woolf 1988b, vol. 2: 189), the author's autodidacticism as disgusting, apparently, as his auto-eroticism.[3] Both of these activities are, as we noted in relation to Huxley's 'savage' in Chapter 1, solitary pleasures, and both take place outside institutions, of learning and of the conjugal relationship respectively. Woolf's is a fascinating conflation of intellectual and class-inflected prejudice with implied accusations of specifically sexual filthiness. Both West and Woolf circle around the topic of the writing/spurting pen and the penis, as well as the metaphorical notion of the 'seminal' text, since they both attempt to account for Joyce's broader literary influence.[4] These are of course topics carefully woven within *Ulysses* itself, most conspicuously when an 'Aeolus' headline declares that 'ITHACANS VOW PEN IS CHAMP' (Joyce 2008: 142). Jacques Derrida has suggested that the writing process, where the labour of the literary hand is employed, is itself masturbatory, regardless of the inclusion of profanities, and that its sacred nature must be preserved by privacy. Questioned as to his working practices, and asked for explicit descriptions, he replies that he is being asked to perform 'a gesture that is quite indecent, a gesture that some would interpret as narcissistic [. . .]. What it entails is talking about [. . .] the moment when, in a highly eroticized space – I would say almost auto-eroticized – we prepare [. . .] a publication' (Derrida, quoted in Attridge 2006: 48). Writing, reading and writing about the writing process (that 'indecent' gesture) are all, it seems, masturbatory matters.

Of the vast cast of *Ulysses*, it is Buck Mulligan's imagination which affords the most direct address to the pleasures of self-love, since he is the voice of a ribald Yeats parody – '*Being afraid to marry on earth / They masturbated for all they were worth*' (Joyce 2008: 207) – and also the claimed author (under the pseudonymous 'Ballocky') of a play offering a hymn to sexual self-sufficiency: '*Everyman His Own Wife or A Honeymoon in the Hand (a national immorality in three orgasms)*' (208). Lydia of the Ormond Hotel is Mulligan's nearest neighbour in this overtly sexual preoccupation: 'On the smooth jutting beerpull laid Lydia hand lightly [. . .]. Fro, to: to, fro: over the polished knob (she knows his eyes, my eyes, her eyes) her thumb and finger [. . .] passed, repassed [. . .] a cool firm white enamel baton protruding' (274). Here the beer pull, used for the tacit acknowledgement of a forbidden intimacy between relative strangers, rather unsubtly joins the pen as a proxy for the penis, yet producing a precious, life-giving liquid of a different order. Mulligan and Lydia may lead us to believe that, seminal pen aside, masturbation functions within Joyce's text as the mere smut and filth of schoolboy humour, or at most as a 'strange necessity' which rules the mind of the male (and may be manipulated by the female). However, considering the namesake of Stephen Dedalus – 'your absurd name, an ancient Greek,' says Mulligan (4) – leads us back once more in the direction of sculpture, the hand-crafted replication of human form, and thence to the look which contains the imagined grasp, the look which (almost, but never actually) touches, and, ultimately, to processes of looking which initiate the appetite for self-touching. In Chapter 1, we noted that Herder posed and answered a crucial question: 'What then is beauty for the sense of touch? It is not colours! [. . .] [It is] bodies!' (Herder, quoted in Gaiger 2002: 14). Via Bloom, Joyce suggests that sculpture, the work of Daedalus and his successors, calls upon the caressing gaze of the viewer, the oculo-tactile mode of appreciation (outlined in Herder's statement that the viewer's 'soul speaks to it [the sculpture], not as if the soul sees, but as if it touches, as if it feels' (Herder 2002: 41)), and leads to the compulsion to self-touch, to masturbate.

Dignam's mortuary grove

Sculpture is of great importance to *Ulysses*. Most obviously, statue forms operate as nodes within the web of characters' paths through the streets of Dublin, reiterating the presence of those long dead, capturing their gestures, and therefore creating a frozen moment in time. Blazes Boylan's path through the city is at one point recorded via the three monuments he passes (Joyce 2008: 265); the city is haunted by the 'hugecloaked Liberator's form' of the statue of Daniel O'Connell; Nelson's Pillar (90) recurs within Stephen's parable of the plums, where the admiral is referred to as a 'onehandled adulterer' (142). Meanwhile, 'Tommy Moore's roguish finger' (155) may be compared with 'the stern, stone hand of Grattan, bidding halt' (219), and even controversially absent statues get a mention: 'the slab where Wolfe Tone's statue was not' (220). These monuments contribute to Dublin's status as a palimpsest city where past and present cohabit, with the tracery of footfall and the telling of tales binding together the temporal layers. Further, and in particular in the form of specifically mortuary monuments, they restate the human incapacity to halt time in their standing in for human flesh, functioning as *memento mori* even as they attempt to indicate immortality. Bloom's mention of 'statues bleeding' (78), intended primarily to refer to reported miracles, also hints toward his interest in the connection between Dublin's sentient and stony inhabitants, the quick and the dead. At Dignam's funeral, Bloom notes the cluster of statues in the yard of Dennany the stonecutter: 'silent shapes appeared, white, sorrowful, holding out calm hands, knelt in grief, pointing. [. . .] In white silence: appealing' (96), with the latter term suggesting both an aesthetic status and an attempt at communication. Following Dignam's burial, 'Mr Bloom walked unheeded along his grove by saddened angels [. . .] stone hopes praying with upcast eyes' (108). This phrasing suggests that he might be walking unheeded by – that is, next to – saddened angels, or that he walks unheeded by saddened angels, with the subtle implication in the latter case that while they pay no attention, they do have that capacity. The term 'grove' has pastoral associations, but also refers to the forest-like layout of statuary that was adopted at Herder's beloved Mannheim collection, a dispersal of the artefacts that, in changing the habit of placing statues along the walls of a long gallery, facilitated the theorist's understanding of this three-dimensional art as outlined in his *Sculpture* of 1778. Herder's own imagination appears to have been forest-haunted, since he used the title *Critical Groves* for a series of essays published in 1769 (Jason Gaiger suggests that in doing so Herder nods toward Quintilian's 'sylvae' (Gaiger 2002: 1)). A further oblique link can be made with Bloom's interest not in groves but in grooves, both the 'mesial groove' of a National Library goddess ('His pale Galilean eyes were upon her mesial groove. Venus Kallipyge [Greek: beautiful buttocks]' (Joyce 2008: 192–3)) and the verb 'to groove', which describes the quarrying of the sculptor's art. The term also, of course, implies habit, and Bloom's nasty habit, his 'strange necessity', often occurs to him following the contemplation of statue forms.

One further ramification of the quick/dead relationship in the consideration of statuary obtains, at least within the mind of Bloom. For him, as for Herder, beauty resides in bodies, and while he is fascinated by the marble forms of the National Library and by a range of real and imagined goddesses of classical sculpture ('*Venus Callipyge, Venus Pandemos, Venus Metempsychosis*' (463)), he also recasts human – that is, potentially bleeding – women as statues. In doing so, Bloom plays with the notion that, just as the figures of the mortuary grove might observe him, so might the women subject to his lascivious look be cast in stone – it might, Joyce implies, be possible to cross that Galatean gulf in either direction.[5] Bloom tackles this topic of tactility and transformation when sitting with a drunken Stephen in the cabman's shelter, where he observes of the National Museum's statuary holdings that they possess 'splendid proportions', going on to complain (using an evocative colloquialism) that 'you simply don't knock against those kind of women here' (592). He clarifies that 'what [he is] talking about is the female form', before proceeding to a habitual complaint about the unsightliness of rumpled stockings and their affront to the feminine ankle (592). Even the discussion of 'opulent curves' cannot rouse Stephen from his alcoholic funk, leaving Bloom to remark largely to himself that 'marble [can] give the original, shoulders, back, all the symmetry. [. . .] whereas no photo could, because it simply [i]sn't art' (607).[6] Bloom, then, is aroused in three dimensions, when looking leans toward touching, when the Herderian glance in the sculptural grove allows the fantasy of actual touch. This appetite applies both to marble sculptures and to fleshly Galateas, reimagined in stony stasis. Crucially, it is those 'opulent curves' that are important to Bloom, since he is aroused not simply by the statueform, but by the statuesque, the latter suggesting the heftiness which makes marble immortalisation worthwhile. We are talking, in particular, of curves, and curves unencumbered by the wrinkle of an ill-fitting stocking, bringing us towards William Hogarth's line of beauty which, as Herder states, 'seeks to raise the figure from the ground and to give wings to the imagination so that it no longer merely *sees*, but *enjoys*, *touches*, and *feels*' (Herder 2002: 64; see also Hogarth 1971: 37–9). It is the imaginative tracing of the curve of the female form, on either side of that Galatean gulf, that leads to Bloom's arousal and, ultimately, to his echoing of the statuary erection with an erection of his own.

Three 'stonecold' women

A trinity of female figures makes visible Bloom's mobilisation of the Herderian grasping look, both when dealing with the curves of statuary and when ogling the living, breathing statuesque: the bathing nymph, Gerty MacDowell and Molly Bloom. The bedroom of the Blooms contains, above the conjugal bed, the 'Bath of the Nymph', an image gleaned from *Photo Bits*. The Nymph appears in the fevered dreams of the 'Circe' episode, when Bloom calls out to her, 'your classic curves, beautiful immortal. I was glad to look on you, to praise you, a thing of beauty, almost to pray' (Joyce 2008: 510), a contemplation of the beautiful line of the female form that sets him off on yet another hosiery-related train of thought (512).[7] The Nymph describes herself as 'immortal', 'stonecold' and 'pure' (514), marking her allegiance to the sculptural, but Bloom is prompted to consider the shape of fleshly women: 'It overpowers me. The warm impress of her warm form. Even to sit where a woman has sat' (515). Here he uses 'form' in a sense related to the form of a hare – the space in which a hare/woman has lain/sat, which retains the imprint of the bodily, an echo of past inhabitation. From ill-fitting stockings, to the perfect fit of hare and grassy form, Bloom is pondering the skin limits of (real or marble) women, a reverie ruined by the fact that the Nymph, '*with a cry, flees from him unveiled, her plaster cast cracking, a cloud of stench escaping from the cracks*' (517). Poetic traditions of the painted woman whose cosmetics mask a death's head are here (see Gwilliam 1994), but more importantly the sculptural beauty of the Nymph is shown to be sepulchral, her skin of plaster containing – we gather from the 'stench' – a rotting body. The sexual nightmare of 'Circe' is therefore the section of Bloom's day where his eroticisation of the bodily border of (stone or fleshly) women both literally and metaphorically comes undone. This is the fall into formlessness, where unveiling or disrobing ceases to be an erotic matter, and becomes an act of flaying or lost line – 'Say a woman loses a charm with every pin she takes out', as it is phrased elsewhere (352).[8] Yet the Nymph allows us to see that Bloom has an interest not simply in shape or form, but in *shapeliness*, closer to *formosa* in that, through aesthetic excitation, it is pleasing in the sensations it creates in the perceiver. While 'shape' denotes that which is available to the geometers, 'shape*ly*' is the province of the aesthetic sense, containing the notion of calculable form *and* the beautiful or good.[9] Thus the loss of shapeliness leads to a loss of desire (and, for Bloom, one further flaccidity). Bloom's mental note of 'shapely bathers on golden strand' (115) in the 'Aeolus' episode suggests that other newspaper readers might enjoy a glimpse of the female line of beauty, and also anticipates his observation of Gerty's 'shapely limbs' (335). As we observed in the foregoing excursus, Bloom remarks upon 'shapely goddesses, Venus, Juno: curves the world admires' (168), a terminology he also applies to his daughter ('Funny she looked soaped all over [when bathing]. Shapely too' (148)), and to both wife and daughter ('prophetic grace of structure, slim shapely haunches' (394)). Lenehan's claim that 'there's a touch of the artist about old Bloom' (225) should be read in this context – he brings his Herderian look, the look which contains a touch, to bear upon the female form, whether tackling stone or flesh, and, providing that shapeliness remains (unencumbered by poor-quality hosiery; fixed with adequate pins), he may be led to crave an act of self-touching.

Gerty's beach scene in the 'Nausicaa' episode is the moment when contemplation of female shapeliness is linked most conspicuously to masturbatory practices.[10] Attention to the novel's explanatory schemata allows us to see that Joyce conceived of 'Nausicaa' as Bloom's 'honeymoon in the hand'. The Gilbert schema records the 'technic' of the episode as 'tumescence, detumescence' (Joyce 2008: 734), putting us on the trail of Havelock Ellis's *Studies in the Psychology of Sex: Sexual Selection in Man* (1905), which commences with the word 'tumescence' and remarks, as if describing Bloom's hungry look on the beach, that 'external stimuli act at every stage' of tumescence, and that 'the process [of masturbation] is never completed without the aid of such stimuli, for even in the auto-erotic sphere external stimuli are still active, either actually or in imagination' (Ellis 1914: 1). The Linati schema lists among the symbols of the episode 'Onanism' (Joyce 2008: 738), a reference to John Marten's *Onania* (c. 1712), which not only coined the term 'Onanism' and outlined the practices of self-love, but also offered quack medicines for the alleviation of the compulsion and its effects (Laqueur 2003: 13–16), a combination of faux-medical advice and salesmanship with which Gerty is familiar from her diet of women's magazines. Both schemata refer to 'nose' as an organ of importance to the episode (Joyce 2008: 735, 738), and Maud Ellmann has suggested that, via Freud's treatment of a fetish of the Wolf Man, we can associate the nose with the penis (Ellmann 2010: 114). We might consider Blazes Boylan's big red 'nose', by which means Bloom is cuckolded, in this light. The other organ listed in the schemata is the 'eye' (Joyce 2008: 735, 738), and it is the aesthetic trigger which forms the connection between the look of the eye and the touch between hand and nose/penis that becomes clearest in Gerty's scene.

The latter's 'snowy slender arms', 'white brow' (350), 'waxen pallor', 'ivorylike purity' and 'Greekly perfect' mouth (333) lead us back, yet again, in the direction of the sculptural. In fact, Gerty's attentions to her appearance upon which we remarked in Chapter 1 can now be understood as an attempt to self-sculpt, to intentionally take on notions of beauty that belong to marble sculpture. (We might note here that Gerty's status as 'Greekly perfect' is echoed in Herder's insistence on referring to his sweetheart, and later wife, Karoline Flachsland as his 'Greek girl' (Breul 1904: 2).) Accordingly, Gerty ensures her shapeliness, choosing a skirt which will capitalise on her 'graceful figure' (Joyce 2008: 335), and of course hosiery that will adequately encase her limbs (335) and remain 'transparent' and free of 'bracks' or faults (344), acknowledging the importance of avoiding stockings which have 'neither shape nor form' (344). In fact, the phrase 'that was what he was looking at, transparent, and not her insignificant ones' (344) leaves the term 'transparent' hovering between the stockings themselves and Bloom, whose look is transparent, blatant and 'passionate' (346). The unattributed narrative voice remains close to Gerty's own phraseology, even as it seems to be remarkably well informed about Bloom's own particular appetites for the shapely. Watching from the rocks, he is 'drinking in her every *contour*, literally worshipping at her shrine' (345, my emphasis). The misuse of 'literally' here indicates that we are in the mind of the comparatively uneducated Gerty, allying her with 'Lily, the caretaker's daughter' of 'The Dead', who is 'literally run off her feet' when attending to the Morkans' party (Joyce 2000b: 175), and whose floral name links her to the Virgin Mary, appropriate given Joyce's intention to deal with Mariolatry in this episode (see Chapter 1). However, since Gerty seems as intent as Bloom upon her transformation into pure white marble, we might also consider the statement of Severin, central protagonist of Leopold (note the name) von Sacher-Masoch's *Venus in Furs* (1870), that he loves Wanda, repeatedly allied or interchanged with a stone Venus, 'passionately [. . .] as insanely as a man can love [. . .] a woman [. . .]. Yes, I literally worshipped her' (Sacher-Masoch 2000: 12). As we are in free indirect discourse here, with the soupiness of the style attributable to Gerty's mental habits of echoing her favourite magazines, we can also speculate that this virginal young woman has been reading Sacher-Masoch. Masochian and masochistic desire are further discussed below. For now, we note that Bloom casts the largely static Gerty as a statue, a fleshly Venus, while she complicitly self-conceptualises, anoints and dresses, to maintain the shapely beauty of statue forms.

When Cissy Caffrey's galumphing along the sands distracts Bloom's gaze, Gerty rather jealously thinks that 'it would have served her just right if she had tripped over something accidentally on purpose [. . .] and got a fine tumble. *Tableau!*' (Joyce 2008: 333–4). While Jeri Johnson notes that this final exclamation relates to a 'parlour game where players strike a pose meant to represent a "message"' (902), and while Bloom's later recollection of the term (352) seems to echo this, the word 'tableau' also brings to mind the titillating practice of the *tableau vivant*, in which often nude women hold poses frequently belonging to classical art, and in which the stillness of statuary is essential in order to skirt licensing laws (see Hindson 2008).[11] Aside from a slow reclining (ostensibly to view the fireworks, but also for the purposes of making the most of the 'three and eleven' (Joyce 2008: 344) expended on good stockings) and a Galatean blush (345), Gerty displays herself as a statue/contributor to a *tableau vivant*, albeit clothed. Her reasons for doing so become clear when she finally moves position on the beach, and her limp is revealed: 'Thought something was wrong by the cut of her jib. Jilted beauty'

(351). Crucially, moving/limping is retrospectively established by Bloom himself to be anathema to his arousal: 'glad I didn't know it [about the limp] when she was on show' (351). It is not quite clear whether Gerty's status as differently abled is the barrier to desire, or whether, as with the Nymph, it is the moment of movement or fleeing, and therefore the crumbling of the plaster of stasis, that ruins Bloom's touching look, and thence his urge to self-touch ('see her as she is spoil all' (353)). In any case, he has moved from tumescence to detumescence ('my fireworks. Up like a rocket, down like a stick' (354)), and is now in possession of a limp penis. 'Limp' here connotes both detumescence, the loss of form (as in Molly's unstarched knickers (607)), and the potential cause of this loss (Gerty's limping gait, her status as '[t]ilted beauty'). Thus when we learn that 'Mr Bloom with careful hand recomposed his wet shirt', and when this thought is followed by 'O Lord, that little limping devil' (353), we are uncertain as to whether it is only Bloom's penis ('the limp father of thousands' (83)) and its devilish drive toward the strange necessity, or additionally Gerty and her wicked display as Venus/Galatea/*tableau vivant* performer, that is the object of the phrase.[12] Contemplation of the 'limp father' brings a new meaning to Bloom's reading of the headline '*Matcham's Masterstroke*' (66), since his contemplation of the shapeliness of the static Gerty has led, to paraphrase rather awkwardly, to the stroking of the master or demanding devil. Bloom is not the first to associate Venus with masturbation, since he recalls 'Wilkins in the high school' being caught 'drawing a picture of Venus with all his belongings on show' (354), a scene which we imagine had a masturbatory rather than simply expository impulse. That Venus should be traced with the pencil brings us back to Bloom, whom we find '*pencilling slow curves*' (525) amongst the prostitutes of Nighttown, an action which in turn recalls Hogarth's line of beauty, which 'being composed of two curves contrasted, becomes still more ornamental and pleasing, insomuch that the hand takes a lively movement in making it with pen or pencil' (Hogarth 1971: 38). Both Gerty and Bloom, along with their creator, demonstrate a preoccupation with the beautiful curves of the statue-form, and both are concerned to have Gerty cast in stone. With this in mind, we can consider 'Nausicaa' to be the most conspicuously ekphrastic of the episodes of *Ulysses*, in that it provides, through Bloom's eyes, a detailed description of (a young woman as) a work of art. Further, the episode follows the convention by which ekphrasis forms a pause in the narrative in order to make room for extended aesthetic contemplation, since Bloom's self-touching is a time-wasting indulgence, confounded when Cissy asks for the hour (Joyce 2008: 345).

Molly Bloom brings this trinity of statue-related female figures to a close in a curious way, since she is at once the possessor of the bodily form most remarked upon by Dublin's citizens ('she has a fine pair, god bless her' (225)) and the only representative of female practices of masturbation in Joyce's novel (although Bloom does, rather lasciviously, imply that the 'ticklish'ness of the potentially menstruating Gerty and her friends could lead in that direction (351)). In the Linati schema, Molly's final word, the extended reverie of the 'Penelope' episode, is denoted not by a time, but by the lemniscate or recumbent figure 8 (739), symbol of 'eternity' (Boheemen-Saaf 2006: 41) or 'infinity' (Ellmann 2006: 101). Joyce once explained, in a letter to Harriet Shaw Weaver, that the 'Penelope' episode was without a linear structure (Ellmann 2006: 98), and the lemniscate does adequately capture endless return (most obviously of Molly's memories), as well as the weaving of Molly's Homeric counterpart. However, the doubled curve can also be taken to represent the female breasts or buttocks, a reading supported by Joyce's identification of breasts, arse, womb and cunt as the 'cardinal points' of the episode (see R. Brown 2006: 118). We should note here that breast, arse and cunt are constituted by curves. However, with the Herderian sculptural caress in mind, we might also read the lemniscate as indicative of the two curves of Hogarth's line of beauty (although doubled again to form the full 8). Further, since Molly herself is prone throughout much of the episode (Maud Ellmann recommends the term 'proneography', as opposed to the erect 'orthography', as an appropriate stylistic label here (2006: 99)), we can make much of the lemniscate's tumbled 8, and read it as depicting a reclining, curvaceous woman – for all its intended indication of infinity, its line traces the *hour*glass, that is, full, female form. In fact, if we read that hourglass as deposed, it neatly combines the rejection of measurable temporality and the central importance of the female physique. 'There is that in [Molly's] reverie which sets before one the image of a recumbent woman', says West (1987b: 48), and that recumbency is rendered in the fallen 8, most statueform of all numerical figures. Given Joyce's interest in the look which touches, and which promulgates self-touching, we might also note that the lemniscate represents unending tactile engagement, in its recurring tracery of the double curve. This unstinting tactile connection also nods toward Merleau-Ponty's 'intertwining' or 'chiasm', moving us, once more, to the reiteration of the bodily border, and thence toward masturbatory self-touching. And we gather that the reclining Molly is masturbating, since she refers to 'the smoothest place', which is 'right there between this bit here how soft like a peach' (Joyce 2008: 720). Further, in touching the double curve of what Bloom refers to as the 'cloven sex' (485), Molly engages with her *mons veneris*, her mound of Venus, associating her with other marble and/or reclining depictions of beautiful goddesses, frequently read in light of their association with sexual self-touching.

We can read Molly, via the title of Pierre Louis Moreau de Maupertuis's peculiarly erotic work of natural history *Vénus Physique* (1745), as a 'Venus Embodied' or 'Earthly Venus'. The first public depiction of the female nude is the Knidian Aphrodite (c. 350–30 bc) who, having bathed, reaches for her drapery. Molly, upon hearing that Bloom has shown her photo portrait to Stephen, makes a mental note that she 'ought to have got it taken in drapery' (724). The image itself is 'slightly soiled' (607), with a hint that it has been used as an aid to masturbation. Pliny the Elder claims that the Knidian Aphrodite's beautiful form is such an erotic inspiration to young men that her bottom bears the stains of the semen of her viewers, since she 'penetrate[s] into the marrow of a youth [so that] he leaves a stain there' (Dolce, quoted in Goffen 1987: 692). These are instances of rear admire-al of which Bloom would approve (and we should note that a naval rear admiral crops up in the 'Cyclops' episode, the single eye of the mythic figure recalling, of course, the penis (Joyce 2008: 329)). However, Molly also appears to echo the *Sleeping Venus* or *Dresden Venus* painted by Giorgione, and finished by Titian (c. 1510), now read as part of the *venus pudica* tradition, in which the gesture of modest self-covering of the genitals can be reinterpreted as an act of self-touching. Writing of Titian's *Venus of Urbino* (1538), Mark Twain famously describes the work as 'the foulest, the vilest, the obscenest picture the world possesses' (Twain 1982: 380). It is the Venus's confrontational look toward the viewer that facilitates the rereading of her self-covering gesture as one of self-touching; the power of that look suggests that modesty is not present. Molly's monologue can be read in the same vein, as a direct appeal to the viewer/reader, through which she refuses to apologise for her sexual appetite, and allows us to know that her recumbency involves not covering but pleasuring. That Twain reads the *Venus of Urbino* as a possession of the world links to Molly's status as a woman of the stage, a situation shared by West's Sunflower – Venus, Molly *and* Sunflower, then, have 'curves the world admires'. Attention to other representations of Venus, to the approach to statuary delineated by Herder, to Bloom's interest in delineation or the tracing of curves, and to two sister figures in the Nymph and Gerty allows us to read Molly as a reclining Venus, belatedly turning the lascivious looks of others to a moment of *venus pudica* self-pleasuring – given her self-reflection, it can be no coincidence that she lusts for Bloom's domestic cast of Narcissus at this point (Joyce 2008: 725). It is in acknowledgement of her place amongst the goddesses that Molly observes of female breasts: 'they're supposed to represent beauty [. . .] like those statues in the museum one of them *pretending to hide it* with her hand' (704, my emphasis). These considerations also allow a rereading of the lemniscate symbol, in curvilinear extrapolations from the notion of the statuesque, as a representation of the reclining female form, of the immortalisation of the hourglass figure, and of acts of tactile engagement both Herderian/imagined and Onanistic/actual.

Ovid, Herder, Sacher-Masoch, Joyce

West invites us to establish just what was 'pressing' on Joyce during the composition of *Ulysses*, a provocation to search for the impetus behind his interest in pressing, i.e. in tactile engagement, and in statuary. It seems that, as with West herself, the Ovidian reading of Pygmalion is of importance to Joyce. Ovid gains an oblique mention in a reference to 'the genius of the elegant Latin poet' (Joyce 2008: 391), and perhaps sits behind Bloom's fretful interpretation of Martha's mistyped phrase: 'I do not like that other world [word] she wrote. No more do I. [. . .] Feel live warm beings near you. [. . .] warm fullblooded life' (110). Myles Crawford nods toward both Ovid and Daedalus in his suggestion that Gumley, working for the city corporation, and stationed near the cabman's shelter, ought to 'mind the stones, see they don't run away' (131). J. J. O'Molloy recreates for a fascinated audience the words of Seymour Bushe, pausing in the defence of the Childs case to describe the 'Moses of Michelangelo in the Vatican [*sic*]' (134), which '*if aught that the imagination or the hand of sculptor has wrought in marble of soultransfigured and of soultransfiguring deserves to live, deserves to live*' (134–5). Stephen, allegedly moved by 'grace of language and gesture' (135), but perhaps also thinking of the extraordinary mimetic capacities of his namesake, offers a Galatean blush (136).[13] Galatea is also present in references to beating veins beneath white skin – 'Lucrece's bluecircled ivory globes' (189); 'an azured harebell like her veins. Lids of Juno's eyes, violets' (269). She is present, too, in the reciprocal nature of a remembered kiss between the Blooms: 'she kissed me. I was kissed. [. . .] Kissed, she kissed me. Me. And me now' (168), which should be read in relation to Condillac's description of Galatea's accession to the world of touch, initiated by a kiss and containing the realisation that 'this is myself, this is still myself' (Condillac 1930: 88). While Bloom is a nominal convert to the idolatrous religion of Roman Catholicism (although primarily interested in what advertising might learn from religious ritual), and while his 'statues bleeding' can be understood in light of the confirmation of faith and the prompt to pilgrimage, his own path through the city involves a decidedly secular, and sexual, view of statuary, making the statue that bleeds a symbol of Daedalusian or Pygmalionesque mimeticism, rather than proof of the existence of a Catholic God.[14]

Given Joyce's interest, via Bloom, in the caressing look and the beauty of bodies in three dimensions, it is reasonable to assume that the work of Herder is significant to *Ulysses*. Herder's *Introduction to the Philosophy of the History of Humanity* (1784–91), in Edgar Quinet's translation, is after all the only book to be engaged with at conspicuous length in *Finnegans Wake* (see Fargnoli and Gillespie 2006: 340). Bloom's day occurs, famously, in 1904, one year after the centenary of Herder's death, when several celebrations of his life and work took place across Europe. His complete works were edited and released at this time. Karl Breul, writing in 1904, asserts that Herder's contribution to European letters is no less than the attempt to 'arrive at a true history of the human spirit in all its manifestations' (Breul 1904: 8), a breadth of intellectual scope that would certainly bring him to Joyce's attention. Buck Mulligan's claim that Kalipedia or the study of beauty will 'soon be generally adopted', a move which will involve 'plastercast reproductions of the classical statues such as Venus and Apollo' (Joyce 2008: 398), seems Herderian, given the latter's *Kaligone* of 1800 and study of reproductions of those figures, amongst many others, in his *Sculpture*: 'Venus steps out of her bath with her beautiful back curved like a dove [. . .]. How can I describe such things?' (Herder 2002: 75). Herder might also have come to Joyce's notice in his treatment, in the first of his *Critical Groves*, of the myth and sculpture of Laocoön, the Trojan priest whose story of fatherhood and castration ties him to *Ulysses*, and whose fate and sculptural depiction (attributed to Agesander, Athenodoros and Polydoros) is explored most comprehensively by Gotthold Ephraïm Lessing, mentor and often intellectual goad to Herder. Lessing's aesthetic treatise *Laocoön: An Essay on the Limits of Painting and Poetry* (1766) fascinated Herder with its contemplation of the relationship between the arts, and its rejection of the thinking of Johann Joachim Winckelmann. Stephen's aesthetics, in *Portrait* dominated by Aquinas and Aristotle, seem in *Ulysses* to have absorbed the advice of Donovan – 'the *Laocoon* interested me very much when I read it. [. . .] idealistic, German, ultraprofound' (Joyce 2000a: 229) – and the interrelationship between the arts is considered in 'Proteus', although we presume that Stephen has clung to his view that 'Lessing [. . .] should not have taken a group of statues to write of' (Joyce 2000a: 232). Joyce may also have come to Laocoön through Quintus Smyrnaeus's *Posthomerica* (c. third century CE), the most grisly evocation of the tale. E. M. Butler, in his *The Tyranny of Greece Over Germany* of 1935, suggests that it is Herder who is the better reader of Homer, overshadowing Lessing in interpreting the poet 'more truly' (Butler 1935: 74), a status that might recommend him to Joyce. Lessing's interpretation of Laocoön crops up again in Joseph Frank's influential but critically disputed essay 'Spatial Form in Modern Literature' of 1945. Frank's interest is, once more, in the interrelationship between the arts, in the wake of the addition of the 'cinematograph'. He attributes to *Ulysses* the label of 'cinematographic' form (Frank 1945: 230–2) for its non-linear, therefore spatialised, approach to the representation of time. Frank's essay is of most use here in reminding us to consider the importance of Lessing and, by association, Herder, and their attention to sculptural renderings of mythic events. Yet it is pertinent to note that, in Servius's reading, Laocoön is punished for conjugal relations with his wife taking place prior to offering a sacrifice to Neptune, and in the presence of a cult image (Brown and Mann 1990: 61) – a situation which recalls the Nymph-hung bedroom of the Blooms, and also points toward a third possible source of sculpture-related influence pressing upon Joyce in the composition of *Ulysses*.

That third source is Sacher-Masoch's *Venus in Furs*. It is William York Tindall who first noted the influence of the latter novel upon the 'Circe' episode of *Ulysses* (Tindall 1959: 207), an observation that has led Steven Marcus to consider that episode in the context of Victorian treatments of flagellation (Marcus 1964: 258–9). Carol Siegel and Frances L. Restuccia have expanded upon Tindall's original statement, arguing that it is Masochian rather than Freudian theorisations of sexual masochism that are pertinent to Joyce's work (Restuccia 1985: 101–16; Siegel 1987: 179–95). However, these critical treatments have tended to read the Masochian influence as connected primarily to Bloom's fantasies of cuckoldry, and to his usurpation by Blazes Boylan in particular – 'a woman's infidelity is certainly a painful stimulus, the supreme voluptuousness', claims Sacher-Masoch's Severin (Sacher-Masoch 2000: 49). It is, as Tindall indicates, in the 'Circe' episode that Bloom's fantasies of shameful domination at the hands of female figures achieve free rein. Severin has been mugging up on Circe, before the cruel and alluring Wanda takes over his existence: 'I was [. . .] reading the *Odyssey*, the part about the attractive sorceress [Circe] who turned her worshipers [*sic*] into beasts. A delicious picture of ancient love' (Sacher-Masoch 2000: 16). Joyce's Mrs Bellingham, giving evidence at the hallucinated semi-trial of 'Circe', reports that Bloom 'addressed me in several handwritings with fulsome compliments as a Venus in furs' (Joyce 2008: 441–2). Meanwhile, Mrs Mervyon Talboys threatens to 'flay him alive' (443), her 'Talboys' (tall boys?) moniker perhaps returning the idea of corporal punishment to its natural, boarding school habitat (although flaying alive goes, of course, far beyond the birch). Bloom is overwhelmed, claiming an interest only in 'refined birching to stimulate the circulation' (443), a phrase returning us to the less sexually loaded environments of the newspaper offices ('But will he save the circulation?' (114)) and, we presume, the Turkish baths (83). The argument for Bloom's masochistic tendencies is, then, firm. However, the importance of statuary in *Venus in Furs* has been neglected. Alongside Ovid and Herder, Sacher-Masoch's stone figures are brought into sharper relief.

Sacher-Masoch's unnamed narrator greets Venus in the opening scene: 'my visitor was the Goddess of Love – in the flesh' (Sacher-Masoch 2000: 3). Venus retains the 'pale face' and 'marble pallor' (4) of her stony self, recalling Gerty's carefully curated waxen complexion, as well as Molly's preparation, forgotten by Bloom in the events of the day, which the chemist notes contains 'white wax' (Joyce 2008: 81). Sacher-Masoch's Venus also has 'white eyes', a reminder of Jacques Derrida's claim (see Chapter 1) that the eyes of statues are 'walled up' or blind. Yet the animated Venus most obviously connects to the tale of Pygmalion, and it is clear that Sacher-Masoch, as well as Joyce, has been reading the *Metamorphoses*: 'there, in front of me, sat Venus [. . .] with warm blood and a throbbing pulse. Yes, she had come alive for me, like that statue that had started breathing for her creator' (Sacher-Masoch 2000: 15).[15] The narrator also remarks that 'her skin was so infinitely delicate that the blue veins shimmered through everywhere' (17), echoing the search for Galatea's pulse. Sacher-Masoch's main protagonist, Severin, shares with Bloom the fantasy of physical domination and cuckoldry, but these enthusiasms are here more explicitly connected to his passion for sculpture; moreover, he shares this passion with the sadistic Wanda. In the narrative's present, an image of the titular 'Venus in Furs' graces Severin's wall alongside Titian's *Venus with Mirror*, one final Venus useful in the analysis of Joyce's Molly, since she refers to her own time in front of the mirror (Joyce 2008: 701), and her moment of self-reflection concludes a book which has begun with the 'cracked lookingglass of a servant' used by Buck Mulligan in his morning ablutions at the Martello tower (7). The 'small Carpathian resort' in which Severin and Wanda meet contains a stone statue of Venus (Sacher-Masoch 2000: 12), of importance to both characters since Wanda declares herself to be allied with the Greeks and against the moderns, due to an upbringing in which fairytales were replaced by 'Venus and Apollo, Heracles and Laocoön' (20), and Severin admits to kneeling before a plaster Venus in his childhood days, and 'recit[ing] to her the prayers that had been inculcated in me, the Lord's Prayer, the Hail Mary, and the Credo' (31).[16] This statement of belief in beauty, the beauty of sculptural bodies, is Bloomian

– as Mulligan notes, 'O, I fear me, he [Bloom] is Greeker than the Greeks' (Joyce 2008: 192). The story of Wanda and Severin plays out amongst classical sculpture, since the former elects to live in a Florentine villa containing 'a kind of loggia, with plaster casts of ancient statues' (Sacher-Masoch 2000: 70), in the garden of which Severin finds a 'small temple' containing yet another iteration of the 'Goddess of Love' (71), whom he views through a chink in the door that may recall Bloom's fantasy of cuckoldry in the person of Blazes Boylan: 'You can apply your eye to the keyhole and play with yourself while I just go through her a few times' (Joyce 2008: 527). Severin continues his sculptural habit, another strange necessity, with a visit to the *Medici Venus* on a rare day of respite from torture and slavery at Wanda's hands (Sacher-Masoch 2000: 88); he makes no attempt to assess her ownership of an anus, meaning his devotional journey has more in common with Mulligan's ('I went to hail the foamborn Aphrodite. [. . .] Every day we must do homage to her' (Joyce 2008: 192)) than Bloom's ('his [. . .] eyes were on her mesial groove' (Joyce 2008: 192)).[17]

Sacher-Masoch has his imperious marble Venus explore the consequences of breaking the Herderian rule and actualising the imagined touch of the eye: 'And if any of you ever has the power to kiss my red lips, he then goes on a pilgrimage to Rome, barefoot and in a penitent's shirt, and expects flowers to blossom from his withered staff' (Sacher-Masoch 2000: 5). While we presume Venus's primary reference is to Tannhäuser, Bloom's blossom-related name and withered (limp) staff (father of thousands) makes him a post-touching penitent in his beach scene with Gerty when read against Sacher-Masoch's earlier text. We know the Blooms to be readers of Sacher-Masoch, since Leopold's trip to the library includes a rejection of the author's *Tales of the Ghetto* as already having been read (Joyce 2008: 226), while *Sweets of Sin*'s 'sable-trimmed wrap' (226) recalls Wanda's customary get-up. While Severin describes himself as 'suprasensual', and reliant upon his imagination for the nourishment of his desires (Sacher-Masoch 2000: 36), it is Wanda herself who comes closest to a description of the Herderian look when she remarks, of the work of Herder's compatriot and (with reservations) friend: 'Those verses from Goethe's *Roman Elegies* have always delighted me [. . .] "Desire followed glance, pleasure followed desire"' (18). Such is the influence, via a common interest in the sculptural, between Sacher-Masoch and Joyce that we can in fact have Goethe's line as a kind of masturbatory manifesto. Bloom is a man for whom the look which touches leads to desire, to self-touching and, as on the beach, to the pleasure of ejaculation.

The three strands of sculptural influence pressing upon Joyce, and drawn through the trinity of female figures composed of the Nymph, Gerty and Molly, become intertwined most conspicuously when Bloom's contemplation of the curving wooden bar of Davy Byrne's pub prompts a riff on the goddesses of the museum:

> Beauty: it curves: curves are beauty. [. . .] Can seen [sic] them library museum standing in the round hall, naked [. . .]. All to see. Never speaking. [. . .] Suppose she did Pygmalion and Galatea what would she say first? Mortal! Put you in your proper place. [. . .] Lovely forms of woman sculped [sic] [. . .]. Immortal lovely. [. . .] They have no. Never looked. I'll look today. (Joyce 2008: 168)

Herder's claim about the beauty of bodies is here, alongside the curve (recalling the curve of the lemniscate, infinite or 'immortal') of Hogarth's line of beauty. The 'round hall' nods toward Mannheim's distribution of sculptural works, while Ovid's tale recurs as refracted through Sacher-Masoch's imperious, pallid Venus. Bloom concludes with the intention of establishing whether or not these goddesses have an anus, a shift from the eye's trace along the double curve of the voluptuous bottom, to matters of bodily circulation. The anus, elsewhere a matter of sexual fetish for Bloom, here becomes fundamental to the goddess/mortal distinction, the indicator of allegiance to perishable enfleshment or otherwor(l)dly immortality. In working with Ovid, Herder (and, through him, Hogarth and Lessing) and Sacher-Masoch, Joyce is able to consider the relationship between forms of art, the distinction between the quick and the dead, the absence of that distinction or possible border-crossing recorded in the Pygmalion myth, human sensory capacities, and aesthetic and sexual responses to beauty.

Sleepy sickness and statuary

It is possible that one particular aspect of life at Joyce's time of writing prompts these densely packed interweavings of three major strands of sculptural influence, and that is the epidemic of von Economo's disease or 'sleeping sickness', now known as encephalitis lethargica (EL) or 'sleepy sickness' (to distinguish it from the 'sleeping sickness' of the Tsetse fly), which took place in Europe, the US and beyond between 1916 and 1927, having first been reported in Vienna (*The Manchester Guardian* 1922: 5). William Pryse-Phillips describes the disease as 'polymorphic', given its varied manifestations, but notes that it is 'marked by fever, pharyngitis [inflammation of the throat], generalized pains, skin rashes, malaise, and gastrointestinal complaints, and by such signs as extreme drowsiness, oculomotor pareses [damage to nerves and muscles controlling the eye], delirium, and catatonia [immobility and stupor]', while its sequelae are a variety of sleep disturbance disorders, including narcolepsy (Pryse-Phillips 2009: 329). Speculation of the period suggested that EL might be connected to the influenza epidemic often referred to as Spanish flu (see Pryse-Phillips 2009; Dale et al. 2003), but subsequent investigation has revealed it to be a 'postinfectious autoimmune [. . .] disorder' (Pryse-Phillips 2009: 329). While EL's polymorphic nature afforded a range of symptoms, those of greatest note because most debilitating were ones associated with catatonic states, reported by newspapers of the time as turning victims into living statues, 'when the patient is conscious of his environment, but is unable to assert himself' (*The Observer* 1922: 7). The epidemic proved a compelling topic for the press and was reported widely, since 'the public's imagination was stirred by pictures of its more striking clinical manifestations' (*The Manchester Guardian* 1922: 5). It is therefore the case that Joyce, a man who shares with his central protagonist an interest in medical matters, having abandoned his medical training (at Cecilia Street Medical School, Dublin) in 1902 (R. Ellmann 1965: 111), composed the sculpture-riddled *Ulysses* at a time when the myth of Pygmalion appeared to have become, in the most frightening way, a reality.

'Sleeping sickness' achieves one brief mention in 'Lotus-Eaters', when Bloom pauses outside the Belfast and Oriental Tea Company (Joyce 2008: 69). However, given the floral preoccupations of that episode, the phrase is most often interpreted as being connected to the use of opiates, and a straightforward piece of Bloom's Orientalist curiosity regarding the East (see Almond 2002). The phrase might conceivably refer to the other, Tsetse-transmitted disease, since confusions between the two were common in the early stages of the outbreak (*The Manchester Guardian* 1922: 5). Yet the bleeding statues of the EL epidemic do make an oblique appearance in Joyce's novel. One of the recorded 'oculomotor pareses' of the outbreak was 'oculargyric crisis' (Dale et al. 2003: 22), the rolling of the eyes, usually upwards, leaving only whites visible. *The Manchester Guardian* of 12 September 1922, writing of a recent report on EL by the British Ministry of Health, notes in bald terms that 'often the eyes "go funny"' (*The Manchester Guardian* 1922: 5). To Bloom, this heavenward glance might be read as arousal or sexual ecstasy ('Whites of eyes swooning up' (Joyce 2008: 227)), but it would also recall the 'walled up' or pallid eyes of Sacher-Masoch's stony Venus, and the pious statuary of Dignam's grove, in which 'stone hopes [are] praying with upcast eyes' (108). In a quirk of medical history, while cases of EL have been observed for hundreds of years, the major epidemic prior to Joyce's time had occurred in 1712 (Pryse-Phillips

2009: 329), that is, immediately prior to another important period of speculation about sculptural forms, in the work of Winckelmann, Hogarth and Herder. While literary and philosophical influences press upon Joyce in his exploration of statuary, it may be the Galateas of his own contemporary moment that prompt the author to make the matter of the look which touches, the pro-masturbatory caress of the eye along the sculptural curve, such a prominent theme in *Ulysses*.[18]

Smashed to atoms

The sculpturally still victim of encephalitis lethargica may also sit behind Bloom's thought patterns regarding the event of Dignam's interment, since the latter is imagined as buried alive ('He is no more dead than you are', says Alf Bergan. 'Maybe so [. . .] they took the liberty of burying him this morning anyhow', replies Joe Hynes (Joyce 2008: 288)), and as making a reappearance through unexpected exhumations: 'Bom! Upset. A coffin bumped out onto the road. Burst open. Paddy Dignam shot out and rolling over stiff in the dust in a brown habit [. . .] the insides decompose quickly. Much better to close up all the orifices' (95).[19] It is the phrase 'burst open' that is of greatest importance in Bloom's mortuary imagination. While the previous section of this chapter concerned itself with the press and trace of the imagined touch along the epidermic lines of statuary and the statuesque, it is equally true that Bloom, and Joyce, take an interest in the counter-pressure: an internal inflation leading to the bursting of the skin. While Molly's full curves are lauded, there is a moment when the 'wellfilled' becomes the 'overfilled', and the skin border, the dermic aegis, is split asunder. The closing up of Dignam's orifices, an act of embalmment that gives his body the continent status of the National Museum goddesses, is a hedge against that bursting which Bloom fears. Throughout the novel, Bloom observes moments when the curve pushes too far, when bloating becomes, potentially, bursting, where one's skin, one's altogether, threatens to fall apart. 'Modern man has an epidermis rather than a soul', wrote Joyce (Berrone 1977: 15; see also Connor 2004: 9; Ellmann 2010: 151). If, via the EL epidemic, we can read the modern epidermis as operating as a bulwark between the living and the (only apparently?) dead, then moments when that bulwark is traduced in terms real or imagined will have the gravest of existential implications.[20]

Simon Dedalus's grim humour imagines the death of Father Coffey, whose almost-funereal surname makes appropriate his presiding over Dignam's funeral, but also anticipates his own demise: 'Burst sideways like a sheep in clover Dedalus says he will. With a belly on him like a poisoned pup' (Joyce 2008: 100). Later, Bloom imagines rats in vats, helping themselves to an excess of porter: 'Drink themselves bloated as big as a collie floating' (145), an analogy that recalls Stephen's sighting of the 'bloated carcase of a dog' during his morning walk on the beach (44). In a later return to the question of Dignam, Bloom again thinks 'belly like a poisoned pup' (266). A preoccupation with the skin fit to burst is also in evidence when Bloom contemplates the long lying-in of Mrs Purefoy: 'Three days imagine groaning on a bed [. . .], her belly swollen out! Phew!' (154). Meanwhile C. P. M'Coy awaits the body of a drowned man (72), whom Stephen remembers as having drowned nine days ago (45), and who is called to mind shortly after the sighting of the dog, suggesting that he too might be found in a bloated state. The tautened skin is also present in the form of the drummer of Micky Rooney's band, whom Bloom thinks may have discovered his vocation through striking his own bloated stomach, following a dinner of 'pig's cheek and cabbage [. . .]. Pom. Pompedy' (277). His drum, remarks Bloom (whose speculations at this point have him living up to his misspelt moniker of 'Boom' (602)), would be made of ass's skin, struck in both life (as a beast of burden) and death (as a drum's surface) (277). Bloom, whose name indicates both natural generation (most conspicuous in his pseudonym of Henry Flower) and the fungal bloom of decay, is concerned with circulation (of newspapers, blood, food and faeces), with decomposition (of bodies, phrases and ads), and with the meatiness or carnality of fleshly existence (Dignam's body, Plumtree's potted meat). However, his primary interest is in 'THE DISSOLUTION OF A MOST RESPECTED DUBLIN BURGESS' (114), as 'Aeolus' has it; not the moral or spiritual dissolution hinted at in the term 'respected', but his bursting and dissolving, the prospect of his carnal explosion. When Dignam is imagined slipping from his coffin, he also slips from beneath the brown habit of his traditional burial garb (95). The habit forms a second skin, echoing the one that Dignam has inhabited in his life, while its cowl apes the hood of the penis, and, perhaps, a natal caul. Having slipped that skin, he might, thinks Bloom, slip the one beneath. In a counterpoint to the tactile trace of the eye, then, Bloom frets repeatedly about dermal incontinence, about skins split apart by internal force. Boom.

The printing presses of the newspaper offices and their 'thumping thump' (114) lead Bloom to wonder what would happen were man to meet machine, not in the cooperative symbiosis of typesetter and mechanism (118), but in a terrible mangling: 'Smash a man to atoms if they got him caught' (114). This atomisation or dissolution – imagined specifically as the fate of Dignam – would occur if the machines 'got out of hand' (114). While the latter phrase is a colloquialism connoting the loss of control, it also refers to the powerlessness that comes from the accession of manual tasks to a mechanical apparatus. Further, we might note that Dignam's conversion to atoms would also move *him* beyond the tactile – we cannot grasp an atom, as will be seen in Chapter 3. We could propose that, as a result of Bloom's morbid fascination with the penetration of the skin, his technology of preference is the X-ray machine; that which leaves the skin intact. Ellmann has noted that the narrator of the 'Ithaca' episode describes Bloom as 'reluctant to shed human blood even when the end justifie[s] the means' (Ellmann 2010: 165; Joyce 2008: 627). Sara Danius apparently concurs, reading the X-ray apparatus as a visual technology that operates as a positive prosthesis, extending the human ocular capacities (Danius 2002: 75–82). While this is quite true, we can also read the X-ray machine as connected to the haptic in important ways, since its status as marvellous is attributable to its access to that which cannot be touched. In addition, the X-ray was first explored and promoted using images of the human hand. A reading of the haptic aspects of the promotion of early X-ray technology allows us to observe some very Bloomian preoccupations, and to challenge the idea that Bloom's chosen technology leaves the human skin rather soothingly in place.

Those naughty Röntgen rays

X-rays gain limited mention in *Ulysses*. Moving towards Dawson Street, Bloom wonders how one might view the full process of food consumption, peristalsis and so on: 'Something green it would have to be [. . .]. Then with those Röntgen rays searchlight you could' (Joyce 2008: 171). As the masticated food takes a 'tour round the body' (171), the rays will make a tour, or visual spectacle, of the digestion process. However, 'the poor buffer would have to stand all the time with his insides entrails on show. Science' (171). This latter reference to embarrassment or indecency, at access to that which ought not to be seen, is present in the public reception of X-rays from their earliest days. Journalist H. J. W. Dam, one of the first to be given access to Wilhelm Röntgen's Würzburg laboratory following the discovery of the rays in 1895, recalls his own X-ray experience in just such terms, while also retaining a touch of the circus, a sense of the show or 'tour':

'Step inside,' said he [Röntgen], opening the door which was on the side of the box farthest from the tube. I immediately did so, not altogether certain whether my skeleton was to be photographed for general inspection or my secret thoughts held up to light on a glass plate. (Dam, quoted in Glasser 1933: 8)

The pose of the naïf is here, a journalistic tactic, alongside the inevitable hesitancy that greets any new technological development. Yet Dam's nervousness regarding specifically mental privacy ('my secret thoughts') is echoed in Edmund Wilson's description of *Ulysses*, in 1922, as 'the most faithful x-ray ever taken of the ordinary human consciousness' (Deming 1970: 228), testament not only to the boundary-pushing power of Joyce's literary experiment, but also to the uncertain scope of the X-ray's capacities.[21] Ideas of exposure haunt the newspaper reports of Röntgen's efforts, seguing into Bloomian fantasies of stripped outfits, flayed or burst skin and crumbled flesh.

Otto Glasser, writing in 1933, looks back upon the treatment of this new discovery beyond the scientific press, and notes that 'the properties of the mysterious rays remained incomprehensible to the layman' (Glasser 1933: 45), resulting in panic, albeit humorous, about just what was going to be displayed by the machine. In 1896, *Punch* was not alone in misdescribing the new technology as an advanced form of photography which could penetrate the flesh, 'giving a picture only of the bones' (Glasser 1933: 41). The poem 'The New Photography' therefore made reference to Röntgen's 'grim and graveyard humour', the reluctance of *Punch* readers to 'take our flesh off and to pose in / Our bones' and, ultimately, a complete ban on 'your worse than "altogether" state / Of portraiture' (Anon., quoted in Glasser 1933: 41). Lawrence K. Russel's 'Lines on an X-ray Portrait of a Lady' (1896), a rather more elegant verse, deploys a lovelorn stance to register disgust in lines such as 'her dorsal vertebrae are not concealed / By epidermis, but are well revealed', also noting that 'Her flesh a halo makes, misty in line' while 'Her noseless, eyeless face looks into mine' (Russel, quoted in Glasser 1933: 42). That 'noseless, eyeless face' may call to mind Stephen's mother in her shredded shroud (Joyce 2008: 539), and the beagle of Nighttown who, feeding on rotting flesh, also has a rotten visage (447). The idea of flesh becoming 'mist' occurred to Sunflower (see Excursus), but the same terminology is used by Woolf's Lily Briscoe of *To the Lighthouse* (1927) who, sitting opposite Charles Tansley at dinner, states that she sees 'as in an X-ray photograph, the ribs and thigh bones of the young man's desire to impress himself lying dark in the mist of his flesh' (Woolf 2008: 74). Woolf's attendance at an 1897 lecture on the power of the rays has informed her writing here (Woolf 2004: 9–10). Russel focuses upon the exposure of the skeleton, the beyond altogether which is a *memento mori* held within the body, as noted by Thomas Mann's Hans Castorp in *The Magic Mountain* (1924), who witnesses Joachim's 'graveyard shape and bony tenement, this lean *memento mori*, this scaffolding' (Mann 1999: 216; see also Kern 2003: 7; Danius 2002: 80). However, other Bloomian interests are in evidence within the saucier responses to this new notion of a penetrating ray. Glasser reports that 'a few weeks after the discovery [of the rays] a firm in London advertised the "sale of X-ray proof under-clothing"' (Glasser 1933: 44). Inappropriate revelation is also played upon in a rhyme attributed to 'Wilhelma', and published in *Photography* in 1896: 'I'm full of daze, / Shock and amaze; / For nowadays / I hear they'll gaze / Thro' cloak and gown – and even stays, / These naughty, naughty Roentgen Rays' (Wilhelma, quoted in Glasser 1933: 44). While Bloom's fascination with unpinning should be read, as above, as a collapse of the shapely line, it can also be considered a series of exfoliations or the slow sloughing of skins (see Ellmann 2006; O'Hanrahan 2006). It is the X-ray apparatus that, as its press reception just prior to Bloom's moment makes clear, was culturally received as an extreme form of striptease – a reminder of the deathly in its offering up of the human skeleton, certainly, but also holding out the promise of access to previously impenetrable layers. For some, the 'epilating effects' (Glasser 1933: 294) and 'roentgen ray dermatitis' (301) brought about by the X-ray procedure may have seemed the thin end of the wedge, the start of a skinning process that would bring them down to bare bones. Between Bloom's fantasy of access to gustatory processes, and his fascination with unpinned knickers (Joyce 2008: 76, 352, 516), sits his interest in the X-ray. Far from leaving the skin in place, it metaphorically (and, through dermatitis, literally) begins to lift it, a horripilation that leads to a comically horrified response in the late nineteenth and early twentieth-century press.

That 'poster boy' of the haptic, the human hand, is the star of the X-ray show. Röntgen's early experiments involved the creation of images of his own hand and, later and more famously, of his wife's. The X-ray 'Hand mit Ringen' (1895) showed Mrs Röntgen's bones and her wedding band, and its title's artistic pretensions perhaps anticipated its republication in scientific and layman's magazines around the globe, as well as its place in the Deutsche Museum, Munich (see Glasser 1933: 25). Danius notes that hand X-rays became sentimental tokens (Danius 2002: 78), presumably playing on the 'I give you my hand' notion contained within Mrs Röntgen's wedding-banded image. The women of New York had X-ray images made of their hands in order to compete with one another regarding the delicacy of their structure (Danius 2002: 78), a fad that puts Sinclair Lewis's Tanis Judique in context (see

Chapter 1). We return to notions of contact and contagion here (root: *contigere*, 'to have contact with', 'to pollute'), since the hand images were, states Glasser, responsible for the unprecedentedly fast spread of news regarding Röntgen's discovery: 'rarely in the history of science has information concerning a new [. . .] invention been disseminated so rapidly or has it made such a deep impression' (Glasser 1933: 29), while 'of all the first roentgen pictures, that of the human hand made the greatest impression upon the public [. . .] [they] contributed their part in demonstrating the important properties of the roentgen rays *ad oculus*' (32). Despite Glasser's claim that the hands 'opened a wide vista for the practical use of the rays [in the study of anatomy]' (32), his tactile terminology of 'impression' and his focus upon the importance of hand images in demonstrations *'ad oculus'* ('with [here, 'for'] the eye') allows a recalibration of our reading of the X-ray apparatus as not only a visual but also a haptic technology, changing the human understanding of what is and is not available to the touch, and leading to fantasies of fallible skin and disloyal flesh, likely to fall away. Röntgen's apparatus is, for the newspaper humourists as, potentially, for Bloom, a *memento mori* machine, reminding us of the inevitable decay of our flesh, revealing the bones beneath. It is also a machine that moves beyond the haptic capacities of the body – we must trust our eyes (and our scientists); we cannot touch that skeleton. Strange, then, that its capacities should be demonstrated repeatedly through the representation of the hand, the bodily element whose skills of verification it trumps – Mrs Röntgen's manual portrait is a picture of the outmoded organ, taken by the technology responsible for its redundancy. When Bloom chooses the X-ray for the investigation of digestive processes he does so in line with his abiding interest in the potential incontinence of the human skin. Joyce's own X-ray experience, at the insistence of Louis Berman (see Armstrong 1998: 89), has been marshalled into one further exploration of the skin border within *Ulysses*.

The blind stripling

Having considered the look that touches, we now turn to its corollary, the touch that looks – the touch, that is, of the blind. While the blind man is, as we will note, a central trope of studies concerned with optics, he is also, by virtue of his loss of vision, thrown upon his haptic resources, and therefore proves a fascinating figure when addressing issues of touch and the tactile. Recalling Condillac's deployment of the Pygmalion myth, in which Galatea gains, by stages, the sensory capacities of the human body, we might consider the blind man to have retreated along that transformational path. For Joyce, such a view is too simplistic and, combining renowned studies of blindness from the seventeenth and eighteenth centuries with his own contemporary experiences of ophthalmic ill health, he explores the possibility that blindness might produce a compensatory access to other modes of 'seeing'. Attridge cautions that we cannot tackle Joyce's work without 'tak[ing] into account his struggle with poor eyesight' (Attridge 2006: 58) and, given the eye problems of Herder and, for that matter, Homer, it seems we must obey and pay attention to this aspect of Joyce's writing life. I connect the author's eyesight to his *writing* life advisedly. As Tim Armstrong has noted, '[Ezra] Pound found in Joyce's focus on [. . .] the text as texture a precise reflection of his worsening eyesight – as if he were too close to the surface of the artwork to gain perspective' (Armstrong 1998: 88). Pound went so far as to consult the American medic and ophthalmological expert George M. Gould on Joyce's behalf (Armstrong 1998: 88), and we can see in Gould's own literary criticism a concern with what he termed 'the poet[ry] of myopia' (Gould 1908: xiii). In his study of the life and literary work of Patrick Lafcadio Hearn, Gould claims that 'his terrible myopia shut him out from every calling except that of a writer' (Gould 1908: 78), and that a myopic literary style results:

> With creative instinct or ability denied, with the poet's craving for open-eyed knowing, and with the poet's necessity of realizing the world out there, Hearn, baldly stated, was forced to become the poet of myopia. His groping mind was compelled to rest satisfied with the world of distance and reality transported by the magic carpet to the door of his imagination and fancy. (Gould 1908: 117)

Hearn had himself considered 'The Artistic Value of Myopia' in a *Times-Democrat* article of 1887 (Gould 1908: 109). Gould's use of the phrase 'open-eyed knowing' reminds us that the etymology of myopia refers, via the Greek *myein* ('to close'), to the closed or shut eye, that which is, to touch once more upon Derrida, 'walled up'. Hearn's passion for the ghost stories and legends of Japan – most in evidence in *Kwaidan: Stories and Studies of Strange Things* (1904) – invokes two other terms from the *myein* root, 'mystery' and 'myth', both of them referring to the prospect of revelation (as in, of course, the mystery plays). *Ulysses*, structured in relation to the *Odyssey* (in a way that West finds unproductive (1987b: 28)), is also mythic in this second sense, as a book of the closed or veiled eye, exploring the limits of vision, and written by another poet of the myopic, another man with a 'groping mind'. Yet myopia as a medical term, and as one of the diagnoses given to Joyce

(R. Ellmann 1965: 66), is 'nearsightedness', bringing us back to Pound's textural reading of Joyce's work, and to the *Nahsicht* that, as we saw in Chapter 1, Aloïs Riegl attributes to Egyptian art.[22] In fact, Riegl's near-sightedness and Pound's claim that Joyce works in the *enchroi* position, right up close to the text, put us squarely in the realm of the haptic. For Laura U. Marks, haptic films

> appeal to embodied memory by bringing vision as close as possible to the image; by converting vision to touch. [. . .] They do this in part by refusing to make their images accessible to vision, so that the viewer must resort to other senses, such as touch, in order to perceive the image. (Marks 2000: 159)

Brought close to textural elements of a scene, the viewer is unable to gain purchase on what is depicted, responding by moving beyond looking and calling upon other somatic resources. Marks's haptic film, requiring the response of the viewer's haptic capacities, finds a near neighbour in the nearsightedness of Joyce's textural text.

Myopia is precipitated or aggravated by eyestrain following an excess of reading, or by the reading of small (close) print in dim light. A habitual proximity to the text results in the necessity of proximity, as nearsightedness eventually demands the close positioning of the book. As in the case of Huxley's savage, we should note that references to the solitary pleasure of reading and that of masturbation often, to use a sub-Joycean pun, come hand in hand. Indulgence in either leads, apparently, to stages of blindness. Robert James's *A Medical Dictionary*, published in London between 1743 and 1745, contains an entry on the topic of 'manustrapratio' which includes the story of a small boy who, as a result of over-indulgence in masturbation, has begun to write in increasingly small script, ultimately ending up nearly blind, and being given the diagnosis of 'amaurosis, impairment of vision, without manifest fault of the eye' (Laqueur 2003: 37). The longstanding association of masturbation with blindness provides one further inflection to Derrida's claim that 'the blind are beings of the fall, the manifestation always of that which threatens erection or the upright position' (Derrida 1993: 21). Setting aside the sexual implication of 'fall' and 'erection', the likely stumble of the blind pedestrian (see below), and the reduction of the blind to the resources of Aristotle's 'base' sense, Derrida's suggestion is that to write of a blind man is, to deploy Ellmann's proposed term for the 'Penelope' episode, to undertake a proneography. While orthography is erect(ion) writing, proneography traces the fallen blind. Molly, reclining in bed and in the dark, shares with the blind that necessary move toward the haptic resources, leading not only to her self-touching and an increased awareness of her other sensory functions in her present moment, but also to the mobilisation of her sensory memory. Her youth in Gibraltar, and a variety of her sexual experiences, are remembered through her body: 'my goodness the heat there [Gibraltar] before the levanter came on black as night' (Joyce 2008: 706); 'I was thinking of him on the sea all the time after at mass when my petticoat began to slip down at the elevation weeks and weeks I kept the handerchief [*sic*] under my pillow for the smell of him there' (713); 'my hole is itching me always when I think of him I want to' (714).[23] This resummoning of past experiences through the invocation of the haptic memory is referred to in Denis Diderot's *Letter on the Blind for the Use of Those Who Can See* (1749), where he notes that, while it is hard to imagine how a blind man experiences and utilises touch:

> I have myself [. . .] had the experience of being in the grip of a violent passion and felt my whole hand tremble as the impressions of bodies that I had touched a long time ago were reawakened in me as vividly as if they were still present to my touch. (Diderot 2011: 182)

It is just such a haptic memory that Molly sets in train. Meanwhile, reversing the customary teleology, she allows the blindness (of night) to lead to masturbation. The shift toward the haptic and toward smell, brought about by the loss of sight, is again connected to the sensual pleasures of Molly's body in a reverie of Bloom's: 'parlour windows plastered with bills. Plasters on a sore eye. [. . .] smell[ing] the gentle smoke of tea [. . .]. Be[ing] near her ample bedwarmed flesh' (Joyce 2008: 59). However, while darkness gives some sense of the sensory shifts initiated by the loss of vision ('dark men they call them [the blind]' (173)), it is through Bloom's encounter with the figure of the medically, permanently blind stripling that Joyce makes explicit his interest in the place of the blind man within the history of philosophies of the senses.

'Seeing' beyond the eye

The thought processes precipitated by the stripling show Bloom to be familiar with several aspects of blind life. Halted at the kerb, and undertaking investigations with his 'slender cane', the former appears to need Bloom's assistance:

> His wall face frowned weakly. He moved his head uncertainly. [. . .] The cane moved out trembling to the left. Mr Bloom's eye followed its line and saw again the dyeworks' van drawn up before Drago's. [. . .] He touched the thin elbow gently: then took the limp seeing hand to guide it forward. (Joyce 2008: 172)

The stripling's 'wall face' is, we presume, a result of his 'walled up' eyes, with the sense that a barrier has been erected, not only keeping out one particular stream of information (the visual), but also preventing communication from within in a customary set of facial responses – the stripling cannot, like Eliot's Prufrock, prepare a face to meet the faces that he meets, since he may initially be unaware that he is meeting them. The 'wall face' is, however, a useful one – Bloom goes on to ask 'How on earth did he know that van was there? [. . .] Seeing things in their foreheads perhaps' (173), a reference to the 'facial vision' or echoloca-tion of the blind (see Paterson 2009: 135). There is a touch of this also in Bloom's speculation that a cat with clipped whiskers can no longer mouse, since the night vision afforded by the hairs will be lost (Joyce 2008: 54). The stripling is later described as having a 'bloodless pious face', presumably because his lack of oculogyric control results in the heavenward turn of his eyeballs, linking him to the 'upcast' eyes of Dignam's mortuary grove. The reading of his face as displaying piety also suggests that he has turned his eyes from the spectacle of 'DEAR DIRTY DUBLIN' (139) – that, unhampered by vision (the vision of a beautiful ankle in a transparent stocking?), he has his mind on higher things.[24]

The stripling's hand, although limp, is a 'seeing' one, a notion reiter-ated when Bloom speculates that he is 'sizing me up I dare say from my hand' (173), a colloquial phrase combining the establishing of size itself with an additional effort to assess the kind or quality of person met (see also 'to take the measure of' someone). That this statement is followed immediately by the thought 'wonder if he has a name' (173) further emphasises that, in addition to putting forward the peculiar idea that a blind man might not be granted the courtesy of self-definition, Bloom is worrying that his own identity and business might somehow be discernible through the braille of his hand – that he might be read. The handshake, that gesture of reciprocity we considered in Chapter 1, here highlights the dissimilarities in the two men's modes of knowing. The reference to 'Mr Bloom's eye' following the line of the stripling's cane reiterates that which Bloom has the use of and the stripling does not, since 'Mr Bloom followed its line and saw' would adequately describe the scene, such is the reader's presumption that all five senses will be in operation unless otherwise stated. The reading of blindness as debilitat-ing and as worthy of pity is attenuated by Bloom's speculations regard-ing the compensatory refinement of the other senses, further advantages to set alongside the 'seeing' hand: 'Sense of smell must be stronger too. Smells on all sides bunched together. Each person too. Then the spring, the summer: smells. Tastes' (173). Such refinements include the increased sensitivity of the haptic sense modality: 'Look at all the things they can learn to do. Read with their fingers. Tune pianos. [. . .] Of course the other senses are more. Embroider' (173). While the finessing of other senses is something of a cliché in representations of blind figures, it has a basis in fact, since 'in a person with long-term blindness, the part of the brain that sighted people use to interpret visual information (the visual cortex) is actually recruited to interpret stimuli received through touch and hearing' (Jablonski 2006: 99), cortical adaptations showing evidence of 'neuronal plasticity' (Jablonski 2006: 203) or the brain's capacity to adapt to shifts in available information streams. While the stripling's hand is 'seeing', however, his feet are not: 'Mr Bloom walked behind his eyeless feet' (Joyce 2008: 173). The knowing hand is assumed to have increased in sensitivity and capacities as a result of the stripling's blindness, yet his situation as a fellow pedestrian is more precarious, and it is this that elicits sympathy from the veteran perambulator Bloom: 'poor young fellow!' (173). Bloom's anxiety on the stripling's behalf proves well founded, since Cashel Boyle O'Connor Fitzmaurice Tisdall Farrell – a man whose own cane proxies of stick and umbrella notably hang from his arm, rather than touching the ground – crashes into the stripling as the latter returns to the Ormond Hotel to collect his tuning fork. Having been 'buffeted', 'the blind stripling turn[s] his sickly face after the striding form. [. . .] You're blinder nor [than] I am, you bitch's bastard!' (240).[25] The clash foregrounds Farrell's peculiar use of city space (here and elsewhere, he has insisted on walking outside the lampposts (152, 240)), and his contravention of a rule established in François de La Mothe Le Vayer's 'Of a Man-Born-Blind' of 1653 that we step into the gutter for the blind (La Mothe Le Vayer 2011: 237). Yet more importantly, it proposes that blindness is not simply a matter of the eye, that those with working eyeballs might very well fail to look, and, by implication, that blindness may simply be another way of seeing: 'Queer idea of Dublin he must have, tapping his way round by the stones' (Joyce 2008: 173).

Cane/pen/penis/prosthesis

That 'tapping' process which provides a 'queer' or alternative idea of the city is facilitated by the use of a cane, a negative prosthesis in that it attempts to compensate for a lack of vision, but a positive one in its extrapolation of the tactile capacities. We might reasonably prioritise the latter reading, not only because the Greek root *prosthenos* refers to extension or putting forward (Paterson 2007: 117), but also because the cane finds correlates in the pen and the penis, two other 'canes' which can be read as positive prostheses. Armstrong has pointed out that the term 'prosthesis' itself is literary in origin and connotes an orthographical supplement, an added letter or syllable (Armstrong 1998: 78). Meanwhile, the penis is the means of Rousseau's 'dangerous supplement', a phrase which places masturbation outside the standard diet of conjugal relations, but which also includes a sense that the penis is itself supplemental or additional, a sexual prosthesis. The penis-as-prosthesis is tackled by Ezra Pound in his 1921 'Translator's postscript' to Rémy de Gourmont's *The Natural Philosophy of Love*, where he connects the penile to the notion of resumable tools (Armstrong 1998: 89).[26] The cane of the pious stripling is, then, trailing the ground as a limp, flaccid penis (echoed in his emasculated, limp hand), and also as a writer of script, a proneographical tracing instrument. The flaccidity of the stripling's cane/penis relates to Bloom's presumption of his piety, and also his incapacity to use the Herderian glance in drawing his eye along female curves. Bloom later notices, in Daly's window, a poster featuring an alluring mermaid, which prompts the thought that the stripling, in passing by, will not be able to see this vision of (presumably, semi-nude) beauty (Joyce 2008: 277). The incident may be an oblique reference to one of La Mothe Le Vayer's doxa in his 'Of a Man-Born-Blind', which states that, since seeing alone is faster than both seeing and hearing, while some men escaped the Sirens (whose words had to be understood), none escaped the vision of the Gorgons – a claim attributed to Lucian (La Mothe Le Vayer 2011: 231). The stripling has, as far as we know, escaped the clutches of the 'Sirens' who give the episode its name, bar staff Miss Lydia Douce and Miss Mina Kennedy. This is a lucky escape indeed given the former's soft touch (*douce* touch) beer pull performance – the stripling should fear for his 'cane'. Bloom eventually decides that sexual encounters would in fact be intensified by blindness, such is the development of the tactile sense in those without the use of the eyes: 'More shameless not seeing. [. . .] Kind of a form in the mind's eye. The voice, temperature when he touches her with his fingers must almost see the lines, the curves' (Joyce 2008: 173). Might the stripling, then, be capable of echoing Bloom's lecherous looks, given that the crucial aspect of the latter is the imagined trace of the hand along the curve? The presence of the stripling in Joyce's text in fact draws out Bloom's haptic approach to female beauty, affording the latter an opportunity to consider the essentials of curve-appreciation, and leading to the conclusion that the grasp, *prehendere*, enables the imaginative conjuring of form, just as the visual contemplation of form enables the fantasy of touch. Diderot offers the chance to link this blind appreciation of form to statuary and, obliquely, to Galatea, suggesting that the stripling could join Bloom in his fetish for women of stone:

> I have no doubt that the feelings they [the blind] would have when they
> touched a statue would be even more powerful than the feelings we have
> when we look at one. How sweet it would be for a man [. . .] to run his hands
> over the charms he could recognize, and experience the illusion [. . .] of them
> being brought back to life. (Diderot 2011: 197–8)

While the extension of tactile capacities predominates in our reading of
the stripling's prosthesis – the sense of touch is put out, both handed
over and extended to the cane's tip – the pen and penis are also, then,
present in the cane.

The stripling's 'seeing hand' and 'idea'-producing, seeing cane are the
sites of his sight supplements, the scenes where his cortical adaptations
to the situation of his blindness are in evidence. René Descartes describes
the ability amongst the blind to use a stick to 'see' in vivid terms:

> consider it [stick use] in those born blind, who have made use of it all their
> lives: with them, you will find, it is so perfect and so exact that one might
> almost say that they see with their hands, or that their stick is the organ of
> some sixth sense given to them in place of sight. (Descartes 1985, vol. 1: 153)

Stephen's use of an ashplant as a walking stick plays with this Cartesian
notion of a sixth sense in that he refers to it as an 'augur's rod' (Joyce
2008: 48, 535), a *lituus* which will read the distribution of birds in the
sky and thus form a prediction of the future. Given Stephen's association, via Daedalus, with the figure of Icarus, and his allegiance with the
'lapwing' (202–3), the use of a *lituus* would be the attempt to read, most
obviously, himself, a gesture echoed in his walk to the coast: 'He walked
on, waiting to be spoken to, trailing his ashplant by his side. Its ferrule
followed lightly on the path, squealing at his heels. My familiar, after
me, calling Steeeeeeeeeeeephen' (20).[27] That which pushes forward, the
true prosthesis, will offer tactile information and provide auguries or
warnings of what is to come. That which trails behind can only call after
or retrace (while that which dangles, as with Farrell, leads to crashes).
This misuse of prostheses is present in West's *Ulysses* review, where she
claims that Joyce 'pushes his pen about noisily and aimlessly as if it were
a carpet-sweeper', while his 'technique is a tin can tied to the tail of the
dog of his genius' (West 1987b: 57).[28] It is not enough to have a touch-
related prosthesis (cane/pen/penis); one must know what to do with it,
and it is the blind who offer a model. When Stephen experiments with
the reduction of one sense in order to emphasise another, he notably
does so with his prosthesis at rest: 'Stephen closed his eyes to hear his
boots crush crackling wrack and shells. [. . .] I am getting on nicely in the
dark. My ash sword hangs at my side. Tap with it: they do' (Joyce 2008:

37). This 'clos[ing] his eyes to hear' finds a parallel in the subsequent claim, which ends Stephen's contemplation of Aristotle: 'If you can put your five fingers through it, it is a gate, if not a door. Shut your eyes and see' (37). While his attention has been upon 'the ineluctable modality of the visible' (37), Stephen concludes with hand knowledge or haptic testing, and reminds himself to extract his 'sword' from its sheathed position, and to use it as a prosthetic extension, tapping in order to 'see'. Stephen, like Molly, and like Bloom's stripling imagined in a sexual encounter, is 'getting on nicely in the dark', given the value he finds in the haptic resources of the human hand and its prosthetic extensions.

Wells's valley of the blind

It is clear that Joyce is well versed in writings on the blind composed in response to the Molyneux question, and in particular he appears to have drawn upon Diderot (whose *Letter* achieved a prominent translation in 1916 (Tunstall 2011: 167)) and La Mothe Le Vayer. That debates on the senses, post-Molyneux, remained a preoccupation in the modernist period is a claim further supported by the publication of H. G. Wells's 'The Country of the Blind', in 1904. In Wells's story, a Columbian mountaineer named Nunez becomes 'lost to the outer world' (Wells 1927: 170) during an attempt on Parascotopetl, a peak in the Andean Cordilleras.[29] The name of the mountain, adapting Popocatapetl to indicate para ('alongside') scoto ('blindness', from 'scotoma' or 'blind-spot'), provides an indication of the story that is to come, for the sighted mountaineer will learn the fallibility of the adage 'In the Country of the Blind the One-eyed Man is King' (174), which runs through his mind as a 'refrain' (174). In common with Bloom's and Stephen's attempts to get to grips with the notion of seeing, beyond the province of the eye, the blind dwellers of the valley into which Nunez wanders have experienced, across the generations, a shift in their vocabulary, and now no longer know either the word 'see' or the word 'blind': 'For fourteen generations these people had been blind and cut off from the seeing world; the names for all things of sight had faded and changed' (177). Like those of the stripling, the senses of the valley dwellers have adapted to their sensory circumstances, with the result that their conceptual framework, echoed in and supported by their language, no longer registers the 'lost' sense, and in addition cortical adaptations have occurred so that they are strangely sensitised within the haptic sense modality – they move with 'their ears directed towards [Nunez]' (174); with 'a hand outstretched' (175); 'touching him with soft, sensitive hands, smelling at him' (176); with senses 'extraordinarily fine' (180). Like Farrell, Nunez proves 'blinder nor I am': 'His senses are still imperfect [. . .]. He stumbles, and talks unmeaning words. Lead him by the hand' (175–6); 'he stumbled [. . .]; stumbled twice as we came hither' (176). The terminology of Nunez's comparative incapacity when moving in the valley is carefully chosen, echoing the words of Shakespeare's Gloucester of *King Lear*: 'I have no way, and therefore want no eyes. / I stumbled when I saw' (xv, 16–17), leading us on to lines which operate as a motto for haptic seeing: 'Might I but live to see thee in my touch / I'd say I had eyes again' (xv, 21–2). Nunez falls in love with the valley-dweller Medina-Sarote who, although beautiful to the eye, is shunned by her own community for what we might term her tactile ugliness, her failure to arouse thigmophilia, since she 'lacks that satisfying, glossy smoothness that is the blind man's ideal of feminine beauty' (186). The mountaineer considers remaining *in situ* to be with his love, but is ultimately forced to flee due to the determination of the local population to correct his 'illness': 'in order to cure him completely, all that we need to do is a simple and easy surgical operation – namely to remove these irritant bodies [eyes]. [. . .] Then he will be perfectly sane, and a quite admirable citizen' (188). The mythic horror of eye-removal here becomes a pseudo-scientific solution, providing amusement for the reader, but also asking that we contemplate the blind spot within our own 'vision' of the world – the possibly erroneous belief in the central importance of vision itself.

Nunez ultimately reinstates the importance of the visual in that he identifies a mountaineer's 'line' or climbing route on the mountainside, and makes his escape. Wells did, however, make many revisions to the ending of his story at the manuscript stage, one of which in fact has Nunez submit to the valley surgeon's scalpel (see Parrinder 1990: 72). Aside from its sharing of common interests with *Ulysses* – in particular the refinement of senses, the transvaluation of sight and touch, and the notion of tactile beauty – Wells's story is also engaged with Joyce's apparent source texts. La Mothe Le Vayer refers, in his 'Of a Man-Born-Blind', to Dreux La Vallée, a man-born-blind or *aveugle* (from *ab oculus*, 'without the eye') who might conceivably be the inspiration behind Wells's 'valley' of the blind. The dox/paradox of Nunez's posited kingship, followed by his stumbling incompetence, also recalls the structure of La Mothe Le Vayer's work. However, Wells is more conspicuously inspired by Diderot's description of a land of the blind into which a sighted man strays: 'If a man [. . .] were to find himself lost in a land of the blind, he would have to decide between keeping quiet and being taken for a mad man' (Diderot 2011: 180). There is an echo of Gloucester here too: ''Tis the time's plague when madmen lead the blind' (xv, 45). Kate E. Tunstall has outlined 'the two great mythical experiences on which the philosophy of the eighteenth century wished to found its beginning: the foreign spectator in an unknown country and the man-born-blind restored to the light' (Tunstall 2011: 6), and Wells's story of Nunez versus the blind is the product of those two poses, modified and reimagined for the modernist period in a way more explicit than Joyce's fragmented glimpses of the blind stripling, but certainly allied in concerns.

More than a brother?

Amongst his lengthy pronouncements upon Shakespeare, Stephen Dedalus claims that 'he has hidden his own name, a fair name, William, in the plays [. . .] as a painter of old Italy set his face in a dark corner of his canvas' (Joyce 2008: 201), and it may be that Joyce intended the blind stripling in a similar way, as a prosthetic extension of his author/ creator, probing his way through the text. His blindness is the most obvious point of connection, linking the 'dark m[a]n' to the benighted Joyce, 'this semidemented zany amid the inspissated grime of his glaucous den making believe to read his usylessly undreadable Blue Book of Eccles, *édition de ténébres*' (Joyce 1992: 179). The relationship of the stripling's cane to the (seminal) penis and the (spurting/creating) pen has already been established. Derrida, writing of the draftsman's attempt to capture the figure of the blind man in the trace of the pencil on paper, notes that each attempt at such a drawing is necessarily an act of self-portraiture:

> Every time a draftsman lets himself be fascinated by the blind, every time he makes the blind a *theme* of his drawing, he projects, dreams, or hallucinates a figure of a draftsman. Or more precisely still, he begins to represent a drawing potency [. . .]. The subtitle of all these scenes of the blind is thus: *the origin of drawing*. (Derrida 1993: 2–3)

We can consider the stripling in these terms – as Joyce's attempt to offer, to a degree, a self-portrait but also, more importantly, to address the business of writing itself, the 'queer idea' of Dublin necessary to write a text which breaks multiple established literary rules. When Bloom shakes hands with '*a blind stripling*' in the 'Circe' episode, and when his greeting is 'my more than Brother!' (Joyce 2008: 459), we can read this as a meeting with, in fact, a father, a Joyce proxy. The function of the blind stripling in *Ulysses* is therefore complex and multi-faceted – he offers a tactile perspective upon or particular grasp of Dublin in his necessarily haptic inhabitation of that space; he offers Bloom the opportunity to muse on the tactile nature of his lascivious look at the curves of the female form; he represents in his averted eyes the pious and the statueform; his 'walled up' eyes anticipate a revelation or the conclusion of a mythic journey; his use of a prosthesis extends the reach of his touch, and draws into debate the pen and penis prostheses of those around him; finally, he functions as a 'dark m[a]n' in a 'dark corner' of Joyce's broad canvas, a signature or tactile trace of the author himself.

Encyclodermia

Diderot may have inspired Joyce in more than his address to the blind, since the former is most famous as the editor and co-author of the ground-breaking *Encyclopédie* (1751–72), an ambitious attempt to capture in book form the knowledge of the Enlightenment (which included entries, we might note, on blindness and on masturbation). Joyce envisioned *Ulysses* not only as a 'damnedest monstrously big novel' but as an 'encyclopedia' (Johnson 2008: xiii), a term which both freed him from expectations of what a novel ought to be, and to a large extent seeded the critical responses to his work in its implication that all of human knowledge might, in one way or another, be here. Italo Calvino has claimed that emerging from the 'great novels of the twentieth century' (great, like *Ulysses*, in scope and in significance) comes 'the idea of the *open* encyclopedia, an adjective that certainly contradicts the noun *encyclopedia*, which etymologically implies an attempt to exhaust knowledge of the world by enclosing it in a circle' (Calvino 1988: 116; see also Danius 2002: 58). While the boundedness of the encyclopedia project could have it be the kin of 'Cyclops', monocular in vision, in works such as *Ulysses* the intertextual nature of the undertaking, its conjuring with myths from across the centuries and its intention to roam between cultures, opens the work, consistently, to others, in proliferating and uncontrollable conversations. That conflict between containment and opening or porousness is also present for the human skin, which – as Bloom and Stephen know – can be continent and shapely, but can also explode or be punctured in a wound. So it was that we established in Chapter 1 that the skin 'both hous[es] and extend[s] communicative interface' (Bruno 2007: 6), forming a 'cultural border between self and the world' (Benthien 2002). Didier Anzieu has noted that

> the primary function of the skin is as the sac which contains and retains inside it [. . .] goodness and fullness [. . .]. Its second function is as the interface which marks the boundary with the outside and keeps that outside out [. . .]. [Its] third function [. . .] is as a site and a primary means of communicating with others, of establishing signifying relations; it is, moreover, an 'inscribing surface' for the marks left by those others. (Anzieu 1989: 40)

This reading of the skin's tripartite function is pertinent to our attempt to approach *Ulysses* as a text which undertakes encyclopedic enclosures, working with the lemniscate's endless return and containing a third section conceived as a counterpart for the Homeric *Nostos* or return home (Johnson 2008: xv), and yet also functions in Calvino's 'contradict[ory]' sense, as a surface of inscription available to the interventions of others in a critical opening out. Joyce's use of the term 'encyclopedia' encourages us to view *Ulysses* not only as a book describing a variety of real or imagined skin conditions and experiences in a litany of epidermic adventures, but also as an encyclodermia, a text which itself partakes of the condition of the skin – merely provisionally binding, and prone to the exfoliations, wounds and inscriptions of multiple readers, authors and critics.

Notes

1. We might sensibly note that the original title of West's essay was 'A Hypothesis' (Hutchinson 1987: vii), a term which nods, as Chapter 1 made clear, toward the hypothetical or sub-story status of the human skin, and therefore anticipates the author's haptic concerns.
2. Wells was of course reviewing Joyce's earlier *A Portrait of the Artist as a Young Man* (1914–15).
3. Woolf also associates *Ulysses* with textual spattering, although in contrast to West's seminal spill *onto* the text, she is concerned with a centripetal blast: 'I feel that myriads of tiny bullets pepper one & spatter one [as one reads]; but one does not get one deadly wound straight in the face' (Woolf 1988b, vol. 2: 200). This book opens multiple apertures in the reader, Woolf implies – a fantasy of penetrated skin she shares with Bloom, as we will see.
4. Derek Attridge points out that pen/penis conflations also occur in Joyce's *Finnegans Wake* (1939), giving the example of Jerry: 'And he has pipettishly bespilled himself from his foundingpen as illspent from inkinghorn' (Attridge 2006: 53).
5. Remember, too, that the conclusion of Joyce's 'The Dead', itself the conclusion of the *Dubliners* (1914) collection, contains the observation that 'snow [i]s general all over Ireland' (Joyce 2000b: 225) and that it is 'faintly falling [. . .] upon all the living and the dead' (225). This 'general' snow may be read as a binding of national identity, a kind of meteorological extrapolation of the theme of paralysis that has run through the collection (general snow and the term 'standstill' never being far apart), a leveller or creator of equivalence between the living and the (statue- or tombstone-marked) dead, or (most useful to us here) as a means of encasing Dublin's, and Ireland's, living citizens in the snow white of marble or stone. Snow, suggests Joyce, makes (mortuary?) statuary of us all.
6. Stephen has 'form' here of another sort – a history of resistance to statue-lust. In *Portrait* he greets Lynch's enthusiasm for the Venus of Praxiteles

at the National Museum with the disdainful words: 'your flesh responded to the stimulus of a naked statue but it was, I say, simply a reflex action of the nerves' (Joyce 2000a: 223). Valerie Benejam has suggested that, in his determination to engage with the rear view of Venus, it is Lynch who is the better sculpture spectator (Benejam 2003: 71–2). This encircling habit (Lynchian, Bloomian, Herderian) I would like to call the 'transit of Venus'. Since Lynch scrawls his name on Venus's arse, we are – via the Knidian Aphrodite – back to ejaculations of the pen/penis once more (although Lynch uses the more Hogarthian pencil (Joyce 2000a: 222)). We should also note that Stephen has been 'shocked' upon his first touch of 'the brittle texture of a woman's stocking' (Joyce 2000a: 168). He is not cut out for this conversation with Bloom.

7. Bloom's interest in hosiery, while straightforwardly an appetite for titillation – the exposure of that which one is not supposed to see – also connects to the notion of a second skin which, in its failure to fit, to trace the line of beauty, creates a textural obstacle to the imagined touch of the lascivious eye. See, for example, 'her wellturned ankle [. . .] *encased* in finespun hose' (Joyce 2008: 335); 'a dream of *wellfilled* hose' (351); 'those curse of God [. . .] yellow stockings, darned with *lumpy* wool' (48); 'Watch! Watch! Silk flash rich stockings white' (71); 'Girl in Eustace street [. . .] settling her garter' (71); 'Her [. . .] stockings are *loose* over her ankles. I detest that' (158); 'that woman [. . .] in the white stockings [. . .]. Always gives a woman *clumsy* feet' (160). All emphases are mine.

8. This suggestion, that to be pinned is to be charming, and to be inadequately pinned is to lose that charm, is present in Woolf's short story 'Slater's Pins Have No Points', in which Fanny Wilmot wonders, of her dowdy piano teacher Miss Craye, 'what need had she of pins? For she was not so much dressed as cased, like a beetle compactly in its sheath' (Woolf 2003b: 209). Miss Craye clothes to cover, while Fanny pins (as here) to attach a flower to complement her loveliness (214), or to reveal her form.

9. We should recall Stephen's quoting of Aquinas here: '*Pulcra sunt quae visa placent*' (Joyce 2000a: 201), from the *Summa Theologica*, 'we call that beautiful which pleases the sight' (Joyce 2000a: 312, n. 58).

10. While not directly relevant to our haptic investigations, we might note that explicit reference to the interference of Bloom's foreskin in his post-ejaculation tidy-up (356) reminds us that he is uncircumcised, in turn asking us to remember his Jewish heritage. It is Bloom's adopted Roman Catholicism that calls for the refounding of a church if the place is polluted by seed (Laqueur 2003: 35). But it is the Jewish faith that, via the anti-Semitic imagination, is most deeply connected with masturbation. Abbé Grégoire describes unassimilated Jews as masturbators, unfit for French citizenship (Laqueur 2003: 62), while Richard Wagner links Jewish 'degeneracy' to masturbation, and claims that the art of the Jews has a masturbatory quality in its self-referentiality and lack of national mission (Laqueur 2003: 62; see also Weiner 1995; Gilman 1991). Setting aside those offensive remarks, since Thomas W. Laqueur describes masturbation as 'disconnected, imaginative, individualist' and claims that 'no form of sexuality is more profligate with time or less linked to family and inheritance' (Laqueur 2003: 22), there is something inherently masturbatory

about Bloom. Profligate with his time during his period of self-touching, he then anxiously fiddles with his watch chain, as Cissy notes (Joyce 2008: 345). Cut off from family due to the suicide of his father, his daughter's distant job and his wife's affair with Boylan, and severed from his Semitic inheritance by his religious conversion, he is left to individualist imaginings. Masturbation, for Bloom, is about more than simple sexual relief.

11. The practice of performers in the *tableaux vivants* of wearing clinging nude stockings in order to give the illusion of absolute nakedness (Hindson 2008: 18) might be one final contributory factor in Bloom's and Stephen's – and Gerty's – interest in 'wellfilled', transparent hosiery.

12. Joyce's motivation for the depiction of a lame Gerty is a puzzle. In *Portrait*, the Dean has a limp, and we are reminded that this puts him in the company of Ignatius Loyola (Joyce 2000a: 201), a man whose wounding prompted his theology. Gerty's limp most obviously makes her 'damaged goods' upon the marriage market, as well as an offender against Hogarthian notions of beauty since she cannot offer 'Uniformity, Regularity, or Symmetry' (Hogarth 1971: 18). However, Gerty may conceivably have been inspired by Montesquieu, whose 'Preface' to his *Persian Letters* (1721) declares the importance of his anonymity via a peculiar metaphor, stating 'I know a woman who walks quite well, but limps as soon as people watch her' (Montesquieu 2008: 3). Originally banned in France (see Cook 1994), the *Persian Letters* would be important reading for Joyce, given his fascination with the near and Middle East, and John Davidson's scholarly translation was published in 1899. While the limping woman's psychosomatic illness puts her in a different camp from Gerty given her Dalkey Hill blighting, both women are spirits conjured when textual controversy is in the air (Montesquieu's analysis of Parisian society; Joyce's masturbatory modernism). Jilted/tilted Gerty needs further attention.

13. West conceives of Stephen himself as statueform: 'he wobbles on his base with suffering, like a Guido Reni' (West 1987b: 21). Since Reni worked on canvas, we presume the reference is to his inspiring of subsequent sculptors, and/or to his depictions of suffering in the lives of the saints.

14. In 'Penelope', Molly's train of thought is interrupted by the realisation that her menstrual bleeding has begun (Joyce 2008: 719). She is therefore a 'statue [. . .] bleeding', connected both to the miraculous bleed of Catholic idols, and to Galatea.

15. The narrator also notes that Venus is wearing a 'white gown [which] shimmered like moonlight (or was it satin?)' (Sacher-Masoch 2000: 15). The presence of white satin here allows us to refine our understanding of Sunflower's transformation at the hands of the sculptor/lover Pitt (see Excursus), since the former, as well as wearing constricting white satin in the novel's closing scenes, has fantasies of submission to her new lover that border on the masochistic.

16. Richard Ellmann, in a rare reference to sculptural links between Joyce and Sacher-Masoch, has proposed that the Blooms' cast of Narcissus and their bedroom Nymph can be seen 'paralleled in the [. . .] cast of Venus to which Severin prays' (R. Ellmann 1965: 381). We might remember at this point that 'Nausicaa' contains a soundtrack in the form of the mass being said at Father Conroy's church – a mass that would include the Credo.

17. As with the Venuses that cluster around the figure of Molly, female self-pleasuring recurs in Sacher-Masoch's text, albeit obliquely, in that the stone Venus who opens the novel is observed by the narrator with 'her white fingers playing in the dark fur' of her coat (Sacher-Masoch 2000: 6). Didier Anzieu, as we noted in Chapter 1 in relation to Huxley, reads fur as, amongst other things, a reference to the genitalia it purports to cover (Anzieu 1989: 45). We are back to the merely ostensible modesty of the *venus pudica*.

18. Will Self's recent novel *Umbrella* (2012) depicts aspects of the EL epidemic at the close of the Great War, and he drew his title from *Ulysses*: 'A brother is as easily forgotten as an umbrella' (Joyce 2008: 203). We might at this point sensibly reread the soma holiday of Huxley's Lenina (see Chapter 1) as reflecting not only the history of narcotics, but also the EL epidemic. The notion of a statue come to life (the reverse of the EL or soma process) is also abroad in the modernist period via Sigmund Freud's reading of the *Moses* of Michelangelo in an essay of 1914. For an account of the connections between Freud's animated statue and the suppositions of psychoanalysis, see Gross 2006.

19. Joyce had one experience analogous to live burial during the writing of *Ulysses*. Having borrowed the Paris flat of Valéry Larbaud, Joyce finds that the small and soundproofed writing room it contains is 'like writing in a tomb' (Attridge 2006: 60), a combination of composition and decomposition which proves anathema to the completion of the work.

20. In Chapter 1 we met one person who knew themselves to be melting, handless and rent apart, and whose sundering is explicitly described in a conflation of physical and psychic reality. This is the anonymous schizophrenic, who states: 'It is as if something is thrown in me, bursts me asunder' (Schilder 1935: 15). Selfhood, then, collapses in concert with the skin.

21. The comparison between literary acuity and the power of the X-ray is also made by Huxley's Helmholtz, who states that 'words can be like X-rays, if you use them properly – they'll go through anything. You read and you're *pierced*' (Huxley 1994: 62), later referring to 'really good, *penetrating*, X-rayish phrases' (168) (emphases mine). As with Wilson's *Ulysses* review, the reference is to the exploration of the hidden, but the uncomfortable sense of psychological exposure remains, foregrounded here in haptic terms through metaphors of wounding. Helmholtz's comparison between scientific apparatus and aesthetic power suggests that Huxley may have named him for Hermann von Helmholtz, German physicist and aesthetician (1821–94).

22. Richard Ellmann's references to Joyce's, and Stephen's, myopia have directed subsequent criticism. However, recent investigations published in the *British Medical Journal* have established that Joyce was in fact hyperopic or farsighted. This alternative diagnosis not only explains the magnifying effect of Joyce's lenses, visible in many photographs, but also 'effectively rul[es] out' the claim of his myopia in youth (Ascaso et al. 2011: 1,295). A letter from Dr Ann McCarthy to the *Irish Times* in December 2011 reveals that she had corresponded with Ellmann in 1985 in order to put forward the hyperopic theory. Ellmann welcomed the note and proposed changes to any future editions of *James Joyce* – editions prevented by his death in

1987 (see McCarthy 2011). Pound's suggestion that *Ulysses* is textural still stands, and is echoed in Dorothy Richardson's review of *Finnegans Wake*: 'Opening, just anywhere, its pages, the reader [. . .] finds himself within a medium whose close texture, like that of poetry, is everywhere significant' (Richardson 1990: 426).

23. Molly's habit of enumerating her bodily parts might ally her with one final Venus: the anatomical Venus, an aid to public education in which a (naked, carefully coifed) wax woman is available for instructive dissection/disembowelment. The sexual or religious swoon of ecstasy in which the Venus was customarily depicted, and the injunction 'Know Thyself' with which she was commonly advertised, are two factors linking her to Molly. For a discussion of the Venus as an instructive aid, see Bates 2006.

24. This association of blindness with piety is related to the concept of blindness as blessing – important to artists selecting blind subjects for their allegorical ramifications, to critics identifying in blind writers a powerful, sightless inspiration, and to blind writers themselves. John Milton's sonnet commonly known as 'On his blindness' (1673) remarks on the 'spent' light of his sight, the 'dark world and wide' (Milton 1993: l.1–2) in which he is now adrift, yet also the blessed opportunity for pious (literary) works which is now his: 'though my soul more bent / To serve therewith my Maker' (l.4–5). For further discussion of the blessed blind, see Flint 2000.

25. Buck Mulligan's borrowed 'cracked lookingglass of a servant' (Joyce 2008: 7) might, in addition to providing Stephen with a metaphor for Irish art (7, 11), represent the blindness at the centre of vision. For consideration of this issue see Ellmann 2010.

26. Pound's 'Postscript' includes a claim that 'the brain itself is, in origin and development, only a sort of great clot of genital fluid held in suspense or reserve' (Pound 1926: 169). Genius and the seminal are, therefore, biologically as well as metaphorically linked.

27. The opening episodes of *Ulysses* are thick with references to prostheses, including Stephen's 'cold steel pen', the 'lancet of [his] art' (Joyce 2008: 7), which is feared by the scalpel-wielding medic Mulligan. Stephen reciprocates that fear, but ultimately suffers 'gaping wounds' from Mulligan's remarks about his mother (8). The pen/scalpel interchange returns us to the notion, explored in Chapter 1, that both writing and surgery are handmade work. There is also the remembered ragging of Clive Kempthorpe, 'chased by Ades of Magdalen with the tailor's shears' (7), which leave his shirt in 'slit ribbons' (7) or tattered rags, recalling both Stephen's mother's grave clothes (539) and horripilated skin.

28. Joyce himself, writing in a letter to Frantisek Shaurek, describes his pen, not as a carpet-sweeper, but as a spade: 'I can't write with this spade of a pen' (Attridge 2006: 52). This description anticipates Seamus Heaney's well-known poem 'Digging' (1966), in which he contrasts his own writing life with his father's rural work. Heaney reverses Joyce's claim, stating in essence 'I can't dig with this pen of a spade', before deciding that, in fact, he will: 'Between my finger and my thumb / The squat pen rests. / I'll dig with it' (Heaney 1999: 4). Heaney, like Joyce, makes use of the interchangeability of prostheses.

29. Despite the Andean location, this valley – with its remote location entirely

encircled by mountains, and with its alternative cosmology and anachronistic beliefs – seems to owe something to modernist understandings of Tibet. This interest was consolidated in the 1920s, as a result of the British expeditions to Everest in 1921, 1922 and 1924, and it was often perceived to be a place out of time, retaining a 'pure' Buddhism that had elsewhere become attenuated. For a discussion of Tibet as historical anachronism, see Lopez 1999.

Chapter 3

Virginia Woolf, Hapticity and the Human Hand

Palm reading

On 11 December 1935, Virginia Woolf paid a visit to Aldous Huxley in his London home, where she had her hand read, or, as she recorded in her diary, 'spent 2 hours over their Dutch writing table under the black lamp being analysed' (Woolf 1988b, vol. 2: 59). Her analyst was Dr Charlotte (Lotte) Wolff who, in her *Studies in Hand-Reading*, published the following year, noted that:

> Virginia Woolf's rectangular palm is divided into two by the Head-line which runs right across the hand and ends in a fork. It is the Head-line of a philosopher. It is not influenced by any other part of the palm, but, self-contained, it forms a barrier between the sensitive and imaginative worlds. [. . .] I do not dare to make any final statement as to whether this division leads to a separation between outward impressions and the experiences of the imagination or whether it acts as a power of resistance refining and subtilising outward and inner perceptions. [. . .] The most striking peculiarity of this hand is the shape and position of the fingers, which are straight, pointed and introverted. (Wolff 1936: 89–90)

Wolff's analysis finds in Woolf's palm and finger-shapes a microcosm of broader questions which have arisen in critical appraisals of the author in recent years, and which also surround her presentation for a hand-reading in 1935: to what extent is Woolf a writer of the imagination, to what extent a recorder of sensory experience, and how might her work be seen as attempting to create a bridge, or forked line, encompassing the two?[1] In her well-known essay 'Modern Fiction' (1925) Woolf suggests of the Edwardians that 'it is because they are concerned not with the spirit but with the body that they have disappointed us' (Woolf 2003a: 147), a rejection of materialism that at first glance makes a focus upon the bodily in the author's work appear a fool's errand. Yet here she is, offering her hand for analysis, and in doing so suggesting that to fully understand the body is an amplification of psychological exploration, rather than an evasion of that modern writer's responsibility. Attending to this scene of Wolff versus Woolf affords an opportunity to investigate the importance of the manual in the author's work, as well as making possible some broader speculations as to the place of palmistry, hand-reading and the physiology of the hand within modernist culture.

Lotte Wolff, of a German-Jewish family from West Prussia, had been brought from Paris to London at the prompting of Aldous and Maria Huxley, to facilitate her investigation of the psychological significance of the human hand. The Huxleys provided a rich seam of social contacts, enabling access to numerous figures of cultural importance – 'No-one escaped', as Sybille Bedford recalls (Bedford 1973: 285). While some analysands chose to remain anonymous (whether due to a fear of psychological exposure or to scepticism about Wolff's methods remains unclear), those named in *Studies in Hand-Reading* include André Breton, Paul Eluard, George Bernard Shaw, Osbert Sitwell, T. S. Eliot, Lady Ottoline Morrell, Maurice Ravel, Cecil Beaton, Man Ray and John Gielgud. Wolff supplemented even this plentiful supply of subjects by studying the 'hands' of the monkeys at London Zoo, under the auspices of Julian Huxley (Bedford 1973: 314), one possible driver in some participants' requests for anonymity. Wolff's work put her literally and metaphorically in contact with a cross-section of European artistic talent, and such contact is carefully nurtured as part of a career constructed in the most strategic manner.[2] Each hand-reading, supported by a full-page photograph of a handprint of her subject, deftly combines extant public perception of that subject, an indication that this network of handshakes has provided Wolff with additional gossip to draw upon and, most importantly, extended passages which clearly use prior personal information regarding the self-conceptualisation of the owner of the hand. So it is that, for example, the paw of her patron is read in admiring terms: 'The particular broadness of the Imaginative Zone expresses the richness of his [Huxley's] artistic genius. The Finger of Apollo is perfectly proportioned and grows quite straight [. . .]. This is a symbol of creative work which aims at intellectual, artistic and ethical perfection' (Wolff 1936: 75). Meanwhile Shaw has a hand of 'the Mars-type. [His] creative powers are nourished by a spirit of combat and opposition. [. . .] The straight, well-shaped Finger of Mercury denotes not only understanding for dramatic art, but creative talent' (Wolff 1936: 87). In this context, Woolf's hand-reading suggests that the author is already known for literary experiments on the mind/body borderland, in turn suggesting that a move toward the bodily in recent Woolfian criticism is in fact a rekindling of debates aflame in her lifetime, at least amongst her social circle. Wolff's readings are, in drawing upon such gossip-sketched portraits of her sitters' personalities, acts of sycophancy. While her analyses maintain the aura of a scientific experiment – and we have no cause to suppose that Wolff herself, a qualified physician, saw her work as anything but a scientific endeavour – she manipulates the social situation of the reading to allow her subjects to use their hand as a flattering mirror, finding there a reflection of that which they would most like to see. In order to support the illusion that it is in the hand that the personality is explained, rather than that the personality is assessed and mapped onto the palm, Wolff makes use of a variety of tactics: systematic analysis (her works are filled with diagrams and terminological appendices), the implied transferability of procedures (in her claims that the books are educative and expository, and her methods available for appropriation), the use of a scientific nomenclature (albeit adulterated by mythological and astrological terminology – Apollo, Mars), claimed support from more established branches of learning (Wolff's introductions often being liberally sprinkled with the names of physiologists, psychiatrists and psychoanalysts), the explicit rejection of other more overtly superstitious practices (palmistry, crystal reading, futurology), and statements of sponsorship and support on the part of her publishers and of her friends.

In the last case, Huxley was called upon, cannily making use of a pose of scepticism to anticipate the concerns of the reader. In his 'Preface' to *Studies in Hand-Reading* he states:

> Here are two sets of given facts. First, a pair of hands, with their peculiar shape, colour, consistency and markings; and, second, the character, medical history and general biography of the person to whom the hands belong. Why should there be any connexion between the two sets of facts? And what, if such a connexion exists, is the mechanism by which one of them exerts an influence on the other? (Wolff 1936: vii)

Whatever the questions remaining within Wolff's practices, Huxley was convinced of her abilities, and persuaded by the potency of the 'chirologist' or hand-reader: 'Master this science, and it will be possible for you, even without the aid of [a palmist's] intuition, to find a whole life hieroglyphically described in the hand. Such is the claim of the chirologist' (Wolff 1936: xi).[3] The invocation of Egyptian culture here cannot be coincidental, returning us to the nearsighted or tactile appreciation of hieroglyphic representation (see Chapter 1), and also combining the statement of a teleological progression from the mysteries of Egypt toward scientific enlightenment with the summoning up of inexplicable powers.[4] These powers must, however, be ordered into a system which suggests scientific rigour – Wolff's marketability as an intellect depends upon that 'science' label, and upon carefully policed boundaries between her own work and that of other practitioners associated with charlatanism. The publishers of *The Human Hand* (1942) claim in their opening note that:

> a clear distinction should be drawn at the outset between the activities of the author of this book, a professional psychologist and physician who interprets hands with a scientific aim, and the activities of people who read hands and dabble in psychology. (Wolff 1942: xi)

In drawing attention to Wolff's near neighbours in pseudo-psychological exploration and the divination of the future in the palm – effectively pointing out the elephant in the room – the publishers in fact thwart her efforts to establish a scientific standing for her work, associating her with sham figures rather than with psychologists/physiologists such as Geza Révèsz.[5] Despite her attempts at systemisation and discipline formation, and her extension into the realms of medicine through clinical studies (she thanks 'the London County Council for having permitted me to carry out research at St. Lawrence's and at St. Bernard's Hospital'[6] in the acknowledgements for *A Psychology of Gesture* (Wolff 1945: unpaginated)), Wolff's work is perhaps most impressive as an exercise in career-building, and as a social performance.

It is Leonard Woolf who cries 'humbug to hand-reading' – a bold intervention into what had clearly become a minor controversy in his milieu. Writing to Julian Bell six days after her own analysis beneath the black lamp, Woolf recalls that:

> we had a crack [debate] on Sunday at Nessas [Vanessa Bell's]. I was glad to find we could still argue with some heat the question of palmistry. [. . .] Leonard said it was all humbug; disgusting humbug; Clive [Bell] said That's not the scientific spirit; you must try things. (Woolf 1994: 452)

Leonard may have had personal motivations for his perceived failure of scientific spirit in this instance, since Woolf had suffered poor mental and physical health in recent months (see Harris 2011: 134–5), was finding revisions for her present novel *The Years* an immense strain ('Never have I worked so hard at any book' (Woolf 1988b, vol. 5: 16)), and might have been negatively affected by too close a belief in any sense of the fated that could arise from an analysis of her palm/personality. Woolf, for her part, was characteristically pleased to be flattered regarding her genius, and yet suspicious of the claimed talents of another: 'some things she got hopelessly wrong; others she guessed amazingly right.

And for two hours poured forth a flood of connected and intense discourse' (Woolf 1994: 452). While 'guessed' implies fairground trickery, Wolff claws back some credit by virtue of the stylistics of her speech. It is clear that this is the reanimation of an ongoing debate and, while Woolf restricts reference to her hand-reading to the diary entry noted above, and to this letter to Julian (the central theme of which is in fact the fun of arguing with Quentin Bell), it is a discussion which occupies her mind and her work at this time. 'I kept my distance', she says of the 'crack', reasoning that 'after all some kind of communion is possible between human beings, that cant be accounted for; or what about my dive into them in fiction? But why [. . .] should deaths or other events indent the palm of the hand?' (Woolf 1994: 452). These questions conspicuously form the basis for Huxley's sceptical pose in his 'Preface' to Wolff's publication, containing the Woolf reading, in 1936.[7] Yet they also have the most fundamental of influences on another work of this period – Woolf's current preoccupation, *The Years*, which, although drafted by the time of her hand-reading, was undergoing sufficiently substantial revisions as to be considered still in the writing. It was finished to the galley stage, to great relief, on 30 December 1936 (Woolf 1988b, vol. 5: 44), and published in 1937. *The Years* is a peculiarly gestural novel; one which chooses repeatedly to alight upon the use of the hands – an ongoing registration of manual action well beyond a simple reading of the manners and manicures of the day. Woolf is engaged throughout her writing with the flow of time and its fraying effects upon personhood and identity. Through meeting Wolff under the lamp, she found a means of illustrating those concerns via the mobilisation of the human hand, as a place where history and heredity are ingrained in skin inscriptions, and as an organ that is superseded in its attempts to know and to control by time's ceaseless flow. While *The Years* is rather a bridesmaid of a book, rarely the centre of attention in a critical assessment of Woolf's work, it can be understood, with the hand-reading 'crack' in mind, as an extended treatment of the abilities and incapacities of the hand, its gestures, and its acts of tactile engagement, and therefore as a vital text for the history of the haptic in the modernist period.

Motorcar kinaesthetics

It is in Woolf's treatment of the motorcar that her concern with philosophies of temporality and her ongoing efforts to describe the experience of selfhood can be seen most intimately intertwined. Originally sceptical about the advantages of this particular mode of mechanised transport (in

1924 she wrote that the country roads of England were being denuded of flowers and charm in becoming 'a mere racing-track for the convenience of a population seemingly in perpetual and frantic haste not to be late for dinner' (Woolf 1988a: 440)), Woolf relented upon the purchase of a second-hand, closed car Singer in July 1927, going on to describe it as 'a great opening up in our lives', since 'one may [. . .] expand that curious thing, the map of the world in ones mind' (Woolf 1988b, vol. 3: 147). Later, it is 'the joy of our lives' (151).[8] The facilitation of travel at great speed puts many friends and locations within reach ('It will I think demolish loneliness' (147)), a recalibration of both map and mental map that also puts the Woolfs themselves within the reach of others (it 'may of course imperil complete privacy' (147)). Yet while Woolf records in her diary the social changes wrought by this new technology, in her fiction it is the existential implications of motorcar travel that are the focus, most famously in *Orlando: A Biography* (1928), when the eponymous hero(ine) makes a dash for her country seat:

> After twenty minutes [of driving] the body and mind were like scraps of torn paper tumbling from a sack and, indeed, the process of motoring fast out of London so much resembles the chopping up small of identity which precedes unconsciousness and perhaps death itself that it is an open question in what sense Orlando can be said to have existed at the present moment. (Woolf 1993b: 212)

It is the rapid movement of the human body, and the concomitant swift pace at which the moments of life are perceived to pass, that forms the association between motoring and death, in that the personal experience of temporality is of 'chopp[ed] up' moments so refined that one cannot say I am living a moment, I know therefore both this moment and myself. Orlando has effectively climbed aboard time's wingèd chariot, although that chariot has become mechanised and lost its horse: 'but how it's done, I can't even begin to wonder. So my belief in magic returns' (Woolf 1993b: 207). The sensation of travel in the horseless carriage requires a physical recalibration to match the mental one of mapping, since the body must find a way to cope with the sensory onslaught offered to the visual sense, whilst also making micro-muscular adjustments to maintain balance on uneven surfaces, when meeting inclines, and when cornering, a development of kinaesthetic and vestibular senses that combines (if the passenger, as Woolf most often was) predominant physical inertia with a registration of the body's apparently magical movement through space.[9] In the episodic structure of *The Years* it is when the story reaches 1914 that the motorcar makes its first conspicuous appearance. Collecting Kitty Lasswade in the household's new car, her driver seems to have made only a partial transition to the latest technology, responding to the faltering car as if he were using a far older mode of transport: 'Kitty saw him jerk his body slightly backward and forwards as if he were encouraging horses. She felt the tension of his muscles' (Woolf 1968: 221). Cole, stating that the local dogs lingering in the road will learn eventually how to avoid motorised vehicles (220), might himself need to do some further learning about the appropriate response of his musculature to the experience of motorcar travel. Those intertwined issues of fleeting time and a sense of self are therefore joined in the motorcar by one final matter for Woolf's contemplation: the human body itself. It is through that body that Woolf seeks to process the experience of travel at speed.[10]

Woolf's motorcar writing is characterised by an attempt to find a literary means of expressing the confounding of the body's senses by travel, and the psychological splitting she believes to occur as a result. In 'Evening over Sussex: Reflections in a Motor Car', posthumously published in 1942 but thought to have been written in 1927, Woolf meditates on 'one's own impotency' when attempting a sensory absorption of all that travel affords to the perceiving mind of the writer: 'I cannot hold this – I cannot express this – I am overcome by it – I am mastered. [. . .] beauty spread at one's right hand, at one's left; at one's back too; it was escaping all the time' (Woolf 1993a: 82–3). 'At one's back' recalls time's wingèd chariot once again, here adapted so that, 'one' having mounted the chariot, it is time that flows behind, ever escaping, rather than gaining in hot pursuit. The passage uses a rhythmic incantation to evoke the experience of scenery and moments flaring past the perceiver, and while the use of dashes lends to the reader's eye that sense of dash, it is in the repetition of the first person pronoun that Woolf establishes a stylistic means of recording the discombobulation of identity: 'But relinquish, I said (it is well known how in circumstances like these the self splits up [. . .])' (Woolf 1993a: 83). The rhythmic representation of travel, and the multiple 'I', are often found when Woolf tackles the transport experience. In *The Years*, Kitty's train journey shows that she too, in her sleeping carriage, registers the rhythm of movement, attempting to pin down the moment by noting the presence of her body in a particular location – a location which changes rapidly: '*Now* where are we? she said to herself. Where is the train at this moment? *Now*, she murmured [. . .] we are passing the white house [. . .]; *now* we are going through the tunnel; *now* we are crossing the bridge' (Woolf 1968: 219). In the 'Present Day' episode, Peggy has similar sentiments while travelling in a cab with Eleanor: 'There were two living people, driving across London [. . .]. But what is this moment; and what are we? The puzzle was too difficult for her to solve it' (Woolf 1968: 269). The apparently precarious position of the human body, facing the inrushing future with a psychologically split self, is most often figured by Woolf with recourse to a plank metaphor, appearing memorably in *Orlando: A Biography*: 'she did not allow these sights to sink into her mind even the fraction of an inch as she crossed the narrow plank of the present, lest she should fall into the raging torrent beneath' (Woolf 1993b: 207). The image also occurs in the mind of Lily Briscoe in *To the Lighthouse* (1927) in remarkably similar terms, although Lily's sea-faring is an imaginative act, as she stands painting on the land: 'Out and out one went, further and further, until at last one seemed to be on a narrow plank, perfectly alone, over the sea. As she dipped into the blue paint, she dipped too into the past there' (Woolf 2008: 141). And Lily also echoes Orlando's 'raging torrent' in her reference to 'step[ping] off her strip of board into the waters of annihilation' (Woolf 2008: 48). The piratical plank serves to indicate the precarious space carved out by the human body, a narrow strip of 'now' facing down wave upon wave of the future.[11]

Woolf herself picks up Peggy's insoluble puzzle in her sketched essay 'The Moment: Summer's Night', where she returns to the notion of the human body as a bulwark against both the inrushing future and the streaming tail of the past:

> Yet what composed the present moment? If you are young, the future lies upon the present, like a piece of glass, making it tremble and quiver. If you are old, the past lies upon the present, like a thick glass, making it waver, distorting it. All the same, everybody believes that the present is something. (Woolf 1947: 9)

Theories of the moment occupy thinkers of the modernist period including Walter Benjamin, Martin Heidegger and Jean Epstein, struggling with, as Leo Charney puts it, 'the evacuation of stable presence by movement and the resulting split between sensation, which feels the moment in the moment, and cognition, which recognizes the moment only after the moment' (Charney 1996: 279). As a result, 'past and future clash [. . .] on the terrain of the body' (Charney 1996: 293), and for Woolf that body stands on a plank above torrents. The moment, as a unit of time theoretically discrete, experientially confirmed, but non-isolatable, was first theorised by Walter Pater in his 1868 conclusion to *The Renaissance: Studies in Art and Poetry*, where he states: 'This at least of [the] flamelike our life has, that it is but the concurrence, renewed from moment to moment, of forces parting sooner or later on their ways' (Pater 1902: 234). Yet, along with Woolf, Pater considers those moments, building blocks of human experience, to be fleeting. We know, he claims, that:

> those impressions of the individual mind to which, for each one of us, experience dwindles down, are in perpetual flight; that each of them is limited by time, and that as time is infinitely divisible, each of them is infinitely divisible also; all that is actual in it being a single moment, gone while we try to apprehend it, of which it may ever be more truly said that it has ceased to be than that it is. (Pater 1902: 235)

This is a statement of human experience as elegy, since the moment can only truly be known, or mentally apprehended, with a retrospective glance. Yet Pater does allow that the body may be able to grasp (*prehendere*) the moment as it occurs. These considerations of self, body, moment and time, often prompted by the unprecedented kinaesthetic experience of motorcar travel, are vital to Woolf's work, including her ambitious attempt to account for the modernist period itself, 1880–c. 1936, in *The Years*. Writing of a summer evening's drive, 15 August 1922, Woolf remarks upon 'beauty abounding & superabounding, so that one almost resents it, not being capable of catching it all, & holding it all at the moment. [. . .] I feel as if I were putting out my fingers tentatively' (Woolf 1988b, vol. 2: 311). In response to the ever-fleeting moment, which may be known only in retrospect, Woolf's characters in *The Years* follow their creator in performing vain but poignant manual gestures of enclosure and grasping which, in their inadequacy, underscore the inherently elegiac nature of a life understood in this Paterian manner as *the forever over*. For Woolf, past and future clash on the crease-riven terrain of the hand.

Carpe diem

As Alexandra Harris has most recently reminded us, *The Years* 'was the fastest-selling of [Woolf's] books and the only one to reach the bestseller lists in America' (Harris 2011: 135), and the author's diary records substantial earnings of '£4,000 about from The Years' (Woolf 1988b, vol. 5: 130). Woolf's critical canonisation has focused on her status as a structural and stylistic innovator, single-mindedly reshaping the novel, and her return to a carefully temporally demarcated story that seems to owe most to Victorian family sagas appears at first a retrogressive move, whatever its commercial spoils. The inspiration behind that move, the impetus to tackle three generations of the Pargiter family, is hinted at within Woolf's essay 'On Being Ill' (1930). In the latter, Woolf's own poor health leads her to note that 'all day, all night the body intervenes' (Woolf 1967b: 193), but that 'of all this daily drama of the body there is no record' (194), and the creation of that record is dependent upon 'a new language [. . .] more primitive, more sensual, more obscene' (194–5). *The Years* may be read in part as an attempt to find a language for the daily drama of the body, and in particular of the hands, but Woolf's essay also supplies a template for the structure of the 1937 novel in her reference to 'Hare and Waterford and Canning' (201), a book to which she has turned in her illness. Augustus J. C. Hare's triple-decker biography *The Story of Two Noble Lives, Being Memorials of Charlotte, Countess of Canning, and Louisa, Marchioness of Waterford* was published in 1893. In Woolf's rendering, the story runs as follows:

> Charlotte married Canning and went to India; Louisa married Lord Waterford and went to Ireland. [. . .] there are the Irish famine and the Indian Mutiny, and both sisters remain to their great, but silent, grief without children to come after them. Louisa, dumped down with Lord Waterford at the hunt all day, was often very lonely; but she stuck to her post, visited the poor, spoke words of comfort. (Woolf 1967b: 202)

In *The Years* it is Eleanor who goes to India (and North to Africa); the Indian Mutiny is responsible for the mutilation of Abel's fingers; Rose, Eleanor and Peggy remain childless, the latter two reflecting upon the matter; Milly marries Hugh Gibbs, who is also 'at the hunt all day'; and Eleanor visits the poor and the sick, although she is frequently too busy with their material needs to offer 'words of comfort'. Woolf appears to have fragmented Hare's subjects and their trajectories, and to have modified his engagement with intergenerational sprawl to her own ends. Hare's humour might conceivably have pleased her, as his epistolary form is full of witticisms: '*Feb.* 4, 1842. – The King of Prussia is gone, pleased with high and low, and having done handsomely in the snuff-box giving line. I am sorry I did not see him' (Hare 1893, vol. 1: 216). However, Woolf laments the fact that 'there, as so often in these fat volumes, we flounder and threaten to sink in a plethora of aunts and uncles' (Woolf 1967b: 201). Yet she concedes that this bewildering array of family connections was essential to Hare, 'for life then was not the life of Charlotte and Louisa. It was the life of families, of groups. It was a web, a net, spreading far and enmeshing every sort of cousin, dependant, old retainer' (Woolf 1967b: 202), and it is precisely this interconnectedness that Woolf utilises in *The Years*, as she tracks the Pargiters (and their own 'old retainer', Crosby) across the decades. The 'net, spreading far' turns up in the novel when North thinks of Milly: 'She cast a net over them; she made them feel all one family; he had to think of their relations in common' (Woolf 1968: 300). Illness and its reminder of fleshly matters, and Hare and his 'plethora of aunts and uncles', should be added to Wolff and her psychological interpretation of the human hand as vital sources for the formulation of *The Years*.

With those sources in mind, my concern here is to offer an overview of the manifold ways in which the manual organs are used to *make manifest* in *The Years*. Etymologically, the word 'manifest' is drawn from the Anglo-Norman and Middle French word *manifeste*, meaning 'confirmed' or 'proven' (*OED*), and so it is that the hands in Woolf's novel may be seen as agents of identity confirmation, and of proof through touch. While we have already considered tactile testing in Stephen Dedalus's Aristotelian attempts to distinguish between gate and door (see Chapter 2), the practice is most famously depicted in the biblical story of 'doubting' Thomas. The latter states that 'unless I see the mark of the nails in [Jesus's] hands, and put my finger in the marks of the nails and my hand in his side, I will not believe [that He is risen]', prompting Jesus to command: 'Reach out your hand and put it in my side. Do not doubt but believe' (John 20:24–9). For Woolf, the hand functions in five ways in order to make manifest – we may count them on our fingers, as Woolf's Nicholas is wont to do – and several are related to that Thomas/Christ confrontation: the broken skin of the scarred or damaged hand connects to memory, confirming a past act; gestures of the hand establish the identity and characters of individuals in private and public contexts; the touching hand verifies the truth of an assertion and/or establishes a relationship; the hand may be used as an outmoded measure to attempt to verify the claims of contemporary science; and, crucially, the grasping hand attempts to halt the ever-fleeting moment.

The human hand

The influence of Wolff on Woolf is perhaps most conspicuous when we are told of Eleanor that 'her middle-aged face was crinkled like an old glove that has been creased into a multitude of fine lines by the gestures of the hand' (Woolf 1968: 235), a statement describing a skin condition, but also suggesting that Eleanor carries with her legible memories, which may be read in either face or hand. Peggy takes further these Wolffian theories, drawing the link between psychology and the palm in her suggestion that both mind and hand are creased by habit, since each person possesses 'a line laid down in their minds [. . .] and along it came the same old sayings. One's mind must be criss-crossed like the palm of one's hand' (Woolf 1968: 288). In her introduction to *A Psychology of Gesture*, Wolff refers to her belief that 'the gestures of the hand are largely responsible for the nature of the crease lines and indirectly for the form of the hand' (Wolff 1945: ix), although no compelling physiological evidence is given in support of this claim. Peggy and Margaret, then, make the case for Wolff's creep into *The Years*, but her influence is in fact extensive, and her concerns structure the book at the deepest level. Woolf's use of free indirect discourse and stream of consciousness writing is less in evidence here than in her previous novels, and it is through the hand that we as readers are, despite our position on the outside of characters' mental spheres, given an insight into their thoughts and personalities. Further, such manual evidence is made use of by other characters; everyone is at the hand-reading game. Given its connection to heredity and futurology, and its vulnerability to scars and scrapes, the hand can also be seen as the place where individual biographies, and their part in the Pargiter family tree, may be found. *The Years* is, in this way, a handbook – a book deeply concerned with the human hand, a guide to the possibilities of hand-reading (and as such a companion piece to Wolff's 1936 publication), and a text which suggests that the hand itself may be read as a form of life-writing.

Abel Pargiter, flawed patriarch, attempts to maintain control over the lives of his children, as his wife Rose ebbs away at the conclusion of a long illness, and as his consolatory affair with the lower-class Mira seems increasingly ridiculous. His tenuous hold on familial power is echoed in his fumbling grasp, since he has lost two fingers in the Indian Mutiny, and 'the muscles ha[ve] shrunk so that the right hand resemble[s] the claw of some aged bird' (Woolf 1968: 13), and yet he will make no mention of the incapacity, nor accept help. Abel's 'curtailed fingers' (86) are mentioned frequently (9, 10, 13, 299), that particular phrasing suggesting that something about his life has been stunted or cut short – possibly his conjugal relations with Mrs Pargiter, the absence of which leads Abel into Mira's arms and, it is mooted, his sister-in-law's as well (199). Other hands are read as equally eloquent in their revelations about the character and history of their owners: Rose's 'thin white scar' (128) recalls a childhood argument with Martin, while her fist clenched on the tea table reminds him of another scene from their youth (129). At Oxford, Gibbs's 'shapeless paw' (303) implies his blunt mind, while his fellow scholar Ashley is his opposite, relying on echolocation and moving amongst the furniture as if making use of 'invisible antennae' (44). Aunt Warburton's great age and status forgive her 'coarse hands, with big finger-joints' (208), while the comparatively young Kitty Lasswade has surprisingly un-Ladylike hands, thinks North, since they are 'rather stubby, and the skin was rough, but she gardened, he remembered' (322). Without the gardening habit to excuse her, Kitty's hands would betray coarseness despite her status, since one expects only domestics to have truly battered hands. North, something of a hand fetishist, and a leerer at the hands of young women in particular, remarks upon 'the regular lodging-house skivvy [. . .] with red hands' (253) who attends Sara's flat. Wolff would join North in his prejudices, since her *Studies in Hand-Reading* includes attention to 'The Hand of a Domestic Servant' and observes that 'the primitive hand of this twenty-six year old woman reveals an interesting combination of a square palm and (in the right hand) pointed fingers', also claiming that 'this is a sign that she is very susceptible to all outside influences' (Wolff 1936: 31). No great statements of palm-evident genius and ethical scrupulousness here. That 'primitive' label conspicuously links the woman in service to the monkeys of the London Zoo, and Woolf also makes this connection between primitivism, poverty and the paw, in referring to the gnarled hand of the ill Mrs Potter whom Eleanor visits as like that of a 'large tousled ape' (Woolf 1968: 88).

North's reading of the ape or monkey association is rather different, seeing in the hand of even his most 'civilised' relatives a hidden claw. Milly and Hugh's concerns are, thinks North, their own property and family, 'which they would protect with the unsheathed claws of the primeval swamp' (304). North has already observed that Milly's clasp is formed of fingers bearing sunken rings: 'flesh grown over diamonds disgusted him' (300); the triumph of the bodily over wealth and apparent civilisation is repellent. Neither is the comparatively popular Maggie divisible from this fleshly tribe:

> They were strong hands; fine hands; but if it were a question, he thought, watching the fingers curl slightly, of 'my' children, of 'my' possessions, it would be one rip down the belly; or teeth in the soft fur of the throat. We cannot help each other [. . .] we are all deformed. (Woolf 1968: 305)

With the primeval claw lurking beneath the surface, and a mere flex of the fingers away from appearing, the Pargiters (whose name, via 'pargeter', refers to plastering or whitewashing (*OED*), and therefore the creation of a skin which masks) are all hiding their deformity. Abel's mangled claw, literally the result of military action, is also spiritually the symbol of the inherent rapacity that North perceives amongst his kin.

Gestural practice

Gesture in *The Years* lends to human speech the quality of oratory through a canon of rhetorical shifts. The hand speaks as it moves.[12] Henri Focillon's 'In Praise of Hands' is recalled here (see Chapter 1): 'From this mimicking of the spoken word, from these exchanges between voice and hands, some trace remains in what the ancients called oratorical gesture' (Focillon 1948: 68). At times the hands and the mouth speak in concert, that is, they are oratorically correct, while at other times hands and mouth thwart one another, or may be read by others in ways unintended by the orator. Digby's wife Eugénie is the possessor of the most eloquent hands in the novel – eloquence which marks her out as a family member only by marriage, as a foreigner, and as potentially sexually incontinent: 'She threw out her hand. She had gestures of extraordinary significance. That's how she rigs things up, [Abel] thought. But he liked her for it' (Woolf 1968: 100). While Abel's wife's hand sits inert on the counterpane of her sickbed, wearing her wedding band (19), Eugénie's hands express a more vibrant world – here she describes the colours of Venice, from whence she is recently returned. Her outward fling of the hand is the characteristic feature by which she is known throughout the novel (107, 115, 124), repeatedly attached to the idea of a life lived vivaciously, and therefore to potential sexual indiscretions. Upon Digby's death, Eleanor suggests that partnership with Eugénie might have been a struggle: '"That manner – " She threw her hand out; but not as Eugénie threw her hand out, Martin thought' (124). While the flung hand indicates all that is unmanageable about the foreign woman, it is also her gesture alone, and cannot be replicated by the spinsterly, disapproving Eleanor. Gestures can be mimicked, then, but not fully incorporated; in the hands of others they are but a mime.

Eugénie has a companion in her use of excessive gesture in the form of Nicholas, also known as Brown, the Polish dentist, who uses his hands 'as people do who find language obdurate' (227), that is, as a foreigner. It is North, as we might expect, who finds these gestures excessive, and he notes that Nicholas talks while 'spreading his fingers out with the volubility of a man who will in the end become a bore' (249), a volubility of finger that becomes a matter for discussion between North and Sara, when the latter tries to echo Nicholas's manual manner (253). His most typical gesture is, as with Eugénie, the outward fling of the hand, and in fact North refers to Nicholas as 'the man who throws his hands out' (259). Nicholas's manual eloquence, and comparative linguistic incapacity, make him the self-appointed orator of the novel, as he uses his hands to capture that which cannot be best conveyed in the English language – his traffic is in that which exceeds language, recognising the latter as, in Woolf's terms, an 'ill-fitting vestment' (Woolf 2003a: 149). At two crucial moments, it is given to Nicholas to attempt to sum up the sentiments of a gathering and, while the insufficiency of his language is attributed to his foreign status, it is in fact the enormity of human existence that is the issue, escaping words and necessitating the mobilisation of the hand. Sheltering in the basement of Maggie and Renny's house during an air raid in 1917, Nicholas begins 'flinging his hand out like an orator' (Woolf 1968: 236) but is told 'we don't want speeches' (236). In the 'Present Day', at Delia's family party which closes the novel, Nicholas tries once again to capture the moment in a speech, and again flings out a hand in 'an oratorical gesture' (336). Having been silenced once more, he is left 'paddling his hands amongst the flower petals' with which Delia has graced the tables (338). The speech that never was is subsequently related, and in stating what he would have said, Nicholas again resorts to gesture, counting his points on his fingers, sweeping the room with a flung hand, and raising his glass (342).

Beyond the realms of the hand-flinging foreigners, whose eloquence lies in their hands, and to whom we therefore turn to express the inexpressible, a Woolfian concern, we find a marked preoccupation with gesture as an indicator of identity. Renny calls for attention in the manner of a 'policeman stopping traffic' (280), and is perceived to be 'commanding i[n] his gesture' (280); Sir William Whatney's younger self is slowly revealed to Eleanor through 'certain words and gestures', since 'there were relics of the old Dubbin if one half-shut one's eyes' (162); Martin spots Maggie in the park after a lengthy separation through 'noticing something about her gesture' (196); and Uncle Edward has 'a way of putting his hand to his head' that recalls him to North's memory (327). Gesture also marks out tribes, for example when North observes a group of youngsters at Delia's party: 'It seemed to him, [. . .] looking at their gestures, [. . .] that they were all of the same sort' (325); North's recent return from Africa makes him peculiarly sensitive to gestural practice – he is for now a manual outsider. And he is not yet free of his hand fetish, noting once the dancing commences that a girl has stopped in his sightline 'and her gesture as she raised her hand, unconsciously, had the seriousness of the very young anticipating life in its goodness that touched him' (305). It is the older women of the novel who, in their understanding of the dictates of the hostess role, make more conscious use of their hands. Mrs Larpent, visiting the Lodge of the unnamed Oxford college which is Kitty's home, gives a wave which is 'dictated by centuries of tradition' (47); the hostess Mrs Malone in her turn waves her hand, and 'there was something authoritative about her action – as if she had done it again and again' (49). These hand-wavings occur in the 1880 episode, but such traditions do not wane: Kitty, taking charge of the women following a dinner in 1914, indicates with an abrupt move of the hand that everyone should take their seats, and we are told that such gestures lead her to be called, 'behind her back, "The Grenadier"'

(208). Delia's own hostessing is successful due to her handsomeness, her presence and her gestures (286), while her husband Patrick has no such manual graces, instead standing 'beside her, dangling his hands in front of him like a bear on which coats are hung in an hotel' (293). The latter might learn from Mr Ramsay of *To the Lighthouse* who, although leaving hostessing duties to his wife in their entirety, is hated by his son James 'for the exaltation and sublimity of his gestures' (Woolf 2008: 33), for which he has 'a gift' (123), using his 'beautiful hands' (126) to draw attention and control emotional power: '[Ramsay] raised his right hand mysteriously high in the air, and let it fall upon his knee again as if he were conducting some secret symphony' (154). Ramsay the philosopher shares with Nicholas the philosopher-dentist a need to express the inexpressible with recourse to the hands.

Woolf's efforts to record the manual gestures of her characters, and her engagement with the readings of those gestures by other cast members of *The Years*, result in a carefully constructed gestural canon which works to separate old from young, the traditional from the innovative, the Briton from the foreigner, the conjugal from the extra-marital, and the orator-philosopher from the man for whom language is enough. The idea of a gestural canon was abroad at Woolf's time of writing, most obviously in Wolff's *A Psychology of Gesture*, but also in Geza Révèsz's *The Human Hand: A Psychological Study*, first published (in German) in 1943, and later translated into English. In a section entitled 'Expressive Movements and Gestures', Révèsz follows Wolff and Woolf in his distinction between the two. 'Expressive movements' are, writes Révèsz, 'simply bodily expressions of psycho-physiological processes [. . .] not innately *directed* and certainly *not intended*' (Révèsz 1958: 101) – see, for example, the raised hand of the dancing girl that North observes. Meanwhile gestures are 'carried out with the aim of achieving *mutual contact* and *intentional co-operation* with another person' (101); as a result, 'most gestures have linguistically expressive value' (101–2). Révèsz goes on to enumerate the many gestures available to the human hand – those with closed fingers, spread fingers, those touching the body (that is, self-touching), which he terms 'autistic' (102–3). A similar attention to gestural canons is discernible in Eleanor's thoughts, particularly when she goes to watch Morris's work in the courtroom:

> One hand was on the edge of his gown. How well she knew that gesture of Morris's, she thought – grasping something, so that you saw the white scar where he had cut himself bathing. But she did not recognize the other gesture – the way he flung his arm out. That belonged to his public life, his life in the Courts. (Woolf 1968: 89–90)

Eleanor here distinguishes between gestures appropriate to public life, and to a situation requiring oratorical command, and those that find a place in the home. We might note that the flinging arm, read as public, is transferred to domestic spaces by Eugénie and Nicholas – their contravention of gestural propriety is therefore about the transference of performance gestures into spaces of ordinary discourse.

The gestural canon of specifically public oratory makes a further appearance when Martin and Rose go to Hyde Park, and pass through Speakers' Corner. One speaker 'crook[s] his finger' (193); another indicates the passing cars with 'a superb gesture of scorn' (194); he speaks of what Martin parrots as 'Joostice and liberty' (194), while his 'fist thump[s] on the railing' (194). Martin is led to wonder: 'What would the world be [. . .] – he was still thinking of the fat man brandishing his arm – without "I" in it?' (195). North, considering the unappealing nature of 'joining societies' and 'signing manifestos' (325), returns to the canon of political oratory, in his description of those who speak from the platform: 'There was the pump-handle gesture; the wringing-wet-clothes gesture; and then the voice [. . .]: Justice! Liberty!' (325). There are twenty-two years between Martin's observations and North's, but little about political communication, in words or in gestures, appears to have changed. For Martin, distinctive gestures (again, of hand-flinging) have brought him towards the question of what an 'I' might be, or how the world might be comprehended without such a notion. North's concerns are, obliquely, connected, in that his rejection of societies, manifestos and the gang of youths at the party, with their gestural similarity marking their bonds, is a rejection of pledging his 'I' to a broader human consort. Wolff tells us that 'gesture comes from the Latin *gerere*, which means to comport oneself or to show oneself' (Wolff 1945: 5), and, while Woolf reads gesture as (conscious or uncontrolled) self-disclosure, North will sign up to no manual manifesto – he will keep his hands to himself.

Doubting Thomas and the atom

Amongst these distinctive hands, self-identifying gestures and political canons of oratorical passes, one manual manoeuvre emerges as of particular importance in *The Years*: the gesture of grasping or enfolding. Wolff notes that 'the first gesture of the hand is the grasping reflex [. . .]. Before children develop an active sense of touch they react by grasping objects [. . .], a proof that prehensile gestures are more ancient than tactile gestures' (Wolff 1945: 34). While we might question the conflation of childhood development and evolutionary theory, Wolff's central point, that the grasp may be of greater significance than the touch with fingers flattened or extended, is vital to a reading of Woolf's novel. For Woolf, the grasp is a means of knowledge-gathering, moving between the literal enfolding gesture of the human hand and the metaphorical grasp of comprehension. This is most conspicuous when Eleanor confronts the atom:

> Atoms danced apart and massed themselves. But how did they compose what people called a life? She clenched her hands and felt the hard little coins she was holding. Perhaps there's 'I' at the middle of it, she thought; a knot; a centre. (Woolf 1968: 295)

For Révèsz this resort to the gesture of grasping when faced with the unknown is typical of human manual behaviour: 'The subject aiming at knowledge wants to make sure of the corporeality of the object' as it 'provides a vivid example of the division between the subject and the physical world; this distinction becomes most marked in the grasping and enclosing touch' (Révèsz 1958: 93). Eleanor, confronted by the indiscernibility of the atoms composing the matter of life, turns to her grasp, with what we presume is a painful pressure upon a hard coin returning her to her body, her perceiving self.[13] Woolf's 'The Moment: Summer's Night' makes a concomitant effort to return to the body when faced with the elusive concept of the essay's title: 'But that [lights coming on in cottages and farms] is the wider circumference of the moment. Here in the centre is a knot of consciousness; a nucleus divided up into four heads, eight legs, eight arms, and four separate bodies' (Woolf 1947: 10). We should note the presence of the language of atomic structure – 'nucleus' – here. While Eleanor conceptually centres herself as a source of radiation or a nucleus, she stabilises her 'I', her perceiving self, by using the grasp of her hand to return herself to bodily measure, and/or to bodily pain.

Alnoor Dhanani has observed that 'Islamic *kalam* philosophers counted touch and sight as the senses providing reliable knowledge, while the other senses perceive only "accidents"' (Dhanani 1994: 124). Since atoms are bafflingly beyond the province of the eye, Eleanor has turned to her other reliable sense, that of touch, and in doing so she follows the adage 'seeing's believing, but feeling's the truth', which, as Mark Paterson has noted, is most often quoted without its qualifying final clause (Paterson 2007: 2). Confronted with the atom, she has recourse to the grasp. We are back to doubting Thomas here, to whom Christ concludes by remarking: 'Blessed are those who have not seen and yet have come to believe' (John 20:29), implying that in his need to see and, crucially, to touch, Thomas has shown himself to lack the blind, unthigmophilic faith of others. In touching in order to know, Thomas does however take part in a long history of the human hand as a means of measure, 'hence the Graeco-Roman notion of cubits (a forearm's length), digits (a finger's breadth, ¾ inch) and so on' (Paterson 2007: 72). Yet the atom is, as well as indiscernible to the eye, well beyond that which may be individually touched, known and believed in through the measuring hand, meaning that the grasp as a reaction to the new or unfathomable is an outmoded gesture. This is a matter that has also concerned Eleanor in the 1908 episode:

> But what vast gaps there were, what blank spaces [. . .] in her knowledge! How little she knew about anything. Take this cup for instance; she held it out in front of her. What was it made of? Atoms? And what were atoms, and how did they stick together? The smooth hard surface of the china [. . .] seemed to her for a second a marvellous mystery. (Woolf 1968: 126)

As an autodidact and avid newspaper reader, we presume that although Eleanor is self-critical with regard to her education (recalling Clarissa Dalloway's lamented 'few twigs of knowledge' (Woolf 1992: 9)), the presence of the atom concept within her imagination has been prompted by the comparatively recent discovery of subatomic particles, negatively charged, by J. J. Thomson on 30 April 1897 (Falconer 1987: 242). Originally labelled 'corpuscles' (a physiological term that keeps the body in play), these later became known as 'electrons', and were a controversial discovery since they suggested the divisibility of the atom, or, as Thomson wrote to Kelvin as early as April 1896, 'a splitting up of the gaseous molecules into finer pieces' (Falconer 1987: 265). Thomson's electron may in this way be seen as comparable to Pater's moment, which recognises the status of time as 'infinitely divisible' (Pater 1902: 235); matter, it seems, is going the same way. Woolf's conflation of temporal and atomic or material refinement, evident in 'The Moment', encourages this otherwise rather eccentric Thomson/Pater connection. Thomson's (unsuccessful) nomination for a Nobel Prize in 1904 (Falconer 1987: 165–6) would have kept him in the European consciousness, and this perhaps explains Joyce's reference to Dignam's atomisation (see Chapter 2), as well as a similar phrasing in Woolf's own *Mrs Dalloway* (1925) when Peter Walsh thinks of his imagined love affair with a woman pursued in the street: 'And it was smashed to atoms – his fun [. . .]; all this one could never share – it smashed to atoms' (Woolf 1992: 59). Eleanor's later description of the sky as composed of 'innumerable grey-blue atoms the colour of an Italian officer's cloak' (Woolf 1968: 165–6) puts a more artistic spin upon these scientific speculations. However, Woolf is most interested in the divisibility of matter that, in its move toward refined particles well beyond the capacities of the eye and of the hand, prompts Wolff's 'primeval' gesture – the outmoded, testing grasp.

Grasping the moment; seizing the day

The grasp's second function in *The Years* is on the Paterian rather than the Thomsonian side, since Woolf makes use of the hand's enfolding capacities to offer a physical correlate to the psychological effort to grasp the moment – to be an alert, coherent body *now*. Woolf's summary of a crucial scene for Hare's Lady Waterford reminds us that it, too, contains a grasp:

> And so it was, that winter's morning; his horse stumbled; he was killed. She knew it before they told her, and never could Sir John Leslie forget, when he ran downstairs on the day of the burial, the beauty of the great lady standing to see the hearse depart, nor, when he came back, how the curtain, heavy, mid-Victorian, plush perhaps, was all crushed together where she had grasped it in her agony. (Woolf 1967b: 202–3)

Beyond simple anguish, the poignancy of the gesture, which has clearly affected Woolf, is in its use of the physical resources no longer available to the dead man, in order to attempt to hold on to him, to halt time and prevent his burial. In Woolf's *Night and Day* (1919) she has used a velvet ('plush') curtain to mark off the Hilbery family drawing room from the private museum dedicated to their great poet forebear, and in this way both hand-marked curtain and grasping hand may be seen to be archive-connected, both being linked to a time-arresting repository of family memory.[14] In *The Years* it is in fact the partial grasp of hollowed hands that is most conspicuously connected to the idea of halted time. Focillon writes: 'As for me, I separate hands neither from the body nor from the mind. [. . .] The gesture that makes nothing, the gesture with no tomorrow, provokes and defines only the state of consciousness' (Focillon 1948: 78). Focillon's claim is poised at the interstices between Wolff's understanding of the hand/mind connection and Woolf's belief (referred to via her own hand-reading experience) that the hand might be mined in a fictional context as a means of psychological exploration and, further, that it might be connected to Kitty's '*now*' in performing gestures with 'no tomorrow'. Nicholas and Eleanor negotiate with the potential of just such an empty or unproductive gesture to define the present moment, a state of human consciousness. Grappling with intractable philosophical questions of how to 'live more naturally . . . better' (Woolf 1968: 238), Nicholas refers to 'the soul – the whole being', and 'he hollow[s] his hands as if to enclose a circle. "It wishes to expand;

to adventure; to form – new combinations?"' (238), a suggestion which Eleanor receives with the realisation that something has been released in her and that she can sense 'a new space of time' (239). Peggy, too, resorts to Nicholas's gesture while contemplating her social awkwardness at Delia's party. While she has a talent for 'fact-collecting', she is baffled by 'what makes up a person – (she hollowed her hand) [. . .] no, I'm not good at that' (284). The hollowed hands indicate, then, the successful encompassing or grasping of a personhood or life ('oughtn't a life to be something you could handle and produce?' thinks Eleanor (294)), and the ability to grasp or carve out a moment from life's ceaseless flow ('I've only the present moment, she thought. Here she was alive, now, listening to the fox-trot' while 'a long strip of life lay behind her' (294)). In *Night and Day*, Katharine Hilbery draws the novel to its conclusion with a similar act of manual shaping:

> it seemed to her that the immense riddle was answered; the problem had been solved; she held in her hands for one brief moment the globe which we spend our lives in trying to shape, round, whole, and entire from the confusion of chaos. (Woolf 1999: 530)

Such gestures recur in Woolf's mind almost twenty years later in the substance of *The Years* itself, but 'wholeness' is also an issue in its composition: 'I see it now, as a whole: I think I can bring it off' (Woolf 1988b, vol. 5: 25).

As an element within the human canon of manual shapes, hollowed hands make most sense as a gesture of community ('new combinations'), as an inept vessel for water or sand (with consequent potential as a rhetorician's metaphor for fleeting life, as these elements escape), and also as the prop for a book.[15] Woolf combines the first two of these possibilities in Nicholas's and Eleanor's uses of the gesture. The third possibility is present in the author's suggestion that it is in fact in the process of literary composition that the hollowed hands may touch upon a stilled moment, a solution to the Nicholas/Eleanor philosophical debate found, in fact, in the pages of *To the Lighthouse*, when Mrs Ramsay's evening of companionable reading with her husband results in a revelation: 'And then there it was, suddenly entire shaped in her hands, beautiful and reasonable, clear and complete, the essence sucked out of life and held rounded here – the sonnet' (Woolf 2008: 98). Pater is here again, in his claim that 'for art comes to you professing frankly to give nothing but the highest quality to your moments as they pass, and simply for those moments' sake' (Pater 1902: 239). These debates are also present in a diary entry of Woolf's from 22 January 1922:

Why do I trouble to be so particular with facts? I think it is my sense of the flight of time [. . .]. I feel time racing [. . .] I try to stop it. I prod it with my pen. I try to pin it down. (Woolf 1988b, vol. 2: 158)

Literature, then, is a kind of time-halting grasp or momentary stillness, a pen-facilitated pinning. In Woolf's last novel published in her lifetime, we might expect to find the author considering literature and immortality. Hare's *The Story of Two Noble Lives* introduces these matters, since the work is, so claims the 'Preface', formed from writings 'preserved as precious memorials by [Charlotte's] mother and sister, when the hand that wrote them was still forever' (Hare 1893, vol. 1: v). Literature as a halt to time is absent from the content of *The Years* – no character contemplates explicitly the link between literature and the immortal – although it remains an issue in the episodic form of the work as a whole, and our final view of the Pargiter family grouping as statues ('[they] wore a statuesque air for a moment, as if they were carved in stone' (Woolf 1968: 347)) does suggest that they have been captured and stilled through literary means. If hollowed hands cannot fully grasp sand, water, character or time, they can at least prop up a text.[16]

Yet it is in one particular composition that Woolf finds a means of ending her sweep through the decades, since I would like to suggest (from root *gerere* – 'to bear or carry'; 'to put forth with the hands') that the conclusion of *The Years* can most helpfully be read as constructed in literary conversation with Horace's Ode 1.11, 'Tu ne quaesieris', which famously includes the injunction 'carpe diem, quam minimum credulo postero' (D. West 1995: 50), commonly translated as 'seize the day, trusting as little as possible in tomorrow'. It is Horace that is Woolf's literary precursor in writing of the link between the embodied experience of the moment and the grasp of the human hand. Given her engagement with just such Horatian notions, we should not be surprised to find that it is Eleanor who moves closest to the ode when she thinks that 'there must be another life, here and now', going on to 'h[o]ld her hands hollowed; she felt that she wanted to enclose the present moment; to make it stay; to fill it fuller and fuller, with the past, the present and the future, until it shone, whole, bright, deep with understanding' (Woolf 1968: 343–4).[17] This is, I would argue, Eleanor's attempt to seize the day. Horace is also in operation when Eleanor poses her final question: '"And now?" she said, looking at Morris, who was drinking the last drops of a glass of wine. "And now?" she asked, holding out her hands to him' (Woolf 1968: 348). Morris, drinking his wine to the dregs, recalls Horace's ode, in which the speaker advises Leuconoë to 'be wise, strain the wine [. . .] / While we speak, envious time will have /

flown past. Harvest the day and leave as little as possible for tomorrow' (D. West 1995: 51). This translation, by David West, remains firmly rooted in the vineyard, translating *carpe* as 'harvest', and we might therefore consider the instruction to 'strain' the wine as being connected to the preparation of the libation, rather than its complete enjoyment (which would be closer to 'drain'). Woolf is herself likely to have been working with the A. S. Aglen translation of 1896, which plumps for the rather unevocative 'snatch' as the meaning of *carpe* (Aglen 1896: 18). In Aglen's hands, Horace advises that we 'wisely pour [our] wine, nor plan / For aught beyond the curtailed hope' (Aglen 1896: 17), moving us back towards Morris's drained drops, and also offering a possible source for Woolf's striking description of Abel's damaged fingers as 'curtailed'.[18]

The latter's gift of a 'dozen of fine old port' (Woolf 1968: 41) to assist his son's examination revision at Oxford results in Edward raising a glass to the light, and seeing his father's own mangled hand superimposed upon his own (43); it is a remembered moment that is seized here, with an imperfect or curtailed grip. North's contemplation of the glass also relates to the place of one's personal identity within temporal flow when he thinks that the ideal mode of existence is to 'be the bubble and the stream, the stream and the bubble [. . .] he raised his glass' (330). Nicholas's two attempts to encompass a moment have been wine-connected, since his first aborted speech occurs in Renny's wine cellar, retreated to during the air raid, and providing a rare opportunity for inebriation in straitened times, while his second takes place at Delia's party, where his raised glass is cruelly ignored. Modernist scholars of Horace were alive to the importance of wine-drinking in the poet's work, with A. D. Sedgwick offering in 1947 a detailed study of the kinds of wine employed, while A. P. McKinlay's 1946 study 'The wine element in Horace' charts exhaustively the interconnections between Horace, booze and the Muse. More recently, Steele Commager has suggested that 'wine seems to represent not so much a subject as a symbol in Horace's thought, a crystallization of attitudes otherwise too abstract to be amenable to poetic development' (Commager 2009: 33), and this is of course Nicholas's territory, as well as Woolf's. Commager also notes that wine and feasting leads toward the Horatian notion of 'floribus et vino Genium memorem brevis aevi' or 'a spirit mindful of life's brevity with flowers and wine' (Commager 2009: 38), and we must remember here that Nicholas, most attuned to the brevity of life, concludes *The Years* not only with a raised glass, but also by 'paddling' his hands amongst the petals on Delia's tables.

Attention to Horace's ode enables us to read him as Woolf's fellow traveller, equally concerned with the escaping moment, recommending the grasp (or snatch, or harvest) as the appropriate gestural response, offering poetry as one means of time control, and turning both to gestures and to wine in order to crystallise profound philosophical questions unamenable to linguistic capture. The poet must therefore sit alongside Wolff to complete the puzzle of hand engagement in *The Years*, and alongside Hare and 'On Being Ill' as its likely sources.[19] In Woolf's novel, then, it is the work of the hand to attempt the grasp of the moment, to establish that it 'is something', to distinguish it from past and future and to place the body on that perilous plank – and yet this is a gesture of futility, one that returns the grasper only to their own body, an outmoded measure and incapable knower, and one which cannot therefore complete Horace's injunction to 'seize the day'. Woolf's most gestural novel repeatedly dramatises this impossibility and yet underscores the strange compulsion to attempt to offer a physical registration of the present. Amongst an extended series of hand-readings and a number of posited gestural canons, Woolf's broader engagement with Paterian theorisations of the moment puts forward for debate the possibility of *carpe diem* as a kind of modernist creed, as 'seize the day' forms an apt injunction for those writers of the *modo*; those, that is, of the ungraspable yet pen-pinnable 'just now'.

Notes

1. Those attending to the bodily in Woolf's work include Maureen F. Curtin (2003), who offers a reading of Clarissa Dalloway's attempts to mask her age and her illness with the application of make-up thought inappropriate to her class; Teresa Fulker (1995), who cautions us to avoid equating Woolf's own evasion of a sexual life with a willed ignorance of the body in her fiction; Maud Ellmann (2010), who addresses the importance of skin experience in *To the Lighthouse* through a psychoanalytical lens; and Alison Light (2008), whose attention to the bodily labours of the Woolfs' domestic servants provides a corrective to the notion that Bloomsbury life was exclusively a life of the mind.
2. Bedford notes that 'soon there were queues' for Wolff's analyses, and that she was 'bidden to [then Duchess of Windsor] Mrs Simpson's' (1973: 314). A hand-reading had clearly become a matter of fashion.
3. The term 'chirology' refers not only to 'the study of the hand', but also to 'the art of speaking by signs made with the hands or fingers' (*OED*), and Wolff's work incorporates both areas of interest, in that she initially began by reading the structure and appearance of the palm and fingers in order to establish the history and personality of her subjects, but moved on, in the mid-1940s, to a consideration of gesture. The etymology of 'chirology' suggests that Wolff's focus is upon 'hand discourse', and this is apt since she is, in tackling gesture, concerned with speech formed by the hands, and, in reading the palm, with hands that 'speak' to the analyst in their revela-

tions about the life of the person to whom they are attached. John Bulwer's *Chirologia: Or, the Natural Language of the Hand* (1644) encompasses these two areas of study, as his title suggests, and he can be seen as one of Wolff's precursors given his interest in gestural rhetoric.

4. The notion that the hands signify 'by Hieroglyphicks what the very thoughts of our Heartes are' is a long-established one, included in Helkiah Crooke's *Mikrokosmographia: A Description of the Body of Man, Together with the Controversies Thereto Belonging* of 1615 (Crooke, quoted in E. Harvey 2011: 396).

5. We should note here, however, the confluence of ideas between Wolff and Henri Focillon, in particular with regard to the latter's claim (discussed in Chapter 1) that we might find in the human hand 'the pattern and as it were the memories of our lives otherwise lost to us' (Focillon 1948: 66).

6. Wolff's access to these institutions was prompted by Huxley's aforementioned 'Preface' which, in attempting to scaffold Wolff's medical credentials, suggested that she might at any moment move into clinical work. The chirologist used the permission granted by the London hospitals to view the gestures of the mentally ill, and *A Psychology of Gesture* takes a particular interest in the manual manoeuvres of the schizophrenic of whom (as we noted in Chapter 1) we might expect an unusual self/skin/hand relationship.

7. Huxley offers a longer address to the mysterious powers of the human hand in his screen treatment *Jacob's Hands*, co-written with Christopher Isherwood (Woolf's 'bright little bird' (Woolf 1988b, vol. 5: 100)) in 1944. The eponymous hero, a war veteran, has an unmanageable and burdensome gift of healing, achieved by the laying on of hands: '"It's not anything I *do*," he keeps repeating, "It just comes into me, somehow. It's as if I can feel it, going out through my hands"' (Huxley and Isherwood 1998: 20). Presumably adapting Woolf's *Jacob's Room* as their title, and playing on contemporary debates regarding palmistry, spiritualism and spiritual healing, the treatment – although schematic – does allow us to note the spiritual questions preoccupying both authors at this time (Isherwood's conversion to Vedantism had occurred in 1939 (see Summers 1980: viii)). The superstitious and sentimental treatment was never made into a film.

8. I consider here a narrow aspect of the motorcar question within Woolf's work. For a broader discussion, see Minow-Pinkney (2000).

9. Elizabeth Bowen offers in *The Death of the Heart* (1938) a memorable rendering of vestibular adjustments in her description of Matchett's taxi journey: 'At corners, or when the taxi swerved, she put one hand out and stiffly balanced herself. Inside her, her spirit balanced in her body, with a succession of harsh efforts, as her body balanced inside the taxi' (Bowen 1962: 315). Matchett's spirit, or psychological self, must find its level within the recalibrating body – it is, in this way, the air bubble within the spirit-level of her wider somatic system. Bowen shares with Woolf the sense that the self struggles in these conditions.

10. Upon her return from India, Eleanor lies on her bed and attends to her body's residual sense of kinaesthesis; her somatic system thinks she's still on the boat and train. Yet she knows that what is passing is not waves, landscape or moments of travel but 'people's lives, their changing lives'

(Woolf 1968: 170). The body's haptic capacities are tied closely to travel and temporal registration here, seguing into Woolf's broader project to track the Pargiters across the decades.

11. The plank becomes a less plausible precipice in Woolf's diary entry for 25 October 1920: 'Why is life so tragic; so like a little strip of pavement over an abyss. I look down; I feel giddy; I wonder how I am ever to walk to the end' (Woolf 1988b, vol. 2: 72). She goes on to note that 'I don't like time to flap around me' (72). The impetus for such thoughts is not related. It was, however, a Monday.

12. It is in the eloquent moment of manual gesture that the hand's operation as synecdoche is clearest. The handshake confirms a mutual contract into which the whole body must enter; the gesture of prayer enters body and soul into contact with God; the raised hand commands attention for the voice and person of the speaker. The 'poster boy' is in action here (see Chapter 1).

13. Observe the similarity of gesture between Eleanor and Bowen's Portia, again of *The Death of the Heart*: 'Portia felt her sixpence for the collection between the palm of her right hand and the palm of her glove. The slight tickling and the milled pressure of the new coin's edge, when she closed her hand, recalled her to where she was – in Seale church, in a congregation of stalwart elderly men and of women in brown, grey, navy, or violet, with collars of inexpensive fur' (Bowen 1962: 172).

14. We should note here that the grasp as a halt to time relates to the notion of forgetting which, via its etymological roots in the Old Teutonic *getan*, means 'to miss or lose one's hold' (Paterson 2007: 59). To grasp is to remember; to release or fail in one's grasp is to forget.

15. The hollowed hands are also, of course, close to the prayerful gesture of self-touching, which (as we saw in Chapter 1) at once alerts the body to its own sensory capacities and reminds the touching-touched that they are but flesh and bone. These concerns – with the sensing body, and the inevitable decay of that body as a result of the accrual of passing moments – are Woolfian. And that fleshly bundle of the passively touched hand might stand as a metaphor for *The Years* as a whole, since Woolf suggests that the completion of the project is like having a 'bony excrescence – [or] bag of muscle [. . .] cut out of my brain' (Woolf 1988b, vol. 5: 3), and that whatever the faults of the book it does have the merit of containing 'more blood & bone' than the rest of her *oeuvre* (38).

16. The notion of the text as an *inept* vessel crops up in Woolf's reading of Arnold Bennett: 'Can it be that [. . .] Mr Bennett has come down with his magnificent apparatus for catching life just an inch or two on the wrong side? Life escapes' (Woolf 2003a: 149).

17. A touch of Horace may also be heard in the poorer streets of London, albeit in a sentimentalised form, since a street singer outside Mira's house reminds passers-by to 'count your blessings, Count your blessings' (Woolf 1968: 10), a related injunction to that given in the ode.

18. D. H. Lawrence's reference to Horatian wine-drinking comes in his essay 'Why the Novel Matters' (1925), where he describes the contemporary positing of a mind/body relationship thus: 'The years drink up the wine, and at last throw the bottle away: the body, of course, being the bottle' (Lawrence

1985b: 193). The passage is of particular interest, since it continues with Lawrence's contemplation of his own hand as that which *knows*.

19. Despite its fascination with the human hand – as marker, as knower, as grasper and as glass-raiser – there is something intangible about *The Years*; something escapes the grasp. While Woolf herself was beset with doubts about the success of the book, Leonard was alert to its intangible beauty: 'The miracle is accomplished. L. put down the last sheet about 12 last night; & could not speak. He was in tears' (Woolf 1988b, vol. 5: 30). Those tears, their specific cause unexplained, are an appropriate response to Woolf's writing in the Paterian-elegiac mode.

Chapter 4

Dorothy Richardson and the Haptic Reader

The licking eye

Dorothy Richardson is the fairy godmother of the haptic. 'Fairy' because she views cinema as an apparatus and an experience that has to do with magical conjuring, with 'enchanted eyes' (Richardson 1998: 177), and 'godmother' because her prescient phenomenology of film spectatorship anticipates in crucial ways the work of Laura U. Marks, who in turn has initiated recent critical interest in the haptic aspects of film, and rehabilitated that 'haptic' term for common use. While Walter Benjamin's reading of Aloïs Riegl, F. T. Marinetti's tactilism manifesto and Aldous Huxley's evocation of the feelies are perhaps the three texts of the modernist period most conspicuously engaged with the haptic (although not hitherto read in concert), it is Richardson that moves closest, through her adroit descriptions of the somatic aspects of film viewing, to the film theory that dominates contemporary discussion of that 'haptic' term. In Chapter 1, we noted that Gilles Deleuze considers the bas-relief of the Egyptian artistic assemblage, brought to modernist attention via Benjamin's engagement with the art history of Riegl, as an opportunity to consider

> the most rigid link between the eye and the hand because its element is *the flat surface*, which allows the eye to function like the sense of touch; [. . .] it confers [. . .] upon the eye a tactile, or rather *haptic*, function. (Deleuze 2002: 99)

When Richardson confronts the flat surface of the cinema screen, she too makes that link between the hand and the eye, echoing Benjamin's belief that modernist cinema is 'primarily tactile, being based on changes of place and focus which periodically assail the spectator' (Benjamin 1999b: 231). Richardson's most Benjaminian reading occurs in her column 'The Front Rows' (1928), part of her 'Continuous Performance' series written for the film magazine *Close Up*, and the title of the latter is apt in this instance, since it is spectatorship in the *enchroi* position, right up close to the screen, that prompts a haptic viewing experience:

> There was indeed no possibility of focusing a scene so immense that one could only move about in it from point to point and realise that the business of the expert front-rower is to find the centre of action and follow it as best he can. Of the whole as something to hold in the eye he can have no more idea than has the proverbial fly on the statue over which he crawls. (Richardson 1998: 172)[1]

The crawling creature has already been read in this study as drawing attention to the haptic – in *Brave New World* via *Troilus and Cressida* in John's confrontation with the semi-sentient Lenina, and (via ants) in Sunflower's experiences of formication in the Forum. The fly undertakes its own exercises in touch, and offers a crawling-skin sensation to any statue with haptic capacities. Yet it is also useful to Richardson here in its sensing of a whole or a form that is known only via perambulatory groping or a travelling grasp, since it cannot be held within the scope of the eye. The statue/fly analogy suggests that the roving eye of the front-rower seems to grasp the screen in its tracking and retracking across an image too expansive to be known in totality. The eye is, as we saw in Chapter 1, epidermic, a particular modification of the skin, since 'the skin provides the medium in which the other sense organs are located, and the element of which we feel they are largely made' (Connor 2004: 34). Those physiological origins are recalled here as the eye crawls its way across the cinematic screen in response to the peculiarities of the *enchroi* position.

This fragmented view afforded only to those seated close to the screen (since watching from a greater distance *would* permit a totalising vision of the image depicted) in fact prompts the front-rower to perceive the film as a form of mess, if we follow David Trotter in noting that the latter:

> enforc[es] upon us sight and touch, sight-as-touch. It shows us matter *radically*: that is, not for the first time, but again (and again) through the displacements worked by spillage, tearing, fragmentation, decay. Mess is always already in close-up. By the time we've noticed it (seen it, touched it, smelt it), it's too late to gain any perspective on it. (Trotter 2008: 139)

While Trotter's point is that mess encourages haptic opticality, Richardson's front row phenomenology allows us to see that if mess is already in close-up, then the front-rower's close-up is always a messy, haptic business.[2] As we noted in Chapter 1, the haptic nature of Egyptian hieroglyphic depictions is attributable to its appeal to *nearsight*, and

Richardson's front-rower should therefore be seen as in the *enchroi* position, engaging with the 'mess' of the fragmented image, and as a nearsighted Egyptian. Marks's description of 'haptic *visuality*' recalls Richardson's groping look when she claims that in this viewing mode 'the eyes themselves function like organs of touch' (Marks 2000: 162). We should note here that Marks leaves responsibility for the haptic quality of film to the film-maker, identifying moments when they create views prompting a haptic response in an audience through the denial of full purchase on that which is depicted. Richardson, by contrast, approaches the haptic through a reading of a particular emplacement within the cinematic theatre. Nevertheless, in recommending haptic visuality, Marks does invoke the fairy godmother of haptic film:

> The ideal relationship between viewer and image in optical visuality tends to be one of mastery, in which the viewer isolates and comprehends the objects of vision. The ideal relationship between viewer and image in haptic visuality is one of mutuality, in which the viewer is more likely to lose herself in the image, to lose her sense of proportion. When vision is like the touch, the object's touch back may be like a caress, though it may also be violent. (Marks 2000: 184)

Richardson's front-rower is similarly 'los[t] [. . .] in the image', crawling across that which cannot be held in the eye, and she is also concerned with 'mutuality', as we will see. Marks extrapolates from her theory of haptic visuality toward questions of the gendered nature of film viewing, and the ethics of both film-making and spectatorship, suggesting interesting equations between post-colonial culture and mastery-resistant haptic films. Her scope, then, is far beyond that with which Richardson is working (although the latter does consider 'The Film Gone Male' in the coming of sound (Richardson 1998: 205–7)). Yet we can claim that Richardson's early appreciation of the haptic aspects of film spectatorship links her not only to her contemporaries, but to twenty-first-century theorisations of the body's response to film. Richardson's touching eye sees (or gropes) a long way into the future of the haptic.

Amongst her contemporaries, Richardson finds a near neighbour in Virginia Woolf, whose concept of the licking eye is outlined in 'The Cinema' (1926), where she writes that 'the eye licks it [the film scenario] all up instantaneously, and the brain, agreeably titillated, settles down to watch things happening without bestirring itself to think' (Woolf 1950: 166). Woolf's business here is to lament the imbecility of the film-viewing 'savages' of her own moment, offered only titillating films of historical events, or simple-minded attempts to parasitically raid the glories of literature and transfer them to the screen. Yet Woolf's claim is interesting in anticipating Richardson's efforts to theorise an eye which functions epidermically, here in 'licking' – both touching and tasting the screen. This 'lick' of the epidermic eye links to Richardson's claim that 'the front-rowers' are a type or a gang, who have been 'initiated' (Richardson 1998: 174), and who have an appetite or taste for the *enchroi* position; the licking eye is gustatory as much as optical. Beyond the optical lick, Woolf's 'The Cinema' is linked to matters haptic via a circuitous route, appearing to be indebted heavily to Shakespeare's *A Midsummer Night's Dream*, and in particular to Theseus's speech in the fifth act:

> More strange than true. I never may believe
> These antique fables, nor these fairy toys.
> Lovers and madmen have such seething brains,
> Such shaping fantasies, that apprehend
> More than cool reason ever comprehends.
> The lunatic, the lover, and the poet
> Are of imagination all compact.
> [. . .]
> The poet's eye, in a fine frenzy rolling,
> Doth glance from heaven to earth, from earth to heaven.
> And as imagination bodies forth
> The forms of things unknown, the poet's pen
> Turns them to shapes, and gives to airy nothing
> A local habitation and a name.
>
> (V, i, 2–17)

A looming tadpole that Woolf observes during a screening of Robert Wiene's *The Cabinet of Dr Caligari* (1920), and which turns out to be a fault of the 'fairy toy' of the cinema rather than an artistic experiment, is nevertheless said to 'embody some monstrous diseased imagination of [Cesare] the lunatic's brain' (Woolf 1950: 169). Woolf echoes Theseus's phraseology here, and joins him in his suggestion that the lunatic might have access to apprehension (*prehendere*, grasping or bodily knowing) rather than distanced, mental comprehension; this is the possibility open to cinema as a form. The tadpole 'bodies forth' the experience of 'fear itself, and not the statement "I am afraid"' (Woolf 1950: 169), and provides Woolf with an intimation of cinema's promise. While the potential indicated by the tadpole is generally taken to be of a psychological stripe, underscoring cinema's ability to render mental experience through abstract visual representation, Jennifer M. Barker suggests that such physical faults in the film and its projection in fact remind us of the bodily nature both of the film, and of our response to it as cinema spectators:

> Cinematic tactility, then, is a general attitude toward the cinema that the human body enacts in particular ways: haptically, at the tender surface of the body; kinaesthetically and muscularly [. . .]; and viscerally [. . .]. The film's body also adopts toward the world a tactile attitude of intimacy and reciprocity that is played out across its nonhuman body: haptically, at the screen's surface, with the caress of shimmering nitrate and the scratch of dust and fiber on celluloid. (Barker 2009: 3)

Woolf's tadpole hints, then, at the haptic aspects of both film spectatorship and film stock. Theseus is of further use in his reference to the poet's eye that, 'in a fine frenzy rolling', undertakes the same optical tracking as Richardson's front-rower. Woolf's reference to the synaesthetic appeal of Shakespeare's sonnets within 'The Cinema' itself makes the claim of the bard's influence on her essay a more plausible one – he 'presents us with impressions of moisture and warmth and the glow of crimson and the softness of petals inextricably mixed and strung upon the lift of a rhythm', she claims (Woolf 1950: 170). Woolf's treatment of the cinema is, in part via Theseus, imbued with the language of touch, referring to the presence of literary characters 'in the flesh', which could be captured by an innovative film director, who would haul in the visual booty 'hand over hand' (170). Woolf also refers to cinema's 'immense dexterity' (171), and its potential to capture 'some secret language which we feel and see' (169). The ostensibly optical medium of the cinema is, for Woolf as for Benjamin and Richardson, a matter not only of seeing but also of feeling; a haptic matter.

In *Samson Agonistes* (1671), John Milton has his hero ask:

> why was sight
> To such a tender ball as the eye confined?
> So obvious and so easy to be quenched,
> And not as feeling through all parts diffused
> That she might look at will through every pore?
>
> (Milton 1990: 513)

Samson's question is, in essence: why can I not have eyes distributed across the surface of my skin, so that my sight cannot be so easily 'quenched' or blinded? Or, more succinctly, why cannot my whole body look? Richardson, Woolf and their fellow modernists ask the other question implied here: why cannot the tender ball of the eye touch? Yet they also ask, alongside Milton, why cannot looking be a whole-body experience? Adolf Hildebrand, a post-Riegl art historian and theorist, writes of sight and touch in *The Problem of Form in Painting and Sculpture* of 1893:

Nature having endowed our eyes so richly, these two functions of seeing and touching exist here [in the eye] in far more intimate union than they do when performed by different sense organs. An artistic talent consists in having these two functions precisely and harmoniously related. (Hildebrand 1907: 14)

The cinema screen's undifferentiated flatness makes it appear at first a strange place to see summoned the haptic responses of the human sensorium; there is no texture here, no braille-like surface to appeal to the touch. Richardson's crawling eye/fly is brought about by a particular seating position; Woolf's haptic tadpole is a mistake. However, Benjaminian/Deleuzian readings of Egyptian hieroglyphics suggest that flatness is a provocation rather than a barrier to haptic engagement with an image. And Richardson does suggest, like Hildebrand, that optical experience can lead to the broader invocation of other experiences within the somatic system. In fact she sees the narrowness of film's appeal to the eye as central to this invoking. Favouring the silent film in an era of the transition to sound, Richardson commends the former in stating that 'the secret of its [silent film's] power lies in its undiluted appeal to a single faculty' (Richardson 1998: 197), since 'sight *alone* is able to summon its companion faculties: given a sufficient level of concentration on the part of the spectator, a sufficient rousing of his collaborating creative consciousness' (197). Silent film therefore 'enhances the one faculty that is best able to summon all the others: the faculty of vision' (197), and through that visual appeal, the cinema asks that the spectator collaborates in the film experience. It is this collaborative relationship, in which the spectator's body is made available to the artistic creations of the cinema, that Richardson transfers to her own literary practice, where she considers reading as a whole-body, haptically engaged act.

Scenes of reading

Richardson's *Pilgrimage* sequence of novels (1915–35) connects to haptic issues in three crucial ways, over and above its author's ongoing fascination with cinematic and proto-cinematic devices as evinced in her 'Continuous Performance' columns: the reading experience is figured within the sequence as a tactile act; Richardson's central protagonist Miriam Henderson finds that her much-needed writing room functions as a kind of ramification of her own epidermic border, a second skin; and the very act of pilgrimage (here, toward the moment of writing) can be considered a fundamentally haptic business.

Being a haptic reader

Jorge Luis Borges has stated that just as 'the taste of the apple [. . .] lies in the contact of the fruit with the palate, not in the fruit itself', so it is that 'poetry lies in the meeting of poet and reader, not in the lines of symbols printed on the pages of a book. What is essential is the aesthetic act, the thrill, the almost physical emotion that comes with each reading' (Borges, quoted in Pallasmaa 2005: 14). From *Babbitt* onwards, this study has addressed the hand's capacity to read, and to be read. Richardson invites us to think about what reading itself, the body/book relationship in Borges's moment of 'meeting', might have to do with touch. As with the cinema, the text enters the body through the portal of the eye, and yet it is imbricated with touch through its summoning up of the body's responses far beyond the fly-crawl of the eye across the page. Writing of the broad cultural impact of the cinema, Richardson notes that 'in literature alone it is creating a new form. For just as the stage play created a public for the written play [. . .] so will the practice of film-seeing create a public for the film-literature' (Richardson 1998: 191). Richardson's statement leaves open the question of just what *practice* of reading might be the correlate to this film-literature, but her comparison with the pairing of page/stage suggests that to read film-literature will be to see before the eyes the world described. In her review of Richardson's *Dawn's Left Hand* (1931), Winifred Bryher claims that 'in each page an aspect of London is created that, like an image from a film, substitutes itself for memory, to revolve before the eyes as we read' (Bryher, quoted in L. Marcus 1998: 153). Bryher's suggestion is that, in Richardson's own attempt at film-literature, she is able to conjure up a scene which revolves, turning before the eye of the reader, and implying a three-dimensional, explorable story space into which the reader can enter and experience bodily sensation, thus participating in Richardson's process of collaborative making. In her memoirs, Bryher undertakes her own act of memory, recalling her experience of reading the *Pilgrimage* sequence: 'Then there was the excitement of her style [. . .] it was stereoscopic, a precursor of the cinema, moving from a window to a face, from a thought back to the room, all in one moment, just as it happened in life' (Bryher 1962: 174). In Chapter 1, we noted that the stereoscope 'is the historically specific visual technology which haptic theory requires to make its case in relation to that phase of the education of the eye which includes early cinema' (Trotter 2004: 41), as a result of its 'illusion of tangibility. The illusion is a product of the assertiveness with which objects in the foreground occupy space: the feeling that one could reach out and touch them, or be touched by them' (41).

If Bryher identifies the illusion of tangibility conjured by Richardson's writing style, then she not only underscores the latter's interest in proto-cinematic devices (most in evidence in the novel *Interim* (1919)), but also makes the first critical claim for Richardson's literary invocation of the haptic sense. For Richardson, 'the [cinematic] onlooker is a part of the spectacle' (Richardson 1998: 176), and an imagined caption from an 'enterprising producer' should instruct the film spectator to '*Cease, in fact, to exist except as a contributing part of the film*' (Richardson 1998: 175). In *Pilgrimage*, Richardson begins to sketch out the ways in which the reader of a text might similarly relinquish being, so as to be fully, haptically incorporated in the spectacle conjured by the text.

While 'the book remains the intimate, domestic friend, the golden lamp at the elbow' (Richardson 1998: 192), the reading process moves one beyond present circumstances, enabling simultaneous existence at the site of reading and at the written site. Miriam observes that 'you are *in* Norway while you read [Ibsen's *Brand*]. That is why people read books by geniuses and look far-away when they talk about them ... What is genius? Something that can take you into Norway in an ABC' (Richardson 2002, vol. 2: 383). In an interview of 1929, when asked 'what should you most like to do, to know, to be?', Richardson replies that she wishes to know 'how to be perfectly in two places at once' (Bronfen 1999: 1). Elisabeth Bronfen has suggested that this dream relates to Richardson's interest in temporality and the operation of memory that, in contrast to Woolf's plank metaphor (see Chapter 3), she sees as piling up around the present in a kind of excrescence of simultaneous moments. Yet the dream of simultaneous existence also works as Richardson's manifesto for 'film-writing', that is, for a form of contemporary literature that, in its appeal to the somatic capacities of the reader through the flat page, echoes the haptic operations of contemporary cinema. In her column 'Narcissus' (1931), she claims that:

> in this single, simple factor rests the whole power of the film [. . .]. In life, we contemplate a landscape from one point, or walking through it, break it into bits. The film, by setting the landscape in motion and keeping us still, allows it to walk through us. (Richardson 1998: 203)

Richardson's dream of simultaneity is, therefore, that the reader undertake two bodily experiences – that of grasping the book beneath the glowing reading lamp, and that of the scene depicted, 'walking through' the haptically responding body, or in its three-dimensional revolving, prompting the reading body to somatically register the scene. Trotter has suggested that 'an account of story's sensuous remaking in the body of the listener might constitute the basis for a theory of haptic narrative' (Trotter 2008: 145) and, by reading her fiction and film-writing alongside one another, we can suggest that Richardson begins to formulate just such a theory.

Skin ego and writing room

Miriam's story, bearing a semi-autobiographical relationship to Richardson's own (see Fromm 1977), is a *Künstlerroman*, in which we track our central protagonist toward the scene of writing, a scene which itself produces the text through which we have passed (or, bearing in mind Richardson's own phenomenology of readership, which has passed through us). Miriam comes to realise, like Woolf, that one must have a room of one's own (Woolf 1993c): 'There must always be a clear cold room to return to. There was no other way of keeping the inward peace' (Richardson 2002, vol. 2: 321). This fictional point of origin for the *Pilgrimage* sequence is interesting in its insistence on a room that functions like a skin, recalling our explorations in Chapter 1 of the notion of the skin ego, a sense of self that is tied crucially to the conceptualisation of one's relationship with a continent, individuated cutis. Miriam's retreat to her writing room affords the material necessities to which Woolf was aiming primarily to refer, and yet it also makes possible the establishment of the individuated ego essential to the commencement of her writing life; it does so through functioning as a skin. In a manner that recalls Eleanor's return to bodily measure and pain when confronted with the mysteries of the atom (see Chapter 3), Miriam uses the skin of the writing room to return her to a centre: 'Once more her room held quietude secure . . . Her being sank perceptibly back and back into a centre wherein it was held poised and sensitive to every sound and scent' (Richardson 2002, vol. 4: 363). Further, this is a room that, like a continent cutis, holds a human being, both caressing and soothing, and holding *together*: 'Coming gently into the room [. . .] instinctively aware of the density of invisible life within a room that holds a human being' (Richardson 2002, vol. 4: 384). Miriam's most oft-cited relationship with her room has the latter function as a kind of apparatus of cinematic projection, in which her memories are cast upon the wall, writing with Herring's 'magic fingers' (see note 1, below):

The walls were traveller's walls. That had been their first fascination [. . .]. They saw her years of travel contract to a few easily afforded moments, lit, though she had not known it, by light instreaming from the past and flowing now visibly ahead across the farther years. (Richardson 2002, vol. 3: 87)

However, if we bear in mind Steven Connor's claim that the human skin's 'fundamental condition is to be that on top of which things occur, develop or are disclosed. The skin is the ground for every figure. [. . .] a setting, a frame, an horizon, a stage' (Connor 2004: 38), then we can read this scene as one in which the wall of the space of writing functions as a skin; a setting within which a life is enclosed, a horizon, and a stage on which one's remembered life is viewed again. Miriam finds this carapace of a skin-functioning room essential to the formulation of the skin ego that is a prerequisite for the business of writing.

Tactile pilgrimages

This insistence on the writing room's skin function is important to a broader reading of Richardson's novel sequence as living up to its name in its relationship to practices of religious pilgrimage. For both the reader and for Miriam, the pilgrimage is 'a spiritual and aesthetic quest which culminates in her discovery of the scene of writing' (Bronfen 1999: 1) and which, in making possible the book through which we pass, forms a loop (something like the Joycean lemniscate; see Chapter 2) into which we may enter at any point. As with pilgrimage, it is the process of travelling, rather than the destination, which is crucial; this is, like the back-to-back repeat projection of a single film programme, a 'Continuous Performance'. Further, since that scene of writing is a skin experience, we look for its echo in the practice of pilgrimage by seeking out instances of touch in the latter. By considering the haptic aspects of this practice of devotional walking, we can identify the ways in which Richardson's novel sequence is invested in touch, the tactile and skin experiences at the deepest levels. While Richardson pays remarkably close attention to hands and their tactile acts (particularly in the case of *Pointed Roofs* (1915) and its many pianists), a haptic reading of the author's work is possible in far broader terms.

Juhani Pallasmaa reminds us that 'in the Islamic belief the five fingers signify proclaiming one's faith, prayer, pilgrimage, fasting and generosity' (Pallasmaa 2009: 39). We considered in Chapter 1 the *chiasmatic* touching-touched gesture of prayer, as well as Thomas's faith confirmed through touch. Generosity too is a matter for the hand, since the gesture of giving is a bringing forth with the hands. Fasting, meanwhile, is the steadfast refusal to put hand to mouth. That pilgrimage takes the fifth finger here indicates that it too might be a tactile matter.[3] In her 1938 'Foreword' to the *Pilgrimage* sequence, Richardson considers her fellow experimental writers and their efforts to work with what others are by now calling 'stream of consciousness' writing, and she makes reference to 'a man walking, with eyes devoutly closed, weaving as he went a rich garment of new words wherewith to clothe the antique dark materials of his engrossment' (Richardson 2002, vol. 1: 10). We can reasonably assume, in part due to the reference to closed (myopic?) eyes and to neologisms, that this devotional walker is James Joyce. The reference to weaving recalls both the Homeric parallel of Joyce's Molly Bloom in the figure of Penelope, and the employment of Riegl as a curator of textiles, a job, as we noted in Chapter 1, concerned with tactility and texture. Contemporary experiments of psychological depiction are, then, a tactile matter, but they are also a pilgrimage, a process of walking for spiritual penance or quest. Ideas of perambulation also structure Richardson's thinking about film spectatorship ('The test of the film on whatever level is that the wayfaring man, though a fool, shall not err therein, though each will take a different journey' (Richardson 1998: 165)), and about novel readership ('And is not every novel a conducted tour? First and foremost into the personality of the author' (Richardson, quoted in Bronfen 1999: 5)). If film viewing and novel reading are, or can be, haptic experiences, and if they are also kinds of pilgrimage, how then is touch invoked and marshalled in the latter case? Peter Brown, in considering *The Cult of the Saints*, has established that 'in the religious life and organization of the Christian church in the western Mediterranean, between the third and sixth centuries a.d.' (Brown 1981: 1), practices of pilgrimage were an essential part of worship. The prompt to pilgrimage was the meeting of heaven and earth, either at the grave of a particular martyr or saint, or at some other location where lay a part of their body, or a 'contact relic', an object they had touched during their lifetime. The notion of *praesentia*, where the spiritual power of the dead saint is said to be in attendance at his or her grave or relic site, is a particularly potent iteration of the force of the haptic. For example, Saint Martin's tomb was inscribed with the words 'here lies Martin the bishop, of holy memory, whose soul is in the hand of God; but he is fully here, present and made plain in miracles of every kind' (Brown 1981: 4). Fingers of saints and martyrs were relics apt to prompt pilgrimage, since these had been the point of earthly contact between saint and world, as well as the primary bodily site of saintly agency (a matter to which we return in Chapter 6). Yet, having walked many miles to visit a grave or shrine, the pilgrim could often be thwarted by the management of the devotional site:

> For the art of the shrine in late antiquity is an art of closed surfaces. Behind
> these surfaces, the holy lay, either totally hidden or glimpsed through narrow

apertures. The opacity of the surfaces heightened an awareness of the ulti-mate unattainability in this life of the person they had traveled over such wide spaces to touch. (Brown 1981: 87)

Brown's reading of a major period of religious pilgrimage underscores the tactile nature of the act itself, as well as the role of touch in both investing *praesentia* and, in the case of enforced abstinence at the shrine, creating a yearning for contact in the pilgrim. For Brown, pilgrimage is a haptic business, putting into context the presence of skin experiences at Miriam's own shrine/writing room. A reading of the tactile aspects of the pilgrimage experience also connects to Richardson's dream of a dual location, *praesentia* seeming to realise that dream in allowing saintly presence 'in two places at once', in both heavenly and earthly realms. Further, Richardson's early attempts to sketch out a theory of haptic narrative mean that the reader's effort to undertake a pilgrimage within Richardson's text, and to follow Miriam on her own pilgrimage toward the moment of writing, is best understood as a tactile act. Toward the end of the reader's pilgrimage, Miriam remarks that:

> whenever something comes that sets the tips of my fingers tingling to record it, I forget the price; eagerly face the strange journey down and down to the centre of being. And the scene of labour, when again I am back in it, alone, has become a sacred place. (Richardson 2002, vol. 4: 609)

The pilgrimage toward the sacred place of writing is a journey toward haptic engagement with the reader through film-literature, in which the flat page allows a collaborative making that affords that reader the opportunity of double-being present in the power of *praesentia*. When we read, and read haptically, Richardson suggests that we can, like the saints, be in two places at once.

Notes

1. *Close Up* and its producer Pool Publishing were founded in Territet, Switzerland, in 1927, by Kenneth Macpherson, Winifred Bryher and H. D. The magazine, with an avowed interest in the question of cinematic art rather than the dazzle of the movies, ran for six and a half years, from July 1927 to December 1933, with regular writers including Richardson and Robert Herring (see Gevirtz 1996: 47). The latter is notably touch-attuned in his suggestion that the cinema projector's beam, in shining its light above the heads of the audience, uses 'magic fingers [to] writ[e] on the wall' (Herring, quoted in Gevirtz 1996: 63).
2. Virginia Woolf makes reference to less haptically engaged experiences of cinema viewing from positions other than the front rows, when she states

that 'The horse will not knock us down. The king will not grasp our hands. The wave will not wet our feet. From this point of vantage [. . .] we have time to feel pity and amusement, to generalize' (Woolf 1950: 167).

3. Richardson views a trip to the cinema as a kind of spiritual pilgrimage, describing the cinema theatre as 'hospice', 'bethel' and 'religion' (Richardson 1998: 171) and stating that 'it offers as many kinds of salvation as all previous enterprises combined' (181), and an opportunity 'to enter into your own eternity' (185). The cinema's operation as a space of collective experience, and as a node within a network of other sites of viewing, supports such a spiritual reading.

Chapter 5

D. H. Lawrence: Blind Touch in a Visual Culture

The 'Unimpeachable Kodak'

Alongside Aldous Huxley's imaginative exploration of the 'feelies', the work of D. H. Lawrence presents the most obvious opportunity to consider questions of touch and the tactile in modernist writing. So it is that, having considered Huxley in Chapter 1, we close with Lawrence. The latter offers a truly corporeal corpus, deeply invested in the experiences of the somatic system, and the philosophical and spiritual insight which consideration of the human body may bring. It is a catalogue of haptic material too vast to rehearse in detail here. Touch establishes male-to-male bonds in the oft-cited naked wrestling scene between Gerald Crich and Rupert Birkin of *Women in Love* (1920), in the bathing scene between George Sexton and Cyril Beardsall in *The White Peacock* (1911), and in Mellors's relationship with his former comrades in *Lady Chatterley's Lover* (1928). It creates betrothal in the story 'Tickets, Please', in 'Hadrian [You Touched Me]' and in 'The Horse Dealer's Daughter' (1922). In 'Odour of Chrysanthemums', a wife touches her dead husband in a belated gesture of care, while both care and spiritual symbolism are communicated by the woman who washes a young miner's feet in 'Daughters of the Vicar' (1914). The poems 'Touch', 'Touch Comes', 'Noli me Tangere' and 'To Let Go or to Hold On' announce their tactile concerns in their titles, but 'Destiny' also makes use of the customary hand metaphor ('I wish you'd show your hand' (Lawrence 1972: 430)), while 'Know Deeply, Know Thyself More Deeply' returns to the theme of darkness, and therefore touch, as a means of epistemological investigation. This group of poems is found in *Pansies* (1929), and Lawrence's introduction to that collection plays with the idea of a posy of poesy, referring to 'this little bunch of fragments', and also to *pensées*, a 'handful of thoughts' (Lawrence 1972: 417). The two hand-connected conceptualisations (bunch, handful) might lead us to expect the touch focus of the book that follows, yet the author also notes 'the other derivation of pansy, from *panser*, to dress or soothe a wound' (Lawrence 1972: 417), and so it is that Lawrence can be seen to link touch to salving, and thence salvation. Acts of touch lead to spiritual revelation denied to the man or woman who merely looks; like doubting Thomas, we touch and we know. In Lawrence's work, the rendering of touch is most consistently used as a counterpoint or, more properly, a corrective to what the author views as a specious valorisation of the visual sense. Vision, for Lawrence, is misleading, and contemporary visual technologies offer only a petrification of the faults inherent in vision itself. He therefore stands opposed to the subject of my previous chapter – while such technologies fascinate Richardson, for Lawrence the camera is sarcastically described as 'the unimpeachable kodak' (Lawrence 1985a: 164); it is, he implies, a mendacious mechanism. Through attention to the short novel *St Mawr* (1925), which concerns itself with contrasts between the visual and the visionary, and to the short story 'The Blind Man' (1922), which depicts a central protagonist who, like Joyce's blind stripling of the same year (see Chapter 2), is thrown upon his haptic resources, we can consider the way in which Lawrence mobilises touch to argue for the place and potency of the knowing hand in what he reads as a predominantly visual culture.

For Lawrence, the Kodak is doubly damned, since it not only reflects the faults within human vision, but also teaches human eyes to operate as if they were a mere apparatus. Contemporary man 'sees what the kodak has taught him to see. And man, try as he may, is not a kodak' (Lawrence 1985a: 164).[1] To evade this cyborgian fate of the mechanistic eye, Lawrence argues that we must reinsert touch in our efforts to see. Henri Focillon, writing in a subsequent decade, echoes Lawrence's concerns regarding the photograph, and also suggests the metaphorical insertion of a hand in the eye:

> The cruel inertia of the photograph will be attained by a handless eye, repelling out sympathy even while attracting it, a marvel of the light, but a passive monster. [. . .] Even when the photograph represents crowds of people, it is the image of solitude, because the hand never intervenes to spread over it the warmth and flow of human life. (Focillon 1948: 73)

Vision with a hand in it, as distinct from the vision offered by the lens, will lead to connection rather than solitude, a more fulsome understanding of human life. Focillon's 'god in five persons' (1948: 73) is powerful because it *knows*: 'It searches and experiments [. . .] it has all sorts of adventures; it tries its chance' (Focillon 1948: 76). Focillon moves close to Lawrence's own hymn to the hand here, since the latter states (as we noted in Chapter 1): 'It [the hand] meets all the strange universe in touch, and learns a vast number of things, and knows a vast number of things' (Lawrence 1985b: 193).[2] Crucially, Lawrence suggests that the untrustworthy and isolating form of seeing, where the retina strives to behave like the camera, is something that has been learned over the course of human development; via shifts in what Aloïs Riegl calls the *Kunstwollen*, contemporary man suffers from Kodak vision, but it was not ever thus. Earlier forms of civilisation saw with the hand, and a trace of this heritage remains in the visual practices of children, whose viewing mode is hieroglyphic – when a child sees a man, they see the 'hieroglyph' (the stick man) that has been used by children 'through all the ages' (Lawrence 1985a: 164). Via Riegl, as we saw in Chapter 1, we can read the hieroglyphic way of seeing as quintessentially haptic, given the conflation of figure and ground offered by Egyptian depictions that do not contain shadow or foreshortening, and therefore invite the touch. Lawrence appears well-versed in Riegl when he states that 'previously, even in Egypt, men had not learned to *see straight*. They fumbled in the dark [. . .]. Like men in a dark room, they only *felt* their own existence surging in the darkness of other existences' (Lawrence 1985a: 165). Such fumbling is of value to Lawrence, since the men not of the dark room (Egyptians) but of the darkroom (contemporaries) have a Kodak picture idea of their own monadic existence, to which 'the universe is just a setting to the absolute little picture of himself, herself' (165). Whatever the implications of an inept grasp contained in that 'fumbl[ing]', Lawrence avers that we have much to learn from this past civilisation which puts itself in con*tact* with other existences: 'Egypt has a wonderful relation to a vast living universe, only dimly visual in its reality' (167). It is from these considerations of our benighted, fumbling, hand-seeing precursors that Lawrence extrapolates a contemporary mode of vision that reinserts the hand – to see darkly and fumblingly is, however counter-intuitively, to see *clearly*.

Lawrence's interest in the haptic aspects of earlier iterations of the *Kunstwollen* is in evidence in his treatment of the artistic representations of the Etruscans, a civilisation that Richard Aldington suggests has affinities with the Egyptians (Aldington 1956: vi). Lawrence's *Etruscan Places*, published posthumously in 1932, was based upon 'a poet's holiday among the relics of that far-distant past' (Aldington 1956: vii) taken in March 1927. It is through the author's engagement with the tactile aspects of the painted tombs of Tarquinia that the Egyptian connection becomes most plausible, and through which we may incorporate the Etruscan studies amongst Lawrence's other tactile texts. Visiting the Tomba dei Vasi Dipinti (Tomb of the Painted Vases), Lawrence finds acts of touch depicted, via a medium which itself invites engagement in the *enchroi* position, right up close, and which offers a manifesto for human contact in the broadest ideological sense:

> Rather gentle and lovely is the way he [a figure depicted] touches the woman under the chin, with a delicate caress. That again is one of the charms of Etruscan paintings: they really have the sense of touch; the people and the creatures are all really in touch. It is one of the rarest qualities, in life as well as in art. There is plenty of pawing and laying hold, but no real touch. In pictures especially, the people may be in contact, embracing or laying hands on one another. But there is no soft flow of touch. The touch does not come from the middle of the human being. It is merely a contact of surfaces. (Lawrence 1956: 45–6)

Metaphors of tactility resonate in Lawrence's overall conception of the Etruscan project. Attempting a non-specialist's view of a civilisation hard to decipher, and hampered by his own failing health in offering a comprehensive view of the relevant historical sites, he states his aim expressly as getting in touch with the Etruscans: 'But who wants object-lessons about vanished races? What one wants is a contact. The Etruscans are not a theory or a thesis. If they are anything, they are an *experience*' (Lawrence 1956: 114). Reaching out from his 'middle', Lawrence touches the painted tombs, and recreates that experience in a study that deploys repeatedly the language of hand engagement. In his essay 'The Five Senses' (1923), the author draws together his thoughts on the problematic nature of vision, and suggests that 'we have a choice' to see with light, or to 'see, as the Egyptians saw, in the terms of their own dark souls: seeing the strangeness of the creature outside, the gulf between it and them, but finally its existence in terms of themselves' (Lawrence 1971e: 62). Dark seeing, Egyptian/Etruscan seeing, and the crossing of a self/other gap through skin contact or a mode of sight that replicates it (echoing F. T. Marinetti's call for 'the perfect spiritual communication between human beings through the epidermis' (Marinetti 2006a: 376)) link together my two central stories here: *St Mawr* and 'The Blind Man'.

St Mawr's dark eye

Lawrence's opposition to the visual technologies which Dorothy Richardson holds dear continues beyond the Kodak in his reading of the cinema as fundamentally insufficient when it comes to grasping life as it is meaningfully, bodily, lived. For Lawrence, the cinema is merely 'a series of inert images, mechanically shaken' (Lawrence 1985a: 168), a view which can be found in various permutations across his *oeuvre*. In *St Mawr*, Lou and her mother, Mrs Witt, retreat from British society to their Texan ranch and find that life there is 'like life enacted in a mirror' (Lawrence 1971c: 137), or 'like a cinematograph: flat shapes, exactly like men, but without any substance of reality, rapidly rattling away with talk, emotions, activity, all in the flat, nothing behind it. No deeper consciousness at all' (137). Lawrence's argument against mirror vision recurs in 'Know Deeply', where he suggests: 'Let us lose sight of ourselves, and break the mirrors' (Lawrence 1972: 477). The poem 'When I Went to the Film' returns to the idea of cinematic flatness, referring not only to the deceiving screen which offers the illusion of three-dimensionality, but also to the flat or affectless images that the cinema projects, unable to connect the human 'middle' to that which is depicted. After five iterations of the film's lack of feeling, the poem concludes with reference to a screen 'upon which shadows of people, pure personalities / are cast in black and white, and move / in flat ecstasy, supremely unfelt, / and heavenly' (Lawrence 1972: 443–4). The cinema offers humans that are in fact disembodied, 'exactly like men, but without any substance' – this is ecstasy in the sense that the true human essence has fled the images that remain; there has (as we saw with Babbitt's manicure in Chapter 1) been an escape from incarnation. In Lawrence's reading, the cinema's vision is flat, not hieroglyphically, but unconvincingly, with no appeal to make to Focillon's five-fingered glance. Yet Lawrence goes further, suggesting that the filmic mechanism is antipathetic toward the flesh, an opinion propounded with greatest force in 'Film Passion', where that poem's title may in part refer to the *paschein* or suffering inflicted on the human body by the film medium – the film 'hated him just because he was a man / and flesh of a man. / For the luscious filmy imagination loathes the male / substance / with deadly loathing' (Lawrence 1972: 538). If the cinema is not, despite its capacities to present bodies, the best way to explore them (or, for that matter, to appeal to them), what then is the province of the flesh? For Lawrence, it is fictional prose.

That these claims about the deathly, disembodied flatness of the cinema crop up in *St Mawr* is puzzling initially, since the eponymous equine hero of that novel is known, first and foremost, for his marvellous eyes – 'big, black brilliant eyes, with a sharp questioning glint' (Lawrence 1971c: 19) and 'flaming, healthy strength' (20) – creating an apparent contradiction in authorial interests. Yet the horse's eyes offer a particular kind of vision, far from the flat and affectless. St Mawr's eyes denote his distance from humanity, his otherworldliness (or other breedliness), and his connection to other times, via the fact that they offer a record of the hurts accrued through the history of the subjugation of the horse (a kind of 'race misery' visible also in the eyes of Phoenix the groom, hence his attempts to live up to his name and, through a good marriage, to rise again (142)). The horse is allied with the tactile (demonstrating 'touchy uneasiness' (20); 'it is as if he was a trifle raw somewhere. Touch this raw spot, and there's no answering for him' (20); he 'needs a special sort of touch' (20)), with the unseeing (he 'look[ed] at her without really seeing her, yet gleaming a question at her' (23)), and, most importantly, with twilight and darkness ('they [horses] moved in a prehistoric twilight where all things loomed phantasmagoric' (27); 'Since she had really seen St Mawr looming fiery and terrible in an outer darkness, she could not believe the world she lived in' (35)). St Mawr, in his darkling look and his touchiness, offers just the kind of tactile vision – the vision that truly *sees* – that Lawrence describes in his non-fiction writing and poetry. In 'Twilight', he refers to the fact that 'the litter of day / Is gone from sight' (Lawrence 1972: 41), again attempting to make a connection between darkness and true seeing. In 'The Five Senses', Lawrence pauses to note that 'the horse's eye is bright and glancing [. . .] the root of his vision is in his belly' (Lawrence 1971e: 61), a claim which chimes with that given above: true touch should come from the 'middle' of the human being (or, as here, the horse). St Mawr's particular species of vision is in fact, as Paul Poplawski has suggested, visionary (2001: 97), a term which sloughs the 'vision' root of its negative connotations, and captures the way in which the horse's look connects to other landscapes and histories, a mode of seeing which operates beyond his immediate sensory surroundings.

The language used to describe St Mawr, eyes included, is the language of fire ('gleaming', 'fiery'), and Lawrence often makes use of the flame to indicate moments when togetherness or communion has been achieved, frequently set in train by tactile acts. In the original first chapter or 'Prologue' to *Women in Love*, the men of the novel conquer a mountain and are 'enkindled in the upper silences into a rare, unspoken intimacy' (Lawrence, quoted in Ingersoll 1990: 7); the climber's notion of the 'brotherhood of the rope' is mobilised here, affording the 'brothers' an opportunity to experience intimacy through shared bodily exertion in a remote, homosocial environment.[3] The connection between touch and enkindling is present also in 'Touch Comes', which seems to promise Marinetti's dreamt-of communion through the epidermis: 'Touch comes [. . .] / slowly up in the blood of men / and women. // Soft slow sympathy / of the blood in me, of the blood in thee [. . .] / covers us / with a soft one warmth, and a generous / kindled togetherness' (Lawrence 1972: 470–1). The latter is useful in reminding us that Lawrence's understanding of touch is one in which tactile sensations are truly situated within the broader haptic sense modality. The shift in the tides of the blood might count as an instance of communion-through-touch, just as such tidal shifts might be prompted by more conspicuous tactile engagement. Blood shifts and instances of touch are often bound together in curious ways within Lawrence's work, not least in 'The Blind Man', as we will see. *St Mawr* contains its own trip to the 'upper silences' in the form of a horse-riding excursion to the Devil's Chair in Shropshire, a location that brings St Mawr within sight of his native Wales. While appetites for the picturesque have motivated the journey – the view is said to be remarkable – the scene prompts both Lou and Mrs Witt to muse on the purposelessness of the beautiful (Rico, Edwards, the Welsh hills) and the power of St Mawr's bodily appeal, as he rears up, crushing his rider Rico, and kicking Edwards in his handsome face. The rearing up has been prompted not only by Rico's semi-competent horsemanship, but also by the sight of a dead snake, and Lawrence makes use of its presence (*et in Arcadia ego*) to suggest that, whatever the beauties of Shropshire, it is the fallen, possibly evil and inherently bodily St Mawr who must triumph. The incident prompts both Lou and Mrs Witt to change their meaningless, cinematically flattened lives. St Mawr's look is, then, one that enkindles, a dark look that contains a touch, and one that connects both with the body of Lewis, his compatriot groom, and with the blood tides of the novel's women.

Back to the blind

St Mawr asks that we reject cluttered day-time seeing since, as Lawrence states elsewhere, 'sight is the least sensual of all the senses' (Lawrence 1971e: 61), and that we create a careful distinction between vision and the visionary, with the latter having more to do with dark (but not misleadingly shadowy) looking – that which sees beyond mere surface appearances – with the flame-like, with a knowing with the hand and the blood and not the retina, and with the sensual. One story of Lawrence's makes most explicit this notion of tactile or sensuous seeing beyond the province of the Kodak eye, and it is one that in this way operates as a companion piece to *St Mawr*: 'The Blind Man'. That Maurice Pervin, central protagonist of the latter tale, moves in the darkness of the stables, amongst horses with whom he has an affinity ('The darkness seemed to be in a strange swirl of violent life' (Lawrence 1971d: 62)), encourages us to forge this link between the two tales – the horses are pieces of darkness, modifications of Maurice's element. The story relates the visit of Bertie Reid, barrister and man of letters, to the country home of his old friend and distant cousin Isabel Pervin, and her husband Maurice, a veteran of Flanders.[4] The conflict has left the latter both blinded and scarred, and the couple have spent the past year in isolation adjusting to this new circumstance. The physical damage suffered by Maurice, which we might presume to have left mental scars as significant as the bodily, seems instead to have brought him a species of peace:

> Life was still very full and strangely serene for the blind man, peaceful with the almost incomprehensible peace of immediate contact in darkness. With his wife he had a whole world, rich and real and invisible.
>   They were newly and remotely happy. He did not even regret the loss of his sight in these times of dark, palpable joy. A certain exultance swelled his soul. (Lawrence 1971d: 55)

However, Isabel is pregnant, and concerned that a kind of emotional equilibrium be maintained in the home. Despite the serenity of his blindness, Maurice also suffers from a surfeit of darkness, too close a connection to the tides of his own blood. Isabel feels at once newly bonded to her husband and distanced by his disability. Bertie is invited to provide her with companionship and intellectual stimulation, and her husband with a friendship that might help him to extract himself from his own inner darkness, metaphorically at least.

In the latter scheme, Isabel is thwarted, for, while Maurice overcomes his initial reservations about Bertie and decides to attempt a bond of friendship, the other man is constitutionally unable to accept such a bond. In the oft-quoted ending of the tale, which Lawrence himself referred to as 'queer and ironical' (Lawrence 1984: 302–3), Maurice enquires about the severity of his scarring, asks permission to touch the barrister, explores his head, shoulder, arm and hand with a 'travelling grasp' (Lawrence 1971d: 73), and finally asks Bertie in his turn: 'Touch my eyes, will you? – touch my scar' (73). Bertie, unable to contrive an escape from this complicated physical and emotional confrontation, complies:

> Now Bertie quivered with revulsion. Yet he was under the power of the blind man, as if hypnotised. He lifted his hand, and laid the fingers on the scar, on the scarred eyes. Maurice suddenly covered them with his own hand, pressed the fingers of the other man upon his disfigured eye-sockets, trembling in every fibre. (Lawrence 1971d: 73)

While the barrister is revolted by this experience, Maurice reads the interaction as a successful sealing of male-to-male friendship, stating: 'Oh, my God [. . .] we shall know each other now, shan't we? We shall know each other now' (74). The story concludes with the real result of this mutual touching between the men, which is filtered through Isabel's observation of Bertie: 'He could not bear it that he had been touched by the blind man, his insane reserve broken in. He was like a mollusc whose shell is broken' (75). We might note that it is less the touching of Maurice's scar that revolts Bertie, more the experience of being the recipient of touch. In this exchange of strengths and senses, Maurice calls out for Bertie's visual report of the extent of his scarring, while the sighted man is forced to make use of touch. Such an exchange, Maurice suggests, completes them in some way; this is a gesture of communion or brotherhood, of knowing through touch. Yet the encounter has, unbeknownst to the blind man, gone horribly awry. With doubting Thomas in mind once more, we can observe that Lawrence suggests, in a modification of Christ's claim, that Bertie fails to believe because he continues to see.[5] The disability of the story is not Maurice's blindness, but Bertie's inability to connect through touch.

Bertie's revulsion corresponds to similar sentiments evinced in Lawrence's poem 'Touch', where a Bertie-esque status as an intellectual, a man of the mind, may be read as a kind of contemporary disease: 'since we have become so cerebral / we can't bear to touch or be touched. // Since we are so cerebral / we are humanly out of touch' (Lawrence 1972: 468). Touch, then, is linked in powerful ways both to disgust and to an essential reassertion of humanity in an age that, in losing touch with the body's tactile capacities, has lost touch with what it means to be human. The former claim is one made by Walter Benjamin, when he states that 'all disgust is originally disgust at touching' (Benjamin, quoted in Barker 2009: 47), a notion that Lawrence expands in order to make the further observation that, even for the anti-tactile Bertie, disgust or revulsion is viscerally felt – Bertie's broken shell reveals a mollusc middle, exposed, raw and itself revoltingly fleshly. That term 'shell' also suggests a thick skin or callous nature, and we should note here the use of those two skin metaphors in colloquial references to emotional unresponsiveness and reserve. Distance from one's fellow humans is, in this way, a skin condition, a reading that makes Marinetti's epidermic communion appear less eccentric. Lawrence makes further use of the link between touch and disgust (see also Trotter 1993) in 'Noli me Tangere': 'O you creatures of mind, don't touch me! / O you with mental fingers, O never put your hand on me!' (Lawrence 1972: 468); 'Great is my need to be chaste / and apart, in this cerebral age. / Great is my need to be untouched' (469). Here, in what seems a confusing further nuance of Lawrence's philosophies of touch, the tactile man begs to be left unmolested by the 'mental fingers' of the excessively mind-driven man. The speaker here rejects the confrontation that Maurice concludes his tale by craving. The statement of the poem is: do not touch me, since you cannot touch me properly; I do not fit with this disembodied age. This is quite a different meaning from 'touch me not', or 'do not hold on to me', the two possible interpretations of Christ's injunction given to Thomas (John 20:24–9), meaning 'have faith without recourse to touch' and 'do not tie me to the world of the body, for I must arise to the Father'. Didier Anzieu translates Christ's words as 'do not hold me back', conforming to the 'formula adopted by the French translators of the so-called Ecumenical version of the Bible' (Anzieu 1989: 143). Tactile engagement here would prevent Christ from leaving his body in the act of ascension. *St Mawr*'s Lou, in considering the way that potential suitor Phoenix leaves her pleasingly in her 'sheath', also exclaims: '*Noli me tangere, homine!* I am not yet ascended unto the Father. Oh, leave me alone, leave me alone!' (Lawrence 1971c: 125). This reading, closer to Anzieu's, suggests that Lawrence returned to this biblical episode several times, and with a flexibility in his interpretation. Maurice, in begging for touch, is therefore requesting a specifically earthly, bodily communion, in line with his creator's belief in the knowledge that comes through commitment to the body. Janice Hubbard Harris has recommended that 'The Blind Man' be categorised a 'resurrection tale' (Hubbard Harris 1984: 129), but Maurice's insistence on touch and the bodily creates both links and dissonances with the resurrection of the touch-resistant Christ.

As we saw in Chapter 2, the figure of the blind man is of great use to the history of the philosophy of the senses, and Lawrence is clearly familiar with this heritage, describing the compensations and adaptations that Maurice's blindness brings – he 'seem[s] to know the presence of objects before he touche[s] them' (Lawrence 1971d: 64); his hearing is 'much sharpened' (65); and there is also 'something else' (70), a compensation to which Maurice cannot put a name, but which has, Lawrence implies, something to do with access to other modes of existence.[6] As we saw with Joyce, beyond the foregrounded exploration of the body's senses, its cortical adaptations to blighted streams of sensory information, and the hint of insight gifted by the loss of sight, the figure of the blind man offers an opportunity to consider other preoccupations of his author. In Lawrence's case, the blind figure is most easily situated within discourses of the bodily damage inflicted by the First World War since, as Santanu Das notes, 'the world's first major industrial warfare ravaged the male body on an unprecedented scale but also restored tenderness to touch in male relationships' (Das 2005: 4). Lawrence's own humiliating assessment and rejection from active service (see Das 2005: 233) can be traced within his *oeuvre* in empathetic attempts to register this bodily ravaging, and within his own private correspondence in his attempts to describe his own physical response to the War: 'The War finished me: it was the spear through the side of all sorrows and hopes' (Lawrence, quoted in Ross 1971: 287). Lawrence's claim is remarkable in its choice of a biblical wound, the decisive conclusion to Christ's *paschein* and, we should note, the specific wound into which Thomas is invited to insert his hand in order to confirm Christ's bodily presence and, by implication, his imminent ascension. The author's bid to claim physical trauma when disbarred from service seems an odd one, but he demonstrates the peculiarity of his position in the blind man's story, since he has Bertie send a note to Isabel, 'speaking of the real pain he felt on account of her husband's loss of sight' (Lawrence 1971d: 49). That Maurice has lost not only his sight but his eyeballs, and that he has additionally been facially scarred, is the most fundamental of blows, since 'the face is of course the great window of the self, the great opening of the self upon the world, the great gateway' (Lawrence 1971e: 57), and Maurice's particular wounding leaves him 'cancelled' (Lawrence 1971d: 66), Isabel thinks. Following Das's reading of the story as conspicuously post-War in its insistence on both bodily damage and tender tactility, Lawrence's decision to scar Maurice's face, his window on the world, is evocative.

In Chapter 2, I linked the 'wall face' (Joyce 2008: 172) of Joyce's blind stripling to Jacques Derrida's claim that the eyes of the blind are 'walled up [. . .] more dead than alive' (Derrida 1993: 44). That connection is pertinent here too, although the building of the wall has gone one step further, in that Maurice is left with empty eye sockets. While absent eyes have mythical associations (most obviously via Prometheus), and while blindness following trauma implies a man that has seen too much, has suffered a surfeit of the visual, the status of the eyes of statuary as 'walled up' also applies to Maurice, in that we can read him as a kind of living monument to the dead and damaged of the War. His witnessing has blinded him, but he remains a kind of corporeal witness, a physical record of suffering. This reading of Maurice as monument is supported by the short shrift Lawrence grants to more conventional stone statuary commemorating the dead. In 'At the Front' he remarks: 'Far-off the lily-statues stand white-ranked in the garden / at home. / Would God they were shattered quickly, the cattle would / tread them out in the loam' (Lawrence 1972: 159). Since Lawrence is engaged here in contemplation of his narrating soldier's domestic life, the 'lily-statues' can be read straightforwardly as flowers, and those with a particular connection to innocence, death and Mary, mother of Christ (see Chapter 2). However, that they are 'ranked' returns us both to the military, and to the establishment of national memorials to the lost of the War. The speaker's prayer is that his home should die in concert with him, and/or that the heavy bodies of the cattle should collapse the insufficient memorial that stands in for the absent body of the fallen soldier. Maurice's monumental status is noted by his wife, of whom we learn that 'she could feel the clever, careful, strong contact of his feet with the earth, as she balanced against him. For a moment he was a tower of darkness to her, as if he rose out of the earth' (Lawrence 1971d: 63). The biblical 'pillar of fire by night' (Exodus 13:22) is here modified as a tower of *darkness* by night, since the benighted insight of Maurice finds its natural habitat amongst dark horses in dark stables. Maurice's earth connection and towering stature have him operate as a living monument, as a conductor (of forces unknown, that 'something else'), and as an erection, in the stone and the fleshly sense.

In contrast with my reading (and Leopold Bloom's reading) of Joyce's stripling as emasculated by his blindness, Maurice's lack of sight has connected him to the tactile, to blood flow and to power in a way that, it is implied, has created an intense sexual relationship between him and his wife. His 'heavy limbs, powerful legs that seemed to know the earth' (Lawrence 1971d: 63) are important to this reading of man-as-erection, since 'The Five Senses' notes that 'the thighs, the knees, the feet are intensely alive with love-desire, darkly and superbly drinking in the love-contact, blindly' (Lawrence 1971e: 56). Derrida suggests that the figure of the blind man collapses three tenses: foreseeing, seeing or not in the present, and that which is not yet seen (Derrida 1993: 5–6). This makes the blind man a creature of pure being, but also a statue, not only in his 'walled up' eyes (Derrida 1993: 44), but in his recognition of what has passed, his present standing witness, and his anticipation of what is to come, the moment when mysteries will be solved, when a mystery (root: *myein*, 'closed') is revealed. The monument, like the blind man, is transhistorical. Further, if Maurice is a monument/erection to the dead of the War, then he is a kind of sepulchre, recalled in John Milton's self-portrait of blindness, *Samson Agonistes*, in which the eponymous hero refers to 'myself my sepulchre, a moving grave; / Buried, yet not exempt, / By privilege of death and burial, / From worst of other evils' (Milton 1990: 513). Maurice is, then, a corporeal witness or mobile monument, a moving grave, and a man who is 'cancelled' or buried. That buried position was of course known to Lawrence through his connection to the mining communities of Nottinghamshire, and the mines themselves offer an experience of premature entombment found also in the trenches and, as Milton suggests, in blindness itself. In fact, Derrida observes that writing in the dark, or with closed eyes, results in an eye that appears at the fingertip (the corollary to Lawrence's/Focillon's look with a hand in it): 'This eye [of the fingertip] guides the tracing or outline; it is a miner's lamp at the point of writing' (Derrida 1993: 3). Through this cluster of associations – war monuments, statuary, conducting rod or erection, blind seer, man of the dark, miner and body dependent upon tactile contact – the figure of the blind man can once again be seen as a touchstone for a range of philosophical and historical concerns. In the context of Lawrence's broader interest in the place of the body within the ontology of the human, his blind man can be read as more conspicuously engaged with the haptic than Joyce's stripling, his fellow creation of 1922.

Given Lawrence's resistance to both the Kodak of still photography and the 'inert images' of the 'mechanically shaken' cinema, we must turn to the literary realm to find the proper place for the rendering of the human body and its experiences, tactile or otherwise. Lawrence's realisation, quoted above, that the hand *knows* is one to which the writer has privileged access:

> that's what you learn, when you're a novelist. And that's what you are very liable *not* to know, if you're a parson, or a philosopher, or a scientist, or a stupid person. If you're a parson, you talk about souls in heaven. If you're a novelist, you know that paradise is in the palm of your hand. (Lawrence 1985b: 193–4)

The scientist anatomises the body, 'he puts under the microscope a bit of dead me', and in doing so reduces the human being to 'a brain, or nerves, or glands, or something more up-to-date in the tissue line' (195). The parson is distracted by the spirit, while the philosopher dreams of going 'off in steam' (194), an escape from his own shirt which, says Lawrence, gives him an erroneous sense of importance. Lawrence is convinced that 'every man [. . .] ends in his own fingertips' (194), and since the writer confronts his own hands whenever he writes, and since he writes, or can write, with a focus upon the body, he has access to the 'man-alive' (194) which evades the other chasers and explainers. When the writer writes about those fingertip livers, the blind man, the miner and the soldier of the trenches, the opportunities to explore the bodily nature of human existence are manifold. In claiming that, while the novel might be seen as a mere tremulation of the ether, such a tremulation '*can* make the whole man-alive tremble' (195), Lawrence, despite their differences, joins Richardson: it is possible to engage the body of one's reader, to make that body tremble and, in trembling, come to know itself. Just as the blind man himself trembles with vital energy, so does 'The Blind Man', his literary rendering, and so, Lawrence hopes, does the reader. Derrida suggests, as we saw in relation to the stripling, that to draw the blind is at once to create a self-portrait and to produce a drawing that scrutinises the business of drawing itself. Lawrence, despite the wide range of uses to which he invites us to put his blind man, is at root engaged in a work of self-portraiture, writing to Bertrand Russell: 'All the time I am struggling in the dark – very deep in the dark – and cut off from everybody & everything' (Lawrence, quoted in Ross 1971: 294). Maurice attempts to deal with his sense of being 'cut off' by attempting contact through con*tact*, the tactile act. Lawrence's strategy is to allow the trace of his writing fingertips to meet the fingertips or end-point of the man-alive of his reader, in a Thomas-inspired attempt to 'know each other now'. In this way, Lawrence makes use of his blind man proxy to consider the business of writing itself, and to propose literature, not photography or cinema, as the natural habitat of the haptic.

Notes

1. This point – that there is something distasteful about the conflation of human sense perception and the camera mechanism – is also made by the theatre critic Walter Kerr, who gives the title 'Me No Leica' (playing upon the famous camera brand name) to his review of the play *I Am a Camera* (1951). The latter is an adaptation of Christopher Isherwood's *Goodbye to Berlin* (1939), which early makes the statement: 'I am a camera with its shutter open, quite passive, recording, not thinking' (Isherwood 1998: 9). For Lawrence, such unthinking looking is deathly, as we will see.
2. Focillon and Lawrence have a fellow hand-advocate in the form of Rainer Maria Rilke, who writes in his study of Rodin that 'we grant them [the hands] the right to have their own development, their own wishes, feelings, moods and occupations' (Rilke 2004: 45). Rilke worked for a time as personal secretary to the great sculptor, who both depended upon manual dexterity for his work, and offered his own hymn to the hand in the subjects of his sculptures themselves – see, for example, *Study for The Secret*, the cover image for the present work.
3. The letters of the most famous climber of the 1920s, George Mallory, coincidentally use metaphors of enkindling to suggest contact and communion. Writing to Marjorie Holmes, whom he had never met but with whom he exchanged several passionate letters, Mallory imagines that the tactile trace of her hand on the letter he reads allows her to burn in his presence: 'What is it all about this fire always wanting to blaze up? Shall we see it blaze or shall we hold the snuffer on it?' (Mallory 1923: 3). This oblique connection to Lawrentian flames is useful in reminding us about the tactile aspects of hand/pen/paper connections, with which Lawrence is often preoccupied, but which find their way into Mallory's mind in the comparatively limited realm of epistolary practice. We might expect such a reliance on embodiment at a distance, and the trace of the hand, from a seasoned military man and expeditioner, often marooned miles from loved ones in the bleakest of circumstances. This theme recurs when we meet another letter writer in Chapter 6.

4. Michael L. Ross has suggested that Lawrence's depiction of Bertie reflects his failed attempt to form a bond of blood brotherhood with Bertrand Russell, with whom he maintained a friendship in 1915–17 and sketched a campaign of anti-war propaganda (see Ross 1971). Paul Delany argues that Bertie is James [J. M.] Barrie, another of Lawrence's mooted blood brothers, and that Maurice is Herbert 'Beb' Asquith, who was 'slightly disfigured by a facial wound' in the War (Delany 1983: 93), and whose subsequent reception by his wife, Lady Cynthia Asquith, forms the basis of Lawrence's story 'The Thimble' (1915). Ross's argument is most useful to us here since, if Bertie is Russell, then Maurice is, logically, Lawrence. As with Joyce, then, the blind man can be seen as a proxy for his creator. Whatever their real-life correlates, Maurice and Bertie form a Manichean dualism, an opposition of forces that drives this tale. Such dualisms, often of this mind/body kind, are also crucial to the work of another of our haptic modernists, Rebecca West (see Schweizer 2002).

5. In Raymond Carver's short story 'Cathedral', which is best understood, although controversially, as a rewriting of Lawrence's tale, it is Robert the visitor who is blind, and he brings to his sighted host a sense that blindness might give access to other modes of seeing. After the two men draw a cathedral together, with Robert's hand riding that of the narrating host, the latter achieves a sort of epiphany: 'I had my eyes closed. I thought I'd keep them that way for a little longer. I thought it was something I ought to do' (Carver 1983: 214). For an account of the controversy regarding the origins of Carver's story, see Cushman 1991. Lawrence's own precursor may be Guy de Maupassant's 'The Blind Man', an argument supported by the mention of the author in Lawrence's 'A Modern Lover' (Lawrence 1987: 33). Maupassant's tale is a memorable one, in which his blind protagonist suffers 'one of the most cruel martyrdoms that could possibly be conceived' (Maupassant 2012: 47), being ostracised by his family and community, and eventually left to die of exposure in a field, his eyes pecked out by 'long voracious beaks' (49). He ends, then, in Maurice's Promethean, blank-socketed state. Maupassant's interest in matters haptic is said to have been prompted by a lunch taken with Algernon Charles Swinburne, after he played a role in saving the latter from drowning (we noted Swinburne's sea-bathing habit in Chapter 1). Swinburne produced the severed, flayed hand of an alleged parricide as a conversation piece, prompting Maupassant's story 'La Main d'Ecorché' of 1875. For more on this bizarre confrontation, see Barnes 2008. Severed hands creep into Chapter 6.

6. Lawrence opens his essay 'Art and Morality' (1925) with the words 'supposing we had all of us been born blind' (1985a: 164), a phrasing that allies him with the philosophical propositions of William Molyneux, and the 'land of the blind' of both Denis Diderot and H. G. Wells (see Chapter 2).

Horrible Haptics

A five-fingered beast

Wilkie Collins joins the ranks of writers tackled in this study who suffer from afflictions of the eye (see Ackroyd 2012), including James Joyce and Johann Gottfried Herder. His 1875 novel *Poor Miss Finch* demonstrates Collins's extensive knowledge of the history of philosophies of the senses, in addition to contemporary ophthalmological innovations. Its story, of blind Lucilla Finch who, despite the titular adjective, is far from 'poor' in her range of compensations and abilities, is told in part through epistolary means. It concludes with a particularly bizarre and extravagant letter-writing scene which invites the reader to contemplate the notion of 'getting in touch' – via the letter, across a great geographical distance, and from realms beyond the living. Nugent, the troubled half of a set of twins intent on winning the heart of Lucilla, closes the novel in the Arctic, where he has dragged his wretched self to take part in a US expedition searching for a fabled polar sea between Spitzbergen and Nova Zembla. His ship goes astray, and is found eventually by the crew of a passing whaler driven off course. Nugent's vessel is discovered to be manned. The whaler captain reports: 'I looked closer, and touched one of his [Nugent's] hands which lay on the table. To my horror and astonishment, he was a frozen corpse' (Collins 2000: 425). In a scenario that combines the notion of legal mortmain with the classic manual synecdoche of 'all hands on deck' (see Chapter 1), Nugent is found writing a letter, his last testament: 'There the hand that held the pen had dropped into the writer's lap. The left hand still lay on the table. Between the frozen fingers, we found a long lock of a woman's [Lucilla's] hair' (Collins 2000: 426).[1] Making two final attempts at contact, via the letter and the grasp of an intimate memento, Nugent makes a sensational end. In writing of 'Fiction Fair and Foul' in 1880, John Ruskin assigns Collins's novel to the latter category, complaining of the catalogue of horrors available in 'novels like *Poor Miss Finch* in which the heroine is blind, the hero epileptic, and the obnoxious brother is found dead with his hands dropped off, in the Arctic regions' (Ruskin 1908: 276). The reader may concur with the thrust of that argument; this is an unexpected lurch to the Pole in a novel of uneven tone and multiple intentions. However, Ruskin exaggerates the lurid aspect of the scene in his claim that both of Nugent's hands have become severed in his icy death. While his right hand has fallen into his lap, and the left lies on the table, there is no reason to suppose that they are not still attached to his arms. In fact, Collins's effort to offer us one final view of Nugent's intentionality, attempting communication and a caress of Lucilla's hair, would be thwarted by the separation of his hands from his body. Those hands do however share a purpose with bodiless *maniculae*, hand illustrations found in the margins of medieval manuscripts that point to text and say 'reader, pay attention here'. That function aside, Ruskin's interpretation is unnecessarily fretful, yet valuable in its insistence upon an early instantiation of a gruesome fantasy central to the modernist imagination: the severed hand.

In the foregoing study, we have explored several facets of the life of the human hand: writers are in daily confrontation with them; they are the 'poster boy' of the haptic; they are the ultimate indicator, as well as the means, of civilisation; they are connected to the hieroglyphic mode of apprehension familiar to the Egyptian and the Etruscan people; they also mark the modernist period's distance from the primitive; they can be read as a handbook, since they tell us many things; they have a complicated relationship with prostheses, which often extrapolate and extend touch capacities. And, as we saw at the very start of this study in relation to *Babbitt*, they can be read as a synecdoche of agency. It is the connection between manual control and human agency that is foregrounded in modernist texts and films that fantasise about severed hands. The liberation of the hand from the human body relieves that body not only of its executive capacities, but also of its primary symbol of intentional selfhood and haptic experience. Meanwhile the attendant notion of the hand that appears without a body, whose original host organism is therefore unknown, is the end-point of D. H. Lawrence's suggestion that the hand flickers with a life of its own (see Chapter 5). While Lawrence's concern is to give Body its due, rather than to conceive of the somatic as a prosthesis of Mind, he also implies that the servant/master relationship between hand and head might be reversed – the hand may have something to teach, or at least have ideas all its own. Henri Focillon, inveterate hand-praiser, pushes Lawrence's observations further still, claiming that 'hands are almost living beings. Only servants?

Possibly. Servants, then, endowed with a vigorous free spirit' (Focillon 1948: 65), and that they store within them 'the will to action' (66), being 'intensely alive' (66). We are one decisive chop away from the hand taking its life elsewhere, and in so doing moving beyond its synecdochic function as part-for-the-whole in making a claim for the status of an independent, gruesome beast. In her study of dead and ghostly hands in the seventeenth and nineteenth centuries, Katherine Rowe suggests that the hand is best understood as both symbol and promulgator of human agency, and that fantasies of ghostly, severed or otherwise recalcitrant hands reflect broader social shifts in just what that 'agency' term means and, further, can be used to marshal 'skeptical intent' in literary efforts to address that concept (Rowe 1999: 2).[2] Rowe observes that:

> Whereas philosophers since Aristotle have seen the hand as the special embodiment of the human ability to manufacture and control the material world, dismemberment relocates this part in that material, instrumental world. Dead hands come to resemble the accessories, tools, and marks they leave behind: as powerful an instrument, but as loosely held as those. (Rowe 1999: 4)

It is the status of the hand as itself a prosthesis, loosely held and tenuously appended to the body, contingent then in its relationship to that body, that makes it a potential source of horror. While Rowe's case is made in relation to prior centuries, severed hands therefore bring together many of the issues considered in this study, and which gain a particular intensity in the early twentieth century: the relationship between self and hand, the hand's admirable but baffling dexterity, the relationship between hand and mechanism and/or prosthesis, and the tantalising possibility of what Gilles Deleuze has called 'manual insubordination' (Deleuze 2002: 125), not simply in term's of Babbitt's manual decorum 'getting out of hand' (see Chapter 1), but of moments when hands display a mind of their own.

That such moments of one's own hands' independent intentionality, or the appearance of a severed hand of *unknown* intentions or origins, are horrifying, and form the basis of tales with an avowed interest in horror, brings us back to Steven Connor's suggestion that horror and horripilation, the lifting of the skin, are linked in etymological and conceptual terms (Connor 2004: 12). The flayed skin forms a second self, of indeterminate relation to the body it flees; in just the same way, the severed hand introduces questions of selfhood, questions that horrify. The phrases 'to have oneself together' and 'to be comfortable in one's own skin' suggest the self is ready to execute actions in a controlled and predictable manner. The severed hand prevents such control, and at the very point of symbolisation where that control is most manifestly present. The idea of the 'discomfiting' is an allied one here. As Jennifer M. Barker tells us, that term suggests both the uncomfortable and the unnerving, since the roots of 'comfiting' are in the Latin *conficere*, 'to put together' (Barker 2009: 7). Thus while the hand can comfort in its caress, and can inflict pain or discomfort, it may also be separated, disaggregated from the body, leading to an unnerving sense of both body and agency gone awry. That 'unnerving' term is also of use to us, since the severed hand both makes one lose one's nerve or composure in its presentation of an unpredictable other, and also 'unnerves' since it carries off a set of vital testing/knowing nerve endings of which frequent use is made by the orienting body. As Elizabeth Bowen has expressed it, 'the senses bound our feeling world: there is an abrupt break where their power stops' (Bowen 1962: 148). Numerous books and films of the modernist period consider an 'abrupt break' at the point of manual sensation and tackle severed, inspirited, grafted or otherwise unbiddable hands that claim power for themselves, a canon of skewed haptic action that brings this study to a horrible end.

Bram Stoker's *The Jewel of Seven Stars* (1904) is a ridiculous but thrilling romp that pits the marvels of contemporary science and policing against the inexplicable powers of ancient Egypt, relating the appearance of the severed hand of the aptly named Egyptian Queen Tera in Stoker's contemporary London. The book's interest in horrible horripilation led to its reimagining as the film *Blood from the Mummy's Tomb* (1971) from the Hammer Horror stable. Maurice Renard's *The Hands of Orlac* (1920) considers the idea of the hand graft, when a superstar surgeon intervenes in the rehabilitation of a pianist whose hands have been mangled in a train crash. It was twice adapted as a film within the modernist period, first by Robert Wiene in 1924 under the same title, and then again by Karl Freund in 1935, the latter rendering renamed *Mad Love*. Freund cast Peter Lorre in the starring role, and Lorre was to confront the issue of severed hands once again in his role in *The Beast with Five Fingers* in 1946. The latter is based upon the humorous short story of the same name, published by William Fryer Harvey in 1928. Harvey draws upon Stoker's novel, and also upon Gerard de Nerval's 'The Enchanted Hand' (1832), itself made into a film in 1942 under the title *The Devil's Hand*.[3] The mention of the devil in the latter again underscores the horror inherent in the severing of the hand, neutering the human potential for dextrous manipulation, and in any confrontation with the severed hand itself, imagined consistently in these tales as possessing the power for independent thought and action. In fact, that 'possession' term is crucial for these instances of modernist manual severance, since it connotes both control (if one owns one's hands in their correct position at the end of one's arms) and loss of control (if one meets a hand 'possessed', or if one's own hands become 'possessed' by a power beyond the self). The five-fingered beasts (or seven-fingered in the peculiar case of Queen Tera) of these texts and films emphasise once again the importance of the 'poster boy' of the haptic sense modality, but they also operate in that *maniculae* role, pointing repeatedly to particular aspects of modernist culture.

Harvey's tale is of blind Adrian Borlsover, whose remarkably deft touch enables his work in botany despite his lack of sight: 'The mere passing of his long supple fingers over a flower was sufficient means for its identification' (Harvey 1928: 3). Like a Lawrentian hero, Adrian touches in order to know, and his specialism is in the fertilisation of orchids, a plant said to be peculiarly fleshly, connected to both death and the sexual ('Their flesh is too much like the flesh of men', says General Sternwood in Howard Hawks's *The Big Sleep* (1946)). His nephew Eustace is at work on a 'great book on heredity' (3), and is considering a conversion to Buddhism (4), two interests that might lead him to consider hand-reading (see the thinking of Charlotte Wolff, Chapter 3) and issues of incarnation and tactile healing, respectively. Adrian reads braille with his left hand, while making notes with his right (4), a strategy that seems initially to be sensible for the purposes of his research work. Yet it appears that Adrian's recent experiments with automatic writing are now interfering with this process, since his right hand is attempting communications all its own: 'Eustace took an empty manuscript-book and placed a pencil within reach of the fingers of the right hand. They snatched at it eagerly' (6). The manuscript or, literally, handwriting book is used by Adrian's hand to complete its own acts of inscription, and Harvey's language reflects this shift of agency: these are fingers belonging to the right hand, and not to Adrian himself. In another play upon the notion of legal mortmain, the right hand revises Adrian's will (which no longer, therefore, lives up to its name as an expression of his intentions), demanding that it be severed from its host after death and sent to Eustace. In this way the hand arranges for its own liberation. This concept has been borrowed from Stoker's earlier story, since Queen Tera plans her own embalmment and mummification to leave her right hand in plain sight. The executive right hand, symbol of her queenly power, must be ready to act in the afterlife. Harvey's version is perhaps more interesting not only in its severance of the physical link between Adrian's body and his hand, but in the clashing intentions that bring about that severance in the first instance. If the hand is not animated by Adrian's mind, by what authority does it operate?

Harvey mines his scenario for comedy, since upon arrival in Eustace's house by post, the hand escapes and runs amok in the library, hurling books around and terrifying Parfit the maid who, when drying her hands in the scullery, finds herself 'drying someone else's hand as well, only colder than hers' (25). The status of the hand as a living entity is questioned through that colder temperature – there has been a change in the hand since its severing, and the means of its ongoing life is disputed. Eustace suggests to his companion-come-secretary Saunders that the hand should be caught, or else 'we shall have to wait until the bally clockwork runs down. After all, if it's flesh and blood, it can't live forever' (26). The mooting of two possibilities for the motor power of the hand – that it is a mechanism, and that it runs according to biological principles – draws on the uneasy status of the manual in automatic writing experiments in which, whilst flesh and blood, the hand is moved as if mechanical. Tim Armstrong has considered the question of automatic writing, a useful companion piece to Rowe's analysis of agency, also addressing questions of the hand as prosthesis or mechanism: 'In automatic writing, it [the hand] becomes a mechanism for the production of data whose authority is less certain' (Armstrong 1998: 188).[4] Uncertain authority and uncertain authorship are two issues interwoven throughout Harvey's story. The hand is certainly malevolent, whatever spirit animates it, and while Eustace and Saunders begin by treating the beast with the objective distance of science (Eustace) and the insouciance of a man of the world (Saunders), they are driven eventually to inflicting a stigmatism (Harvey 1928: 30), covering it with an antimacassar (31), and locking it in a safe (31). After fleeing to Brighton, and then a further unnamed location, the beast ultimately catches up with Eustace, intent on revenge for its sufferings. Harvey leaves the reader to decide whether Eustace dies by beastly strangulation or by a fire he has started himself in his attempt to keep the hand at bay in its scuttle down the chimney. Morton, the butler who has attended Eustace, concludes the story, having been found by the surviving Saunders and our unnamed narrator, on a plaintive quest in the zoological gardens for the titular 'beast with five fingers' (44), a quest Saunders for one thinks is purposeless: 'The poor chap is a born materialist' (44). The story is conspicuously of its historical moment in tackling issues of automatism, heredity, agency, spiritualism, advances in botany and zoology, and the notion of mortmain and the will. However, there may be one further touch-associated issue here, since the unmarried Eustace and his companion Saunders, of undisclosed status and ill repute, may, it is subtly implied, be lovers. While Eustace's home is spacious enough to leave sleeping arrangements a mystery, the rooms taken at Brighton are separate but interlinked, while those in the final location have no dividing doors. While Rowe's agency and Armstrong's automatism are in play, it may be the creep towards other forms of tactile connection, the touch that dare not speak its name, that in fact underlies Harvey's tale of the bestial hand.

Pianists and surgeons

Perhaps inevitably, given our focus on touch and the tactile, we have met several pianists in the course of this study: Rebecca West's Harriet Hume, Dorothy Richardson's Miriam and many of her charges, Virginia Woolf's Miss Craye and Fanny, Wilkie Collins's Lucilla and her tutor Madame Pratolungo, Sinclair Lewis's Tanis, James Joyce's blind stripling, and now Maurice Renard's Steven Orlac. *The Hands of Orlac* is a particularly interesting iteration of the hand/piano relationship, because (as implied in its title) it stakes out the hands as a terrain fought over by two men of remarkable manual capacities – not only the pianist himself, but also the surgeon. The latter's efforts are a form of manual labour, since *chirurgie* comes (as we saw in Chapter 1) 'from the Greek *kheir* (hand) and literally means the "work of the hands"' (Derrida 1993: 5). Both professions, pianist and surgeon, are fundamentally concerned with delicacy and precision of touch, both make use of a positive prosthesis (the piano and the scalpel, respectively) which extrapolates human powers, and both are said to strike their patient/audience to the core (literally in the case of the invasive cut of the surgeon, metaphorically in the case of the pianist's attempt to convey musical and emotional vibration).[5] The two figures contrast, however, in that the pianist's touch is associated with the caress, and with a judiciousness of manual connection that is often said to be found in the cortically adapted blind person (the stripling and Lucilla are examples here). The pianist even has a particular musical form, the toccata, in which to demonstrate his or her capacity to control touch, although the etymological origins of the word in the Italian *toccare* indicate both touch or stroke (*tocca*) and knock, strike or the hammer blow (*tocco*), suggesting that the pianist must not always be delicate. In fact, in its early twentieth-century manifestation, the toccata asks the performer to transform his or her hands into multiple hammers, echoing the mechanism of the piano itself, and the pianist is aiming to demonstrate the close connection between will and fingers via the rapid onslaught of notes. Meanwhile, the surgeon's touch is associated not with the caress but with the cut or cutaneous intervention, and not with blindness but with the letting in of light. Walter Benjamin associates the cinematic camera and the surgeon figure, since both gain access to new realms through processes of incision (Benjamin 1999b: 226–7), but the illumination is of course literalised when the surgical operation is an ophthalmic one, such as that performed upon Lucilla by Grosse the German 'oculist' who 'h[o]ld[s] in his hands [. . .] the restoration of [her] sight' (Collins 2000: 190). Collins's rendering of this surgical intervention attends to the prospect held out by the cataract operation for the solving of the Molyneux question (see Chapter 2), but also makes the interesting suggestion that Lucilla's formidable piano-playing ('She was a born musician, with a delicacy and subtlety of touch such as few even of the greatest *virtuosi* possess' (Collins 2000: 71)) will be ruined by her coming sight: 'She accompanied them [the words 'I shall see him'] with hands that seemed to be mad for joy – hands that threatened every moment to snap the chords of the instrument' (230). This is the toccata gone too far.

Renard's story of Orlac and his surgeon Cerral is positioned in a conceptual field that considers the marvels attributable to the medical touch, and also the cluster of issues surrounding the hands of the pianist. Franz Liszt, piano prodigy, used the term 'finger virtuoso' disparagingly (Gerig 1976: 187) in order to suggest that dexterity alone is not enough, and that too close a resemblance to a mechanism undermines the musician's attempt at emotional communication. An automatism of the hand affects Harriet Hume when her mind is distracted by political gossip during a performance: 'it was not I who played my part in Mozart's Water Music, but my fingers which found their way home like dogs whose masters have fallen dead by the wayside' (West 1980a: 191), again both invoking and troubling the master/servant, head/hand relationship. Given the capacity of the pianist's hands to have a mind of their own, if not carefully monitored and controlled to convey emotion to the audience, they are rich pickings for an author who wishes to introduce horrible questions of agency through an address to the severed and grafted hand. Orlac, like Liszt, is a 'celebrated virtuoso pianist' (Renard 1981: 14) who, like his instrument, is 'highly strung' (20), quivering with musical emotion and conveying that emotion through his hands:

> Ah, his hands, his beautiful white hands, fine, supple, so nimble and so nervous, his virtuoso's hands, two magical beings dancing over the keyboard, bestowers of joy, of fame and of abundance! . . . Ah! if he must be mutilated, rather than struck down by fate, would it not be a hundred times better if he were blind, like so many musicians! [. . .] But his hands! No . . . no . . . not that! That would kill him! (Renard 1981: 34)

Here, the anxious thoughts of Orlac's wife Rosine anticipate her husband's dreadful diagnosis, since his hands have been badly damaged in the train wreck, and he is left at the mercy of medical science. A doctor Rosine encounters at the crash site recommends Cerral who, while carrying a reputation for ill-sketched immoralities concerning the grafting of body parts, is nevertheless described via a volley of terms that denotes his superhuman status. He is 'a magician with the scalpel' (27), undertaking 'surgical conjuring tricks' (27) through his dextrous sleight-of-hand; he is 'master', 'prince', 'hero', 'athlete' (29) and 'pioneer' (31) in his place at the forefront of medical innovation, and yet his power is so mysterious that he is also a 'priest [. . .] of the spirit' (30) whose dazzlingly white consulting rooms are a 'snowy temple' (30).[6] In a plot more convoluted than a fingerprint, Renard allows the reader to suspect that Orlac has been the duped subject of a hand-grafting experiment, unwittingly given the hands of the criminal Vasseur, and enraged not only by his inability to retrain his mangled hands and regain his career-defining tactility, but also by his bodily possession by the spirit of the evil man. The story offers the opportunity to consider questions of medical ethics and the peculiar priesthood of contemporary surgeons, and also the issue of agency, through this suggestion that Orlac has not only lost physical dextrousness, but has in fact become unable to exercise mental control over his digits, given the mooted attribution of unscrupulous hands to his own body. Steven's desperate attempts to use various manicurists and mechanisms to rehabilitate and refamiliarise his own hands (95–7) is a tour through the hand-related innovations of the period. His inability to write in his own legible 'hand' is experienced as a loss of identity, and Steven's resorting to a typewriter is read by Rosine as the first of many capitulations to his ill health (102). The switch from one set of keys to another in the move from piano to typewriter indicates that, while both are positive prostheses, the former provides a more symbiotic relationship which allows the expression of the self *through* the mechanism, while the latter removes the possibility of unique expression through the imposition of a standardised typeface. Rosine's elderly companion Monsieur de Crochans introduces a further set of tactile issues in his connection to a network of spiritualists and experimenters in automatic writing and drawing. Crochans's cronies suggest not only the power to get in touch with other realms (see also Chum Frink's efforts to contact Dante, Chapter 1) but also the sleight-of-hand involved in the trickery of magic/cod-science – 'these people made a profession of artfulness and dexterity' (219). Deft hands in a surgeon or a pianist are vaunted; in a spiritualist they are to be suspected. Renard's use of the term 'magician' to describe Cerral in fact makes him a near neighbour of Crochans et al. *and* of his talented patient, whose hands are 'magical beings'. Cerral might be superman or charlatan.

Renard, then, offers an overview of the hand-connected realms of the 1920s, noting the peculiarity of Steven's unique musical touch being mediated through the deceiving gramophone (93–4), discussing the personhood implied by a fingerprint or a handwriting sample (238), and indulging in a range of manual puns regarding gaining the 'upper hand' (275), taking matters in hand (277) and so forth. Ultimately, the psychologically overwrought Orlac is assured that his hands, although damaged and unfamiliar in their clumsiness, are his own. The criminal Vasseur appears, claiming to have had his hands stolen away, but is revealed to have been wearing fine metal gloves which give to his as yet attached hands the appearance of mechanical prostheses.[7] The book closes with the words spoken to Orlac: 'Your hands are undefiled' (301), suggesting that the contact experiences and/or deeds of the hands can pollute their host body and mind. Renard's story is memorable not only for its catalogue of hand technologies and debates, but also for the power of its central imaginative conceit, in which two men of handiwork, the pianist and the surgeon, appear to be battling for control of a single set of hands. The tenor of the novel can be described in the German term *hautnah*, connoting both a relationship as close as skin (as close as Vasseur's pseudo-prosthetic gloves) and, in a literary context, the dramatic or gripping; Renard's tale is one that grabs you. It is situated amongst a range of texts and films of the modernist period that tackle similar issues of touch and the tactile with recourse to severed, grafted and straying hands, seeking ultimately to explore the idea expressed pithily by Focillon: 'Hands are almost living beings. Only servants? Possibly.'

Hands and acts of hand-to-hand contact play a central role in my conceptualisation of this study, as *Haptic Modernism* is ordered according to a number of 'presiding spirits' who, in relay formation, have led me through the writing process. The 'spirits' term is perhaps inapt, since my interest in them is determinedly as incarnated beings, creatures of the flesh dependent, for a variety of reasons, upon the haptic sense modality. The first is poor, bewildered Babbitt, adrift in a world in which his hands will not behave. Next is Huxley's Savage, whose anachronistic allegiance to the deferral of desire – the right to touch or not to touch according to one's appetite – is equally at odds with his surrounding society. Galatea follows, the protagonist of Ovid's 'Pygmalion' whose transformation from marble into flesh is a move into haptic subjectivity. She hands on (I use the metaphor advisedly) to the masturbator, with whose self-touching activities she can identify, and who might very well be moved to engage in his 'strange necessity' by the sight of such a Greekly perfect goddess. The masturbator hands on (after a wipe with his shirt, in Bloom's case) to the blind man, with whom he is apocryphally associated, but whose averted eyes suggest a pious superiority to such carnal instincts. The blind man taps his cane, his prosthetically extended touch, against the would-be geometer, whose redundant hands retain the gestures of grasping previously central to her epistemology. The geometer then grasps at the front-rower and the reader, who make a somatic response to screen and text. The haptic reader hands on to a second blind man, damaged in the horror of war, and seeking to reinstantiate brotherhood through strategies of touch. He hands on to the surgeon, whose scalpel echoes the camera, and who may or may not have the capacity to let light in to the world of the 'dark m[a]n'. The surgeon pauses to interfere with the expressive touch of the pianist, whose toccata contains the caress and the hammer blow, before, in a final flourish, severing the hands that have made this tactile relay possible. The hands – horribly – scuttle off by themselves.

Notes

1. Mortmain should be understood as 'the testamentary clutch of the past on the present, a concept drawn loosely from the legal term "dead hand" (from medieval Latin *manus mortua*)' (Rowe 1999: 16).

2. With the exception of a quick note on gloves (below), I do not address ghostly hands in this study. However, the idea of a 'phantom hand' does connect to the history of the haptic. The acronym PHANToM refers to a 'personal haptic interface mechanism', the result of research work undertaken within the contemporary field of haptics (with that crucial 's'). Haptics explores the possibilities of tactile, kinaesthetic and proprioceptive manipulation of computer technology users, as well as contributing to computer-aided design and manufacture. For a discussion of this field, and more about the PHANToM, see Paterson 2007. We can also note that the phrase 'phantom hand' is used in contemporary parlance to denote a particular masturbatory practice where the participant restricts blood flow to their hand in order to numb manual sensations, using that temporarily insentient hand for the purposes of self-touching, to provide the illusion of touch by the body of another. The practice is interesting in its attempt to bypass the experience of Merleau-Ponty's *chiasmatic* self-touching (see Chapter 1), and in its illusion of the short-circuiting of the will/manual link – while the mind tells the numb hand what to do, the hand offers no surface sensory indication that it is animated by that mind, suggesting instead that it responds to an alternative agency.

3. Nerval's story also gains a mention in *The Hands of Orlac* (Renard 1981: 288). Nerval was diagnosed as suffering from a cluster of symptoms later identified as schizophrenia (Sass 1998: 6), and given the problematic relationship between the schizophrenic and specifically manual agency (see Chapter 1), we can speculate that the author's own episodes might have influenced his tale.

4. The Surrealists under André Breton made most programmatic use of automatic writing and drawing experiments, and their additional interest in questions of chance is also, if more obliquely, related to the hand. As Benjamin has stated, 'there can be no game without the quick movement of the hand by which the stake is put down or a card is picked up. The jolt in the movement of a machine is like the so-called *coup* in a game of chance' (Benjamin 1999a: 173). Surrealist manual automatism is, then, about channelling, agency, mechanistic data production, and the chance or contingent (the latter, as used in Chapter 1, is a hand word through its root in *contigere*, meaning to touch, pollute or befall). For the role of the hand in Surrealist thinking, see the fascination with the eponymous heroine's hands and gloves in Breton's *Nadja* (1928). For more on automatic writing, see Armstrong's chapter 'Distracted Writing' (Armstrong 1998: 187–219). In tackling theories of the body recalibrated in the modernist period, particularly in response to new forms of mechanical apparatus, Armstrong also moves toward a further implication of the severed hand: that it stands in for the mysteries of the machine. Mass production techniques create dextrous mechanisms of indiscernible power and direction, prompting just the same anxieties as the human hand gone rogue. Surrealist hands could, space permitting, have taken up a chapter of the present study, tying in with the belief of other modernists that the hand 'exploits also an unpredictable element beyond the realm of spirit, that is to say, accident' (Focillon 1948: 74). Remember too that Breton was subject to one of Charlotte Wolff's hand-readings (see Chapter 3).

5. The notion that the audience is 'touched' by the pianist, in terms of emotional responses to the physical resonances passed through the instrument as a result of his or her tactile acts, is central to the concept of the virtuoso. This is clear in Henry Reeves's description of a recital by Franz Liszt (1811–86) in Paris in 1835: 'My chair was on the same board as the piano when the final piece began. [. . .] As the closing strains [of 'a work of his own'] began I saw Liszt's countenance assume that agony of expression, mingled with radiant smiles of joy, which I never saw in any other human face except in the paintings of Our Saviour [. . .] his hands rushed over the keys, the floor on which I sat shook like a wire, and the whole audience was wrapped with sound, when the hand and frame of the artist gave way. He fainted in the arms of the friend who was turning over the pages for him, and we bore him out in a strong fit of hysterics. [. . .] As I handed Madame de Circourt to her carriage we both trembled like poplar leaves, and I tremble scarcely less as I write this' (Reeves, quoted in Gerig 1976: 172–3). While the piano is a positive prosthesis manipulated at will, it is often read in the context of the virtuoso as an incorporated part of both body and spirit of the performer. This reading applies to Harriet Hume, whose piano responds to her voice and emotions. For Liszt and Harriet, the body extends its power through the mechanism. The alternative, or contrapuntal, reading is that the body becomes automaton through association with the piano mechanism. Orlac's story lies closer to the latter interpretation, since he doubts his power of control over his hands, and retrains them via a series of mechanised contraptions.

6. It is likely that Renard has in mind here the work of Dr Alexis Carrel (1873–1944), who in 1912 was awarded a Nobel Prize in recognition of his

research in the suturing of blood vessels, work that paved the way for human grafts and transplants. See Friedman 2008.

7. The empty glove of course gives the appearance of a severed hand, and abandoned gloves with their implication of an inhabitant are another part of the story of horrible haptics. Giuliana Bruno has suggested that 'an empty dress is a specter' (2007: 323); so too is an empty glove. In *Harriet Hume*, Condorex reads Harriet's abandoned gloves as shed skins (West 1980a: 53). Meanwhile, Elizabeth Bowen's short story 'Hand in Glove' (1952) has Ethel Trevor strangled by the abandoned glove of the dead aunt whose clothing supply she is trying to pilfer (Bowen 1999: 775). 'Hand in glove' operated within the modernist period as a phrase suggesting a confederacy or suspiciously close friendship, sometimes with a hint as to sexual goings-on. The phrase crops up in Bowen's own *The Death of the Heart* (1938) (Bowen 1962: 294), and in *The Hands of Orlac* (Renard 1981: 273).

Appendix: Tactile Terminologies

Many of the following terms are central to contemporary scholarship addressing touch and the tactile and/or the haptic. Others are central to the present study in particular. All are fascinating – in their etymologies, in the experiences they describe, and in the conversations they establish about the touch-point between language and somatic experience itself. This appendix is a provocation to further investigation, rather than an exhaustive list of definitions. My sources are those listed in my bibliography, cited if quoted directly.

Automatic writing   A scriptive practice poised at the interstices between spirit-summoning, allowing one's body to function as a machine, invoking the powers of chance and contingency and, crucially, exploring the connection between manual practices and human agency. The automatic hand and the severed hand are conceptual bedfellows (see Chapter 6).

Blessed blindness   A notion of long provenance in which blindness is read as indicating piety, a non-sexual aversion to the flesh, closeness to God, and selection for spiritual insight beyond the province of the eye.

Blindness   The absence of sight, either literal/physical, or metaphorical/ psychological. Useful to the history of the haptic since the blind man is thrown upon his haptic resources, and the cortical adaptations of blind figures make the haptic aspects of their sensoria particularly acute.

Brand   The imposition of a mark upon the flesh, connoting identity and/ or ownership, and useful here in its suggestion that the skin can be inscribed and, subsequently, read. Branding, as with Nathaniel Hawthorne's Hester Prynne, might be a punishment or, as with Algernon Charles Swinburne, a masochistic pleasure. Both experiences are felt in the flesh.

Callous   A skin condition of hardening through a build-up of additional skin cells, often in response to friction. Also an emotional condition which makes one untouchable, peculiarly resistant both to emotional hurt and/or to an empathetic response to the hurt of others.

Caress   A touch that communicates love or sexual desire. Also one species of the travelling grasp which, in its explorations, makes known that which is touched.

Carnal   Of the flesh, returning the sentient being to its status as *carné* or meat.

Carpe diem   The Horatian injunction to 'seize the day', which both functions as a modernist manifesto and offers the body as one means of temporal registration. Contains within it the idea of the body's power but also, through its invocation of fleeting time, functions as a *memento mori*, anticipating that body's decay.

Chiasm   Describes the crossed nature of the touching-touched gesture of self-touching, in gestures such as prayer. Also describes the status of the skin as registered by the mutual constitution of self and world, and imbricated in the establishment of both.

Conjuring   An act of summoning up, useful here in that haptic texts might conjure somatic experiences, prompting an incarnated response to the flat page. Also related to the haptic via Surrealist and spiritualist interest in the power of the hand, since such summoning is usually a manual matter. The *impression* of summoning is achieved through sleight-of-hand.

Contact   An act of connection, a meeting of any part of the human skin with any aspect of the world external to it. Contains both the notion of meeting ('con') and that of 'tact', which in turn indicates both tactile acts and social niceties.

Contactilations   F. T. Marinetti's coinage that denotes contact experiences, while also conveying their titillating effects.

Cutaneous   Of or having to do with the skin of man or beast.

Dermis   The layer of skin beneath the epidermis (see below) that, alongside the latter, forms the cutis.

Doubting Thomas   A haptic figure in his insistence upon touching the risen Christ in order to confirm his identity.

Ecstasy   Colloquially a state of joy or bliss, particularly religious or sexual, but also related to *ecstasis*, the state of being beside oneself. Of use to describe those who slip their skins or escape their incarnations.

Ectoderm   The germ cell layer of the human embryo that most closely relates to and resembles the human skin. Paul Valéry suggests that we attend to it in order to understand the nature of human existence (1957: 214–16).

Epidermis   The upper layers of the skin; those presented, therefore, to the outside world.

Exfoliation   The active or passive removal of skin layers, revealing newer skins beneath. Therefore the slipping of skins. Via folio, a connection is possible to the literary page.

Formication   The sensation of crawling skin, from *formic*, 'of the ant'. In its classic manifestation, the sensation of the ant crawl on the skin. Can beset the schizophrenic, whose relationship with his or her skin both responds to and exacerbates a failed sense of ipseity, or the understanding of somatic experiences as one's own.

Gesture   The act of speaking with the hands. Part of oratorical performance. From *gerere*, to bring forth with the hands. In this way linked to 'suggestion', another form of offering.

Grasp   A practice of the hand associated with knowledge-gathering, tool use and the communication of emotion. Also the successful psychological effort to understand.

Hand   The 'poster boy' of the haptic sense, the synecdochic symbol of the complicated interrelationship between the quartet of somatic experiences that we can label 'haptic'. (Severed hand: a five-fingered beast that haunts modernist texts and films, pointing at (or crawling over?) issues of human agency.)

Handiwork   Manual labour or craft practice. Additionally any work of the hands including, as we have seen here, writing, piano-playing and surgery.

Haptic   A sense modality combing touch, kinaesthesis, proprioception and the vestibular sense. A term applied to literature or film describing and/or evoking that sense modality.

Haptic criticism   Literary criticism attending to the operation of the haptic sense modality in texts of any kind.

Haptics   A field of computer technology working toward the manipulation of the haptic sense modality of tech users, through force feedback interfaces, rumble packs etc. Important to the gaming industry, and to computer adaptations for the blind and visually impaired. The field also includes computer-aided design and manufacture (CAD/CAM).

Haptomorphs   Stonecutters, masons, sculptors etc., who undertake the work of shaping with the hands (Paterson 2007: 71).

Hexis   The durable sense of one's body and its operation in the world (see Thompson 1991: 13).

Horripilation   The lifting and/or shaping of the human skin. Shares an etymology with horror, underscoring the horrifying nature of any tampering with the human skin (Connor 2004: 12).

Incarnation   The state or process of enfleshment, at once ascribing life to meat, and suggesting that a spirit exists beyond the *carné* and may move and possess other fleshly vessels.

Infrangible   Unbreakable or inseparable. Applies to the relationship between the experience of touch and the human body.

Kinaesthesis   The body's sense of its own movement, recalibrated in the modernist period in response to travel experiences by mechanised transport, and viewing experiences in the cinematic theatre in particular.

Licking eye   Virginia Woolf's iteration of the notion of the eye as epidermic, a particular modification of the skin. Occurs in her 1926 essay 'The Cinema'.

Manicure   Care for the hands; a nail-shaping and polishing process of particular popularity in the modernist period; the practitioner who undertakes such a process.

Nearsight   The close look prompted by the Egyptian artistic assemblage which, with its conflation of figure and ground, asks the eye to undertake imagined strategies of touch.

Noli me tangere   Christ's statement to Mary of Magdala (see above), meaning both do not touch me, and do not hold on to me/hold me back, for I am not yet arisen to the Father (John 20:17; Mark 16:9).

Prehension   The act of grasping or seizing, and the experience of coming to know.

Prestidigitator   Skill in manual performance, particularly in relation to sleight-of-hand, and therefore to acts of conjuring (see above).

Proprioception   The body's sense of its orientation in space.

Proximal senses   Those operating in a way stubbornly adhered to the body (touch, taste and smell) rather than those extending far beyond the body (the distance senses of sight and hearing). Of increasing interest to the academy at the present time.

Psychodermatology   A twenty-first-century field exploring the complicated connections between human psychology and the human skin.

Salve   An unction that calms or heals the skin, and the act of its application. Often connected in haptic texts to the idea of salvation or of spiritual insight, concomitant with the touching/soothing application of the salve.

Scar   An indelible mark upon the skin that can confirm identity, and which also offers an epidermic record of past acts. A skin inscription.

Schizophrenic skin   The problematic relationship between the schizophrenic and his or her own skin was observed in the modernist period.

Skin   The 'cultural border between self and the world' (Benthien 2002), and the point at which self and world can be seen to be mutually constituted.

Skin ego   A sense of selfhood contingent upon the sensation and psychological recognition of a continent cutis.

Somatic   Of the body.

Surgery   Best understood in the modernist period as a form of handi-work (see above), and a means of passing the hand through the cutis, opening up the body's interior to the eye.

Tact   Social ability to comport oneself and one's body in an appropri-ate manner.

Tactile   Of the touch; appealing to the touch; a person with an appetite for touch.

Textiles   Important here since Aloïs Riegl, early theorist of the haptic, was a curator of textiles, perhaps leading to his understanding of near-sight (see above), texture and the tactile.

Texture   Offering to the hand a differentiated surface. In texts, offering to the body of the reader haptic experiences.

Thigmophilia   Hunger for touch.

Touch   The act or experience of skin-meets-world.

Touched   On the receiving end of a tactile act; emotionally affected; psychologically damaged or abnormal.

Travelling touch   A touch that moves, giving the best guide to overall shape. An exploratory caress useful to the blind.

Vestibular sense   The body's sense of balance, reliant upon the inner ear.

Bibliography

Ackroyd, Peter (2012), *Wilkie Collins*, London: Chatto and Windus.

Aglen, A. S. (1896), 'Tu ne quaesieris', in *The Odes and Carmen Seculare of Horace Translated into English Verse*, Glasgow: James Maclehose and Sons, pp. 17–18.

Aldington, Richard [1932] (1956), 'Introduction', in D. H. Lawrence, *Mornings in Mexico and Etruscan Places*, London: Heinemann, pp. v–viii.

Almond, Ian (2002), 'Tales of Buddha, dreams of Arabia: Joyce and images of the East', *Orbis Literrarum*, 57, pp. 18–30.

Anon. (1904), 'Beauty and the toilet: answers to correspondents', *Lady's Pictorial*, 47: 1,216, p. 1,162.

Anzieu, Didier (1989), *The Skin Ego*, trans. Chris Turner, New Haven, CT: Yale University Press.

Aristotle (1907), *De Anima*, trans. R. D. Hicks, Cambridge: Cambridge University Press.

Aristotle (2001), *On the Parts of Animals*, trans. James G. Lennox, Oxford: Clarendon Press.

Armstrong, Tim (1998), *Modernism, Technology and the Body: A Cultural Study*, Cambridge: Cambridge University Press.

Ascaso, Francisco, and Jan L. van Velze (2011), 'Was James Joyce myopic or hyperopic?', *British Medical Journal*, 343, p. 1,295.

Attridge, Derek (2006), 'The body writing: Joyce's pen', in Richard Brown (ed.), *European Joyce Studies 17: Joyce, 'Penelope' and the Body*, Amsterdam: Rodopi, pp. 47–62.

Barker, Jennifer M. (2009), *The Tactile Eye: Touch and the Cinematic Experience*, Berkeley: University of California Press.

Barnard, Frederick M. (2001), *Democratic Legitimacy: Plural Values and Political Power*, Montreal: McGill-Queen's University Press.

Barnes, Julian (2008), 'Brits abroad', *The Guardian*, 18 October 2008, p. 20.

Bates, A. W. (2006), 'Dr Kahn's museum: obscene anatomy in Victorian London', *Journal of the Royal Society of Medicine*, 99, pp. 618–24.

The Beast with Five Fingers, film, directed by Robert Florey. US: Warner Brothers, 1946.

Bedford, Sybille (1973), *Aldous Huxley, Vol. I*, London: Chatto and Windus.

Benejam, Valerie (2003), 'Stephen and the Venus of Praxiteles: The backside of aesthetics', in Richard Brandon Kershner (ed.), *European Joyce Studies 15: Cultural Studies of James Joyce*, Amsterdam: Rodopi, pp. 59–76.

Benjamin, Walter [1939] (1999a), 'On Some Motifs in Baudelaire', in *Illuminations*, trans. Harry Zorn, London: Pimlico, pp. 152–96.

Benjamin, Walter [1936] (1999b), 'The Work of Art in the Age of Mechanical Reproduction', in *Illuminations*, trans. Harry Zorn, London: Pimlico, pp. 211–44.

Benthien, Claudia (2002), *Skin: On the Cultural Border between Self and the World*, trans. Thomas Dunlap, New York: Columbia University Press.

Berrone, Louis (1977), *James Joyce in Padua*, New York: Random House.

The Big Sleep, film, directed by Howard Hawks. US: Warner Brothers, 1946.

Billings, John Shaw (1890), 'Haptic', in Billings (ed.), *The National Medical Dictionary*, Edinburgh and London: Young J. Pentland, p. 620.

Blood from the Mummy's Tomb, film, directed by Seth Holt. UK: Hammer Horror, 1971.

Boheemen-Saaf, Christine von (2006), 'Joyce's answer to philosophy: writing the dematerializing object', in Richard Brown (ed.), *European Joyce Studies 17: Joyce, 'Penelope' and the Body*, Amsterdam: Rodopi, pp. 31–46.

Bowen, Elizabeth [1938] (1962), *The Death of the Heart*, London: Penguin.

Bowen, Elizabeth [1952] (1999), 'Hand in Glove', in *Collected Stories*, ed. Angus Wilson, London: Vintage, pp. 767–75.

Bowers, Fredson (2002), 'Hamlet's "sullied" or "solid" flesh: a bibliographical case-history', in Allardyce Nicoll (ed.), *Shakespeare Survey 9: Hamlet*, Cambridge: Cambridge University Press, pp. 44–8.

Breton, André [1928] (1999), *Nadja*, trans. Richard Howard, London: Penguin.

Breul, Karl (1904), 'In memory of Johann Gottfried Herder', *The Modern Language Quarterly (1900–1904)*, 7: 1, pp. 1–10.

Bronfen, Elisabeth (1999), *Dorothy Richardson's Art of Memory: Space, Identity, Text*, trans. Victoria Appelbe, Manchester: Manchester University Press.

Brown, Jonathan, and Richard G. Mann (1990), *Spanish Paintings of the Fifteenth Through Nineteenth Centuries*, Oxford: Oxford University Press.

Brown, Peter (1981), *The Cult of the Saints: Its Rise and Function in Latin Christianity*, London: SCM Press.

Brown, Richard (2006), 'Body words', in Brown (ed.), *European Joyce Studies 17: Joyce, 'Penelope' and the Body*, Amsterdam: Rodopi, pp. 109–27.

Bruno, Giuliana (2007), *Atlas of Emotion: Journeys in Art, Architecture and Film*, London: Verso.

Bryher, Winifred (1962), *The Heart to Artemis: A Writer's Memoirs*, London: Collins.

Buber, Martin (1955), *Between Man and Man*, trans. Ronald Gregor Smith, Boston, MA: Beacon Press.

Bulwer, John [1644] (1974), *Chirologia: Or, the Natural Language of the Hand, and Chironomia: Or, the Art of Manual Rhetoric*, ed. James W. Cleary, Carbondale: Southern Illinois University Press.

Butler, E. M. (1935), *The Tyranny of Greece over Germany: A Study of the Influence Exercised by Greek Art and Poetry over the Great German Writers of the Eighteenth, Nineteenth and Twentieth Centuries*, Cambridge: Cambridge University Press.

The Cabinet of Dr Caligari, film, directed by Robert Wiene. Germany: Decla-Bioscop AG, 1920.

Calvino, Italo (1988), *Six Novels for the Next Millennium*, trans. Patrick Creagh, Cambridge, MA: Harvard University Press.

Carver, Raymond (1983), 'Cathedral', in *Cathedral*, London: Vintage, pp. 196–214.

Charney, Leo (1996), 'In a moment: film and the philosophy of modernity', in Leo Charney and Vanessa R. Schwartz (eds), *Cinema and the Invention of Modern Life*, Berkeley: University of California Press, pp. 279–94.

Classen, Constance (1993), *Worlds of Sense: Exploring the Senses in History and Across Cultures*, London: Routledge.

Classen, Constance (ed.) (2005), *The Book of Touch*, Oxford: Berg.

Classen, Constance (2012), *The Deepest Sense: A Cultural History of Touch*, Champaign: University of Illinois Press.

Collins, Wilkie [1875] (2000), *Poor Miss Finch*, Oxford: Oxford University Press.

Commager, Steele (2009), 'The function of wine in Horace's odes', in Michèle Lowry (ed.), *Oxford Readings in Classical Studies: Horace – Odes and Epodes*, Oxford: Oxford University Press, pp. 33–49.

Condillac, Etienne Bonnot de [1754] (1930), *Condillac's Treatise on the Sensations*, trans. Geraldine Carr, Los Angeles: University of Southern California Press.

Connor, Steven (2004), *The Book of Skin*, London: Reaktion.

Cook, Elizabeth Heckendorn (1994), 'The limping woman and the public sphere', in Veronica Kelly and Dorothea von Mücke (eds), *Body and Text in the Eighteenth Century*, Stanford: Stanford University Press, pp. 23–44.

Crary, Jonathan (1992), *Techniques of the Observer: On Vision and Modernity in the Nineteenth Century*, Cambridge, MA: MIT Press.

Curtin, Maureen F. (2003), 'Skin eclipses in Virginia Woolf's *Mrs Dalloway*', in *Out of Touch: Skin Tropes and Identities in Woolf, Ellison, Pynchon, and Acker*, New York and London: Routledge, pp. 15–40.

Cushman, Keith (1991), 'Blind, intertextual love: "The Blind Man" and Raymond Carver's "Cathedral"', in Keith Cushman and Dennis Jackson (eds), *D. H. Lawrence's Literary Inheritors*, Basingstoke: Macmillan, pp. 155–66.

Dale, Russell C., A. J. Church, R. A. Surtees, A. J. Lees, J. E. Adcock, B. Harding, B. G. Neville and G. Giovannoni (2003), 'Encephalitis Lethargica syndrome: 20 new cases and evidence of basal ganglia autoimmunity', *Brain: A Journal of Neurology*, 127: 1, pp. 21–33.

Danius, Sara (2002), *The Senses of Modernism: Technology, Perception, and Aesthetics*, Ithaca, NY: Cornell University Press.

Das, Santanu (2005), *Touch and Intimacy in First World War Literature*, Cambridge: Cambridge University Press.

Dean, Tim (2004), 'T. S. Eliot, famous clairvoyante', in Cassandra Laity and Nancy Gish (eds), *Gender, Sexuality and Desire in T. S. Eliot*, Cambridge: Cambridge University Press, pp. 43–65.

Deane, Seamus (2000), 'Introduction', in James Joyce, *A Portrait of the Artist as a Young Man*, London: Penguin, pp. vii–xliii.

Delany, Paul (1983), 'Who was the blind man?', *English Studies in Canada*, 9: 1, pp. 92–9.

Deleuze, Gilles (2002), *Francis Bacon: The Logic of Sensation*, trans. Daniel W. Smith, Minneapolis: University of Minnesota Press.

Deleuze, Gilles, and Félix Guattari (1983), *Anti-Oedipus: Capitalism and Schizophrenia*, trans. Robert Hurley, Mark Seem and Helen R. Lane, Minneapolis: University of Minnesota Press.

Deming, Robert H. (1970), *James Joyce: The Critical Heritage, Vol. I*, London: Routledge and Kegan Paul.

Derrida, Jacques (1993), *Memoirs of the Blind: The Self-Portrait and Other Ruins*, trans. Pascale-Anne Brault and Michael Naas, Chicago: Chicago University Press.

Derrida, Jacques (2000), *On Touching – Jean-Luc Nancy*, trans. Christine Irizarry, Stanford: Stanford University Press.

Descartes, René (1985), *The Philosophical Writings of Descartes*, 3 vols, trans. John Cottingham, Robert Stoothoff and Dugald Murdoch, Cambridge: Cambridge University Press.

The Devil's Hand, film, directed by Maurice Tourneur. France: Continental Films, 1942.

Dhanani, Alnoor (1994), *The Physical Theory of Kalam: Atoms, Space and Void in Basrian Mu 'tazili Cosmology*, Leiden and New York: E. J. Brill.

Diderot, Denis [1749] (2011), *Letter on the Blind for the Use of Those Who Can See*, in Kate E. Tunstall (ed.), *Blindness and Enlightenment: An Essay*, London: Continuum, pp. 163–227.

Diodorus Siculus (1939), *Library of History*, 12 vols, ed. and trans. C. H. Oldfather, Cambridge, MA: Harvard University Press.

Donne, John (1950), 'The Flea', in *Selected Poetry*, ed. John Hayward, London: Penguin, p. 48.

Drobnick, Jim (ed.) (2006), *The Smell Culture Reader*, Oxford: Berg.

Ebisch, Sjoerd J., Anatolia Salone, Francesca Ferri, Domenico De Berardis, Gian Luca Romani, Filippo M. Ferro and Vittorio Gallese (2012), 'Out of touch with reality? Social perception in first-episode schizophrenia', *Social Cognitive and Affective Neuroscience*, <http://scan.oxfordjournals.org/content/early/2012/01/24/scan.nss012.full.pdf+html> (last accessed 16 November 2012).

Eliot, T. S. [1922] (1963), 'The Waste Land', in *Collected Poems 1909–1962*, London: Faber, pp. 61–79.

Ellis, Havelock [1905] (1914), *Studies in the Psychology of Sex: Sexual Selection in Man*, Philadelphia: F. A. Davis.

Ellmann, Maud (2006), '"Penelope" without the body', in Richard Brown (ed.), *European Joyce Studies 17: Joyce, 'Penelope' and the Body*, Amsterdam: Rodopi, pp. 97–108.

Ellmann, Maud (2010), *The Nets of Modernism: Henry James, Virginia Woolf, James Joyce, and Sigmund Freud*, Cambridge: Cambridge University Press.

Ellmann, Richard (1965), *James Joyce*, New York: Oxford University Press.

Falconer, Isobel (1987), 'Corpuscles, electrons and cathode rays: J. J. Thomson and "the discovery of the electron"', *The British Journal for the History of Science*, 20: 3, pp. 241–76.

Fargnoli, A. Nicholas, and Michael Patrick Gillespie (2006), *Critical Companion to James Joyce: A Literary Reference to his Life and Work*, London: Infobase.

Faulkner, William [1929] (1995), *The Sound and the Fury*, London: Vintage.

Ferri, Francesca, Francesca Frassinetti, Francesca Mastrangelo, Anatolia Salone, Filippo Maria Ferro and Vittorio Gallese (2012), 'Bodily self and schizophrenia: The loss of implicit self-body knowledge', *Consciousness and Cognition*, <http://www.sciencedirect.com/science/article/pii/S1053810012001304>(last accessed 17 October 2012).

Flint, Kate (2000), 'Blindness and insight', in *The Victorians and the Visual Imagination*, Cambridge: Cambridge University Press, pp. 64–92.

Focillon, Henri (1948), 'In Praise of Hands', in *The Life of Forms in Art*, trans. S. L. Faison Jr, New York: Wittenborn Schultz, pp. 65–78.

Frank, Joseph (1945), 'Spatial Form in Modern Literature: Part 1', *Sewanee Review*, 53, pp. 221–40.

Freud, Sigmund [1923] (1995), 'The Ego and the Id', in *The Freud Reader*, ed. Peter Gay, London: Vintage, pp. 628–59.

Friedman, David M. (2008), *The Immortalists: Charles Lindbergh, Dr. Alexis Carrel, and their Daring Quest to Live Forever*, New York: Harper Perennial.

Fromm, Glora G. (1977), *Dorothy Richardson: A Biography*, Urbana: University of Illinois Press.

Fulker, Teresa (1995), 'Virginia Woolf's daily drama of the body', *Woolf Studies Annual*, 1, pp. 3–25.

Gage, John (1993), *Colour and Culture: Practice and Meaning from Antiquity to Abstraction*, London: Thames and Hudson.

Gaiger, Jason (2002), 'Introduction', in Johann Gottfried Herder, *Sculpture: Some Observations on Shape and Form from Pygmalion's Creative Dream*, ed. and trans. Jason Gaiger, Chicago: University of Chicago Press, pp. 1–28.

Gance, Abel (1927), 'Le temps de l'image est venu', in *L'Art cinématographique, Vol. II*, Paris: Librairie Felix Alcan, pp. 100–1.

Gaudreault, André, and Philippe Marion (2002), 'The cinema as a model for the genealogy of media', *Convergence*, 8: 4, pp. 12–18.

Gay, Peter (2006), *Freud: A Life for our Time*, New York: W. W. Norton.

Gerig, Reginald R. (1976), 'Liszt and virtuoso technique', in *Famous Pianists and their Technique*, London: David and Charles, pp. 171–95.

Gevirtz, Susan (1996), *Narrative's Journey: The Fiction and Film Writing of Dorothy Richardson*, New York: Peter Lang.

Gilman, Sander (1991), *The Jew's Body*, New York: Routledge.

Glasser, Otto (1933), *Wilhelm Conrad Röntgen and the Early History of the Roentgen Rays*, trans. Otto Glasser, London: John Bale, Sons & Danielsson.

Glendinning, Victoria (1986), 'Afterword', in Rebecca West, *Sunflower*, London: Virago, pp. 268–76.

Glendinning, Victoria (1987), *Rebecca West: A Life*, London: Weidenfeld and Nicolson.

Goffen, Rona (1987), 'Renaissance dreams', *Renaissance Quarterly*, 40, pp. 682–706.

Gould, George M. (1908), *Concerning Lafcadio Hearn*, London: T. Fisher Unwin.

Gross, Kenneth (2006), 'The thing itself (which does not move)', in *The Dream of the Moving Statue*, Pennsylvania: Penn State University Press, pp. 167–99.

Gwilliam, Tassie (1994), 'Cosmetic poetics: coloring faces in the eighteenth century', in Veronica Kelly and Dorothea von Mücke (eds), *Body and Text in the Eighteenth Century*, Stanford: Stanford University Press, pp. 144–59.

The Hands of Orlac, film, directed by Robert Wiene. Austria: Pan-Film, 1924.

Hare, Augustus J. C. (1893), *The Story of Two Noble Lives, Being Memorials of Charlotte, Countess of Canning, and Louisa, Marchioness of Waterford*, 3 vols, London: George Allen.

Harris, Alexandra (2011), *Virginia Woolf*, London: Thames and Hudson.

Harvey, Elizabeth D. (2011), 'The portal of touch', *The American Historical Review*, 116: 2, pp. 385–400.

Harvey, William Fryer (1928), 'The Beast with Five Fingers', in *The Beast with Five Fingers and Other Tales*, London: Dent, pp. 1–44.

Hawthorne, Nathaniel [1850] (1986), *The Scarlet Letter*, in *The Scarlet Letter and Selected Tales*, ed. Thomas E. Connolly, London: Penguin.

Heaney, Seamus [1966] (1999), 'Digging', in *Death of a Naturalist*, London: Faber, pp. 3–4.

Herder, Johann Gottfried [1778] (2002), *Sculpture: Some Observations on Shape and Form from Pygmalion's Creative Dream*, ed. and trans. Jason Gaiger, Chicago: University of Chicago Press.

Hildebrand, Adolf [1893] (1907), *The Problem of Form in Painting and Sculpture*, trans. Max Meyer and Robert Morris Ogden, New York: G. E. Stechert and Co.

Hindson, Catherine (2008), *Female Performance Practice on the Fin-de-Siècle Popular Stage of London and Paris: Experiment and Advertisement*, Manchester: Manchester University Press.

Hogarth, William [1753] (1971), *The Analysis of Beauty*, Menston: The Scolar Press.

Homer (1946), *The Odyssey*, trans. E. V. Rieu, London: Penguin.

Howes, David (ed.) (2005), *Empire of the Senses*, Oxford: Berg.

Hubbard Harris, Janice (1984), *The Short Fiction of D. H. Lawrence*, New Brunswick, NJ: Rutgers University Press.

Huget, Virginia (1928), 'Molly the Manicure Girl', in the Caroline and Erwin Swann Collection of Caricature and Cartoon, Library of Congress, Washington, DC.

Hughes, Ted (1997), 'Pygmalion', in *Tales from Ovid: Twenty-Four Passages from the Metamorphoses*, London: Faber, pp. 144–50.

Hutchinson, G. Evelyn (1987), 'Introduction', in Rebecca West, *The Strange Necessity: Essays and Reviews*, London: Virago, pp. vii–xii.

Huxley, Aldous [1932] (1994), *Brave New World*, London: Flamingo.

Huxley, Aldous, and Christopher Isherwood [1944] (1998), *Jacob's Hands*, London: Bloomsbury.

Ingersoll, Earl (1990), 'Lawrence in the Tyrol: psychic geography in *Women in Love* and *Mr Noon*', *Forum for Modern Language Studies*, 26: 1, pp. 1–11.

Irigaray, Luce (1986), *The Sex Which Is Not One*, trans. Catherine Porter with Carolyn Burke, Ithaca, NY: Cornell University Press.

Isherwood, Christopher [1939] (1998), *Goodbye to Berlin*, London: Vintage.

Iversen, Margaret (1993), *Alois Riegl: Art History and Theory*, Cambridge, MA: MIT Press.

Jablonski, Nina G. (2006), 'Touch', in *Skin: A Natural History*, Berkeley: University of California Press, pp. 97–111.

Johnson, Jeri (2008), 'Introduction', in James Joyce, *Ulysses*, Oxford: Oxford University Press, pp. ix–xxxvii.

Josipovici, Gabriel (1982), *Writing and the Body*, Brighton: Harvester.

Josipovici, Gabriel (1996), *Touch: An Essay*, London: Yale University Press.

Joyce, James (1966), 'Letter to Frank Budgen', in Stuart Gilbert (ed.), *James Joyce Letters, Vol. I*, New York: Viking Press, p. 135.

Joyce, James [1939] (1992), *Finnegans Wake*, London: Penguin.

Joyce, James [1914–15] (2000a), *A Portrait of the Artist as a Young Man*, London: Penguin.

Joyce, James [1914] (2000b), *Dubliners*, London: Penguin.

Joyce, James [1922] (2008), *Ulysses*, ed. Jeri Johnson, Oxford: Oxford University Press.

Kern, Stephen (2003), *The Culture of Time and Space, 1880–1918*, Cambridge, MA: Harvard University Press.

Koo, John, and Andrew Lebwohl (2001), 'Psychodermatology: the mind and skin connection', *American Family Physician*, 64: 11, pp. 1,873–8.

La Mothe Le Vayer, François de [1653] (2011), 'Of a Man-Born-Blind', in Kate E. Tunstall (ed.), *Blindness and Enlightenment: An Essay*, London: Continuum, pp. 229–38.

Lant, Antonia (1995), 'Haptical cinema', *October*, 74, pp. 45–73.

Laqueur, Thomas W. (2003), *Solitary Sex: A Cultural History of Masturbation*, New York: Zone Books.

Lawrence, D. H. [1932] (1956), *Etruscan Places*, in *Mornings in Mexico and Etruscan Places*, London: Heinemann.

Lawrence, D. H. [1915] (1968), 'The Thimble', in *Phoenix II: Uncollected, Unpublished and Other Prose Works*, ed. Warren Roberts and Harry T. Moore, London: Heinemann, pp. 53–63.

Lawrence, D. H. [1922] (1971a), 'Hadrian [You Touched Me]', in *England, My England*, London: Penguin, pp. 107–24.

Lawrence, D. H. [1924] (1971b), 'Nathaniel Hawthorne and *The Scarlet Letter*', in *Studies in Classic American Literature*, London: Penguin, pp. 89–107.

Lawrence, D. H. [1925] (1971c), *St Mawr*, in *St Mawr and The Virgin and the Gypsy*, London: Penguin, pp. 11–165.

Lawrence, D. H. [1922] (1971d), 'The Blind Man', in *England, My England*, London: Penguin, pp. 55–75.

Lawrence, D. H. [1923] (1971e), 'The Five Senses', in *Fantasia of the Unconscious and Psychoanalysis of the Unconscious*, London: Heinemann, pp. 51–63.

Lawrence, D. H. [1922] (1971f), 'The Horse Dealer's Daughter', in *England, My England*, London: Penguin, pp. 157–74.

Lawrence, D. H. [1922] (1971g), 'Tickets, Please', in *England, My England*, London: Penguin, pp. 41–54.

Lawrence, D. H. (1972), *The Complete Poems of D. H. Lawrence, Vol. I*, ed. Vivian de Sola Pinto and Warren Roberts, London: Heinemann.

Lawrence, D. H. [1911] (1983), *The White Peacock*, ed. Andrew Robertson, Cambridge: Cambridge University Press.

Lawrence, D. H. (1984), *The Letters of D. H. Lawrence, Vol. III: October 1916–June 1921*, ed. James Boulton and Andrew Robertson, Cambridge: Cambridge University Press.

Lawrence, D. H. [1925] (1985a), 'Art and Morality', in *Study of Thomas Hardy and Other Essays*, ed. Bruce Steele, Cambridge: Cambridge University Press, pp. 163–8.

Lawrence, D. H. [1925] (1985b), 'Why the Novel Matters', in *Study of Thomas Hardy and Other Essays*, ed. Bruce Steele, Cambridge: Cambridge University Press, pp. 193–8.

Lawrence, D. H. [1933] (1987), 'A Modern Lover', in *Love among the Haystacks and Other Stories*, ed. John Worthen, Cambridge: Cambridge University Press, pp. 28–48.

Lawrence, D. H. [1928] (1993), *Lady Chatterley's Lover*, London: Penguin.

Lawrence, D. H. [1914] (1995a), 'Daughters of the Vicar', in *The Prussian Officer and Other Stories*, ed. Brian Finney, London: Penguin, pp. 40–87.

Lawrence, D. H. [1914] (1995b), 'Odour of Chrysanthemums', in *The Prussian Officer and Other Stories*, ed. Brian Finney, London: Penguin, pp. 181–200.

Lawrence, D. H. [1920] (2008), *Women in Love*, ed. David Bradshaw, Oxford: Oxford University Press.

Léger, Fernand [1925] (1973), 'The machine aesthetic: geometric order and truth', in *Functions of Painting*, ed. Edward F. Fry, trans. Alexandra Anderson, London: Thames and Hudson, pp. 62–6.

Lessing, Gotthold Ephraïm [1766] (1930), *Laocoön: An Essay on the Limits of Painting and Poetry*, London: Dent.

Lewis, Sinclair [1922] (1950), *Babbitt*, New York: Harcourt, Brace and World.

Light, Alison (2008), *Mrs. Woolf and the Servants: An Intimate History of Domestic Life in Bloomsbury*, New York: Bloomsbury.

Locke, John (1976–89), *The Correspondence of John Locke*, 9 vols, ed. E. S. de Beer, Oxford: Clarendon Press.

Lopez, Donald S. (1999), *Prisoners of Shangri-La: Tibetan Buddhism and the West*, Chicago: University of Chicago Press.

McCarthy, Ann (2011), 'Letter to the Editor', *Irish Times*, 21 December 2011.

McKinlay, A. P. (1946), 'The wine element in Horace', *Classical Journal*, 42, pp. 161–8.

Mad Love, film, directed by Karl Freund. US: MGM, 1935.

Mallory, George (1923), 'Letter to Marjorie Holmes 7 November', London: Royal Geographical Society, LMS/M48.

Man, Paul de (1983), 'The rhetoric of blindness: Jacques Derrida's reading of Rousseau', in *Blindness and Insight: Essays in the Rhetoric of Contemporary Criticism*, London: Methuen, pp. 102–41.

The Manchester Guardian (1922), 'An obscure malady: ministry of health's report', 12 September 1922, p. 5.

The Manicure Girl, film, directed by Frank Tuttle. US: Famous Players-Lasky Corporation, 1925.

Mann, Thomas [1924] (1999), *The Magic Mountain*, trans. H. T. Lowe-Porter, London: Vintage.

Marcus, Jane (1983), 'A speaking sphinx', *Tulsa Studies in Women's Literature*, 2: 2, pp. 150–4.

Marcus, Laura (1998), 'Introduction', in James Donald, Anne Friedberg and Laura Marcus (eds), *Close Up 1927–1933: Cinema and Modernism*, London: Cassell, pp. 150–9.

Marcus, Laura (2007), *The Tenth Muse: Writing about Cinema in the Modernist Period*, Oxford: Oxford University Press.

Marcus, Steven (1964), *The Other Victorians*, New York: New American Library.

Marinetti, F. T. [1921] (2006a), 'Tactilism: A Futurist Manifesto', in *Critical Writings*, ed. Günter Berghaus, trans. Doug Thompson, New York: Farrar, Straus and Giroux, pp. 370–6.

Marinetti, F. T. [1924] (2006b), 'Tactilism: Toward the Discovery of New Senses', in *Critical Writings*, ed. Günter Berghaus, trans. Doug Thompson, New York: Farrar, Straus and Giroux, pp. 377–82.

Marinetti, F. T. [1909] (2006c), 'The First Manifesto of Futurism', in *Critical Writings*, ed. Günter Berghaus, trans. Doug Thompson, New York: Farrar, Straus and Giroux, pp. 11–17.

Marinkova, Milena (2011), *Michael Ondaatje: Haptic Aesthetics and Micropolitical Writing*, London: Continuum.

Marks, Laura U. (2000), *The Skin of the Film: Intercultural Cinema, Embodiment and the Senses*, Durham, NC, and London: Duke University Press.

Marks, Laura U. (2008), 'Thinking multisensory culture', *Paragraph*, 31: 2, pp. 123–37.

Maupassant, Guy de (2012), 'The Blind Man', in *Short Stories, Vol. II*, trans. Albert M. C. McMaster, A. E. Henderson and Mme. Quesada, Pennsylvania: Penn State Electronic Classics, pp. 47–50, <http://www2.hn.psu.edu/faculty/jmanis/maupassant/deMaupassant-ss-2.pdf> (last accessed 17 October 2012).

Merleau-Ponty, Maurice (1968), 'The Intertwining – The Chiasm', in *The Visible and the Invisible*, ed. Claude Lefort, trans. Alphonso Lingis, Evanston, IL: Northwestern University Press, pp. 130–55.

Merleau-Ponty, Maurice [1945] (2004), *Phenomenology of Perception*, trans. Colin Smith, London: Routledge.

Metropolis, film, directed by Fritz Lang. Germany: UFA, 1927.

Metzger, Bruce M. (ed.) (1991), *The New Oxford Annotated Bible*, New York: Oxford University Press.

Milton, John [1671] (1990), *Samson Agonistes*, in *Complete English Poems, of Education, Arcopagitica*, ed. Gordon Campbell, London: Everyman, pp. 505–55.

Milton, John [1673] (1993), 'When I Consider How My Light Is Spent', in M. H. Abrams, E. Talbot Donaldson, Alfred David, Hallett Smith, Barbara K. Lewalski, Robert M. Adams, George M. Logan, Samuel Holt Monk, Lawrence Lipking, Jack Stillinger, George H. Ford, Carol T. Christ, David Daiches and Jon Stallworthy (eds), *The Norton Anthology of English Literature, Vol. I*, New York: W. W. Norton, pp. 1,472–3.

Minow-Pinkney, Makiko (2000), 'Virginia Woolf and the age of motor cars', in Pamela L. Caughie (ed.), *Virginia Woolf in the Age of Mechanical Reproduction*, New York and London: Garland, pp. 159–82.

Montagu, Ashley (1978), *Touching: The Human Significance of the Skin*, New York: Harper & Row.

Montesquieu [1721] (2008), 'Preface', in *Persian Letters*, ed. Margaret Mauldon and Andrew Kahn, Oxford: Oxford University Press.

Musil, Robert [1930–32] (1979), *The Man Without Qualities*, 4 vols, trans. E. Kaiser and E. Wilkins, London: Picador.

My Fair Lady, performance, directed by Alan J. Lerner. Mark Hellinger Theater (Broadway), 1956.

The Observer (1922), 'The new malady: "Encephalitis Lethargica" and its causes', 10 September 1922, p. 7.

O'Hanrahan, Paul (2006), 'The geography of the body in "Penelope"', in Richard Brown (ed.), *European Joyce Studies 17: Joyce, 'Penelope' and the Body*, Amsterdam: Rodopi, pp. 189–95.

Ovid (2008), *Metamorphoses*, trans. A. D. Melville, Oxford: Oxford University Press.

Pallasmaa, Juhani (2005), *The Eyes of the Skin: Architecture and the Senses*, Chichester: John Wiley and Sons.

Pallasmaa, Juhani (2009), *The Thinking Hand: Existential and Embodied Wisdom in Architecture*, Chichester: John Wiley.

Parrinder, Patrick (1990), 'Wells's cancelled endings for "The Country of the Blind"', *Science Fiction Studies*, 17: 1, pp. 71–6.

Pater, Walter [1873] (1902), 'Conclusion', in *The Renaissance: Studies in Art and Poetry*, London: Macmillan, pp. 233–9.

Paterson, Mark (2005), 'The forgetting of touch', *Angelaki*, 10: 3, pp. 115–32.

Paterson, Mark (2007), *The Senses of Touch: Haptics, Affects and Technologies*, Oxford: Berg.

Paterson, Mark (2009), 'Introduction: re-mediating touch', *Senses and Society*, 4: 2, pp. 129–40.

Poplawski, Paul (2001), '*St Mawr* and the ironic art of realization', in Poplawski (ed.), *Writing the Body in D. H. Lawrence: Essays on Language, Representation, and Sexuality*, Westport, CT: Greenwood Press, pp. 93–104.

Pound, Ezra [1921] (1926), 'Translator's postscript', in Rémy de Gourmont, *The Natural Philosophy of Love*, trans. Ezra Pound, London: Casanova Society, pp. 169–80.

Pryse-Phillips, William (2009), 'Encephalitis Lethargica', in *Companion to Clinical Neurology*, Oxford: Oxford University Press, p. 329.

Rainey, Lawrence S. (2004), 'Fables of modernity: the typist in Germany and France', *Modernism/Modernity*, 11: 2, pp. 333–40.

Renard, Maurice [1920] (1981), *The Hands of Orlac*, trans. Iain White, London: Souvenir Press.

Restuccia, Frances L. (1985), 'Molly in furs: Deleuzian/Masochian masochism in the writing of James Joyce', *NOVEL: A Forum on Fiction*, 18: 2, pp. 101–16.

Révèsz, Geza (1950), *Psychology and Art of the Blind*, trans. H. A. Wolff, London: Longmans, Green and Co.

Révèsz, Geza [1943] (1958), *The Human Hand: A Psychological Study*, trans. John Cohen, London: Routledge and Kegan Paul.

Richards, Thomas (1990), 'Those lovely seaside girls', in *The Commodity Culture of Victorian England: Advertising and Spectacle, 1851–1914*, London: Verso, pp. 205–48.

Richardson, Dorothy [1939] (1990), 'Adventures for readers', in Bonnie Kime Scott (ed.), *The Gender of Modernism: A Critical Anthology*, Bloomington: Indiana University Press, pp. 425–9.

Richardson, Dorothy [1927–33] (1998), 'Continuous Performance', series, in James Donald, Anne Friedberg and Laura Marcus (eds), *Close Up 1927– 1933: Cinema and Modernism*, London: Cassell, pp. 150–209.

Richardson, Dorothy [1915–35] (2002), *Pilgrimage*, 4 vols, London: Virago.

Riegl, Aloïs [1901] (1985), *Late Roman Art Industry*, trans. Rolf Winkes, Rome: G. Bretschneider.

Riegl, Aloïs [1902] (1988), 'Late Roman or Oriental?', in Gert Schiff (ed.), *German Essays on Art History*, trans. Peter Wortsman, New York: Continuum, pp. 173–90.

Riegl, Aloïs [1893] (1992), *Problems of Style*, trans. Evelyn Kain, Princeton: Princeton University Press.

Rilke, Rainer Maria [1919] (2004), *Rodin*, trans. Daniel Slager, New York: Archipelago Books.

Ross, Michael L. (1971), 'The mythology of friendship: D. H. Lawrence, Bertrand Russell, and "The Blind Man"', in S. P. Rosenbaum (ed.), *English Literature and British Philosophy*, Chicago: University of Chicago Press, pp. 285–315.

Rowe, Katherine (1999), *Dead Hands: Fictions of Agency, Renaissance to Modern*, Stanford: Stanford University Press.

Ruskin, John [1880] (1908), 'Fiction Fair and Foul I', in E. T. Cooke and Alexander Wedderburn (eds), *The Works of John Ruskin, Library Edition, Vol. 34*, London: George Allen, pp. 276–9.

Sacher-Masoch, Leopold von [1870] (2000), *Venus in Furs*, trans. Joachim Neugroschel, London: Penguin.

Sass, Louis A. (1998), *Madness and Modernism: Insanity in the Light of Modern Art, Literature, and Thought*, Cambridge, MA: Harvard University Press.

Sass, L. A., and J. Parnas (2003), 'Schizophrenia, consciousness and the self', *Schizophrenia Bulletin*, 29, pp. 427–44.

Schilder, Paul (1935), *The Image and Appearance of the Human Body*, London: Kegan Paul, Trench, Trubner.

Schweizer, Bernard (2002), *Rebecca West: Heroism, Rebellion, and the Female Epic*, Westport, CT, and London: Greenwood Press.

Scott, Bonnie Kime (1991), 'Refiguring the binary: Rebecca West as feminist modernist', *Twentieth Century Literature*, 37: 2, pp. 169–91.

Sedgwick, A. D. (1947), *Horace*, Cambridge: Cambridge University Press.

Serres, Michel (1998), *Les Cinq Sens*, Paris: Gallimard.

Shakespeare, William (1987), *Troilus and Cressida*, ed. R. A. Foakes, London: Penguin.

Shakespeare, William (1995a), *Macbeth*, ed. G. K. Hunter, London: Penguin.

Shakespeare, William (1995b), *A Midsummer Night's Dream*, ed. Stanley Wells, London: Penguin.

Shakespeare, William (1997), *Romeo and Juliet*, ed. Brian Gibbons, Surrey: Arden/Methuen.

Shakespeare, William (2003), *Hamlet, Prince of Denmark*, ed. Philip Edwards, Cambridge: Cambridge University Press.

Shakespeare, William (2008), *King Lear*, ed. Stanley Wells, Oxford: Oxford University Press.

Shaw, George Bernard [1912] (1972), 'Pygmalion', in *The Bodley Head Bernard Shaw: Collected Plays with their Prefaces, Vol. IV*, ed. Dan H. Laurence, London: Bodley Head, pp. 655–823.

Shaw, George Bernard [1912] (1985a), 'Letter to Ellen Terry', in *Bernard Shaw:*

Collected Letters 1911–1925, ed. Dan H. Laurence, London: Max Reinhardt, pp. 110–12.

Shaw, George Bernard [1913] (1985b), 'Letter to Mrs Patrick Campbell', in *Bernard Shaw: Collected Letters 1911–1925*, ed. Dan H. Laurence, London: Max Reinhardt, pp. 184–5.

Siegel, Carol (1987), '"Venus Metempsychosis" and Venus in furs: masochism and fertility in Ulysses', *Twentieth Century Literature*, 33: 2, pp. 179–99.

Sobchack, Vivian (2004), *Carnal Thoughts: Embodiment and Moving Image Culture*, Berkeley: University of California Press.

Stoker, Bram [1904] (1996), *The Jewel of Seven Stars*, Oxford: Oxford University Press.

Stoller, Paul (1997), *Sensuous Scholarship*, Philadelphia: University of Philadelphia Press.

Summers, Claude J. (1980), *Christopher Isherwood*, New York: Frederick Ungar.

Swinburne, Algernon Charles [1859–68] (1952), *Lesbia Brandon*, ed. Randolph Hughes, London: The Falcon Press.

Swinburne, Algernon Charles [1888] (1995), *The Whippingham Papers*, Ware: Wordsworth Editions.

Thompson, John B. (1991), 'Editor's introduction', in Pierre Bourdieu, *Language and Symbolic Power*, ed. John B. Thompson, Cambridge, MA: Harvard University Press, pp. 1–32.

Tindall, William York (1959), *A Reader's Guide to James Joyce*, New York: Farrar.

Trotter, David (1993), 'Disgust', in *The English Novel in History, 1895–1920*, London: Routledge, pp. 214–29.

Trotter, David (2004), 'Stereoscopy: modernism and the haptic', *Critical Quarterly*, 46: 4, pp. 38–58.

Trotter, David (2008), 'Lynne Ramsay's *Ratcatcher*: towards a theory of haptic narrative', *Paragraph*, 31: 2, pp. 138–58.

Tunstall, Kate E. (2011), *Blindness and Enlightenment: An Essay*, London: Continuum.

Twain, Mark (1982), *A Tramp Abroad*, London: Century.

Valéry, Paul [1933] (1957), 'L'Idée fixe: ou, Deux hommes à la mer', in *Oeuvres complètes, Vol. II*, Paris: Gallimard, Pleiade, pp. 214–16.

Weiner, Marc A. (1995), *Richard Wagner and the Anti-Semitic Imagination*, Lincoln, NE: University of Nebraska Press.

Wells, H. G. [1904] (1927), 'The Country of the Blind', in *The Time Machine and Other Stories*, London: Ernest Benn, pp. 167–92.

West, David (1995), 'Carpe diem', in West (ed.), *Horace Odes I: Carpe Diem – Text, Translation and Commentary*, Oxford: Clarendon, pp. 50–2.

West, Rebecca [1929] (1980a), *Harriet Hume*, London: Virago.

West, Rebecca [1922] (1980b), *The Judge*, London: Virago.

West, Rebecca (1986), *Sunflower*, London: Virago.

West, Rebecca [1928] (1987a), 'Sinclair Lewis introduces Elmer Gantry', in *The Strange Necessity: Essays and Reviews*, London: Virago, pp. 269–80.

West, Rebecca [1928] (1987b), 'The Strange Necessity', in *The Strange Necessity: Essays and Reviews*, London: Virago, pp. 13–198.

West, Rebecca [1918] (2010), *The Return of the Soldier*, London: Virago.
Wolf, Naomi (1991), 'Religion', in *The Beauty Myth: How Images of Beauty Are Used Against Women*, London: Vintage, pp. 86–130.
Wolff, Charlotte (1936), *Studies in Hand-Reading*, trans. O. M. Cook, London: Chatto and Windus.
Wolff, Charlotte (1942), *The Human Hand*, London: Methuen.
Wolff, Charlotte (1945), *A Psychology of Gesture*, trans. Anne Tennant, London: Methuen.
Woolf, Virginia (1947), 'The Moment: Summer's Night', in *The Moment and Other Essays*, ed. Leonard Woolf, London: Hogarth Press, pp. 9–13.
Woolf, Virginia [1926] (1950), 'The Cinema', in *The Captain's Death Bed and Other Essays*, ed. Leonard Woolf, London: Hogarth Press, pp. 166–71.
Woolf, Virginia [1941] (1967a), 'Ellen Terry', in *Collected Essays, Vol. IV*, ed. Leonard Woolf, London: Hogarth Press, pp. 67–72.
Woolf, Virginia [1930] (1967b), 'On Being Ill', in *Collected Essays, Vol. IV*, ed. Leonard Woolf, London: Hogarth Press, pp. 193–203.
Woolf, Virginia [1937] (1968), *The Years*, London: Penguin.
Woolf, Virginia [1931] (1977), 'Introductory letter to Margaret Llewelyn Davies', in Margaret Llewelyn Davies (ed.), *Life As We Have Known It, By Co-operative Working Women*, London: Virago, pp. xvii–xxxxi.
Woolf, Virginia [1924] (1988a), 'The Cheapening of Motorcars', in Andrew McNeillie (ed.), *The Essays of Virginia Woolf, Vol. II: 1919–1924*, London: Hogarth Press, p. 440.
Woolf, Virginia (1988b), *The Diary of Virginia Woolf*, 5 vols, ed. Anne Olivier Bell and Andrew McNeillie, London: Penguin.
Woolf, Virginia [1925] (1992), *Mrs Dalloway*, London: Penguin.
Woolf, Virginia [c. 1927] (1993a), 'Evening over Sussex: Reflections in a Motor Car', in *The Crowded Dance of Modern Life*, ed. Rachel Bowlby, London: Penguin, pp. 82–5.
Woolf, Virginia [1928] (1993b), *Orlando: A Biography*, London: Penguin.
Woolf, Virginia [1929] (1993c), *A Room of One's Own*, in *A Room of One's Own and Three Guineas*, ed. Michèle Barrett, London: Penguin, pp. 3–103.
Woolf, Virginia (1994), *Collected Letters, Vol. V: 1923–35: The Sickle Side of the Moon*, ed. Nigel Nicolson and Joanne Trautmann Banks, London: Hogarth Press.
Woolf, Virginia [1919] (1999), *Night and Day*, Oxford: Oxford University Press.
Woolf, Virginia [1925] (2003a), 'Modern Fiction', in *The Common Reader, Vol. I*, ed. Andrew McNeillie, London: Vintage, pp. 146–54.
Woolf, Virginia [1928] (2003b), 'Slater's Pins Have No Points', in *A Haunted House: The Complete Shorter Fiction*, ed. Susan Dick, London: Vintage.
Woolf, Virginia (2004), *A Passionate Apprentice: The Early Journals and 'Carlyle's House and Other Sketches'*, ed. Mitchell A. Leaska, London: Pimlico.
Woolf, Virginia [1927] (2008), *To the Lighthouse*, ed. David Bradshaw, Oxford: Oxford University Press.
Worringer, Wilhelm (1928), *Egyptian Art*, trans. Bernard Rackham, London: G. P. Putnam's Sons.

Wyschogrod, Edith (1981), 'Empathy and sympathy as tactile encounter', *The Journal of Medicine and Philosophy*, 6, pp. 25–43.

Zola, Émile [1883] (2008), *The Ladies' Paradise*, trans. Brian Nelson, Oxford: Oxford University Press.

Index